Next Steps

Improving Management in Government?

Edited by
BARRY J. O'TOOLE
University of Liverpool
and
GRANT JORDAN
University of Aberdeen

Dartmouth

Aldershot • Brookfield USA • Singapore • Sydney

Published by
Dartmouth Publishing Company Limited
Gower House
Croft Road
Aldershot
Hants GU11 3HR
England

Dartmouth Publishing Company
Old Post Road
Brookfield
Vermont 05036
USA

British Library Cataloguing in Publication Data
Next Steps: Improving Management in
    Government?
    I. O'Toole, Barry J. II. Jordan, Grant
    354.4107

Library of Congress Cataloging-in-Publication Data
Next steps : improving management in governement / edited by Barry J.
    O'Toole, Grant Jordan.
        p.   cm.
    Includes bibliographical references and index.
    ISBN 1-85521-491-1 : $57.95
        1. Administrative agencies–Great Britain–Management–Evaluation-
    -Congresses. 2. Civil service reform–Great Britain–Congresses.
    I. O'Toole, Barry J., 1959-   . II. Jordan, Grant.
    JN324.N49   1994
    354.41–dc20   94-33081
                                                               CIP

ISBN 1 85521 491 1

Printed in Great Britain by Ipswich Book Co. Ltd., Ipswich, Suffolk.

JN1

NEXT STEPS

Contents

Preface

This book is the product of a seminar held on 29 May 1992 at the Civil Service College in London. We are grateful to the College for providing excellent facilities. Michael Duggett, who made the arrangements, was his usual unflappable, hospitable and generous self, and we are extremely grateful to him for his help and support.

The idea for the seminar arose from the fact that at that time there was no important critical study of the operation of Next Steps agencies. The Public Administration Committee (PAC) of the Joint University Council was aware of this deficiency and the Research Sub-Committee of the PAC decided to sponsor a workshop on Next Steps agencies. Again, we are very grateful to the Sub-Committee for its support and encouragement. The result of that sponsorship was the Next Steps seminar referred to above.

In addition to the assistance and interest of the PAC and its Research Sub-Committee we also received invaluable support from the Nuffield Foundation. The Foundation was, in effect, the co-sponsor of the seminar. We wish to express our gratitude to the Foundation.

The seminar participants included senior academics undertaking research into the Next Steps agencies and senior practitioners, including members of the Efficiency Unit Next Steps team itself. Their contributions were invaluable and we wish here to thank formally all who took part.

All the papers were especially commissioned for the seminar, apart from that by O'Toole and Chapman on Parliamentary Accountability. Originally the paper on accountability was presented by Barry Winetrobe, then of the University of Aberdeen. However, Mr Winetrobe now works in the House of Commons and it was thought that it would not be proper for him to contribute to the book. However, Richard Chapman was the discussant of the original paper and provided extensive comments which have been included in the chapter. Though the Carter-Greer paper was commissioned by the editors of this book for the seminar, it first appeared in *Public Administration*, Volume 71, Summer 1993, and we acknowledge the permission of Blackwell's to publish that contribution.

The seminar took the normal pattern of such events, with papers being presented by their authors, comments from a discussant and then general discussion. Each of the papers has been turned into a chapter for this book, and each author was encouraged to take into account the comments of the discussants and of the wider audience when rewriting their contribution. The editors and authors are grateful to the discussants and other seminar participants for the very helpful comments. The chapters were also rewritten during the summer and autumn of 1993 to take account of the most recent changes. This means that this book is as up-to-date as is possible. The editors and contributors are especially grateful for the role of Hettie Ras in turning disparate chapters in a motley collection of types into a well presented whole. Ms Pam Strang prepared the final version with admirable efficiency.

Barry J. O'Toole, Liverpool
Grant Jordan, Aberdeen   May 1994

PART ONE
THE CONTEXT OF
THE NEXT STEPS

The Next Steps: Origins and Destinations

GRANT JORDAN AND BARRY J. O'TOOLE

Introduction

In February 1988 the Government published what some regard as a revolutionary document. *Improving Management in Government: The Next Steps* (Efficiency Unit, 1988), is the twentieth century's equivalent of the famous Northcote-Trevelyan report of the nineteenth century. The *Next Steps* report set in motion enormous organizational and, as importantly, constitutional changes. This book attempts to catalogue, to analyze and to assess these changes and to address their implications for the government of the United Kingdom.

The *Next Steps* proposals were the next steps in the Conservative Government's long-running Efficiency Strategy. That strategy had been set in place almost immediately the 1979 Ministry took office, when the new Prime Minister, Mrs Margaret Thatcher, ordered a freeze on all recruitment to the civil service as the first step in 'rolling back the frontiers of the state'. Mrs Thatcher went on to appoint Sir Derek (now Lord) Rayner, who was then the joint managing director of Marks and Spencer, to spearhead the drive for efficiency as her 'efficiency adviser'. In turn he was responsible for the establishment of the Efficiency Unit, and it was this Unit which has been in the vanguard of what might be termed the 'Value for Money' (VFM) movement.

The subsequent reforms have all been catalogued elsewhere (see for example

Chapman, 1991b; Metcalfe and Richards, 1987, 1990), and need only be mentioned in passing here. They mainly arose from so-called efficiency scrutinies, or departmental self-examination of activities, directed by the Rayner Unit. Most famously, they included the Financial Management Initiative (FMI), which sought to:

> Promote in each department an organization in which managers at all levels have
> a) a clear view of their objectives, and means to assess and, wherever possible, measure outputs and performance in relation to those objectives;
> b) well defined responsibility for making the best use of their resources, including a critical scrutiny of output and value for money; and
> c) the information (particularly about costs), the training and the access to expert advice that they need to exercise their responsibilities effectively (Cmnd. 8616, 1982).

These principles are, of course, verging on the banal. However, they may be seen as being inconsistent with the then realities of British government. After all ministers and senior officials set policy and financial frameworks. They interfered constantly in operational matters and it was unreasonable for them to have expected individual officials to be held accountable in quite the ways envisioned by these principles. Perhaps it was these realities which eventually led to the Efficiency Unit, under its new Director, Sir Robin Ibbs, Chief Executive of ICI, to be asked by Thatcher at the end of 1986 to consider the next generation of organizational change in Whitehall.

Improving Management in Government: The Next Steps

The *Next Steps* report was itself the product of a Rayner style efficiency scrutiny. The study took 90 days and cost £50,000. Its terms of reference were:

> to assess the progress achieved in managing the civil service;
> to identify what measures had been successful in changing attitudes and practices;
> to identify institutional, administrative, political and attitudinal obstacles to better management and efficiency that still remain; and
> to report to the Prime Minister on what further measures should be taken (Efficiency Unit, 1988, Annex C) .

The report produced in consequence of the scrutiny was, arguably, lightweight, especially given these terms of reference which more or less imply the complete re-organization of the civil service. It had seven main findings:

> First, the management and staff concerned with the delivery of government services (some 95 per cent of the Civil Service) are generally convinced that the developments towards more clearly defined and budgeted management are positive and helpful.
>
> Second, most civil servants are very conscious that senior management is dominated by people whose skills are in policy formulation and who have relatively little experience of managing or working where services are actually being delivered.
>
> Third, senior civil servants inevitably and rightly respond to the priorities set by their Ministers, which tend to be dominated by the demands of Parliament and communicating Government policies.
>
> Fourth, the greater diversity and complexity of work in many departments, together with demands from Parliament, the media and the public for more information, have added to Ministerial overload.
>
> Fifth, the pressures on departments are mainly on expenditure and activities; there is too little attention paid to the results to be achieved with the resources.
>
> Sixth, there are relatively few external pressures demanding improvement in performance.
>
> Seventh, the Civil Service is too big and too diverse to manage as a single entity. With 600,000 employees it is an enormous organization compared with any private sector company and most public sector organizations (Efficiency Unit, 1988, paras. 3-10).

In addition to these specific findings the report described how the freedom of an individual manager to manage effectively and responsibly in the civil service was circumscribed. It said that managers were controlled not just on resources and objectives but also in the ways in which objectives could be managed, that is through recruitment and dismissal, choice of staff, pay, promotion, hours of work, grading, organization, accommodation, and the use of information technology. All this was attributed by the report to the fact that rules were established centrally - and changing the rules was beyond any one manager. The report argued that:

In our discussions it was clear that the advantages which a unified civil service are intended to bring are seen as outweighed by the practical disadvantages. We were told that the advantages of an all embracing pay structure are breaking down, the uniformity of grading frequently inhibits effective management and that the concept of a career in a unified Civil Service has little relevance for most civil servants, whose horizons are bounded by their local office (Efficiency Unit, 1988, para. 12).

The major recommendation to rectify the problems identified in this analysis was that 'agencies should be established to carry out the executive functions of government within a policy and resources framework set by a department' (Efficiency Unit, 1988, para. 19). The report proposed that the civil service should be restructured so that as far as possible the delivery of services is separated from policy work and executed by agencies operating under business style regimes. It said that such agencies could be part of government and the public service or could be more effective 'outside of government'. According to Sir Peter Kemp, the first Next Steps Project Manager:

> Each service needs to be examined and regularly re-examined, to see if it is best delivered by the private sector; is deemed a vital part of departmental responsibility; or, lying somewhere between the two, whether it can be farmed out at arm's length to an Executive Agency (Kemp, 1993, p. 19).

Kemp was central in the practical implementation of the Next Steps concept. He argued that agencies fill a gap in arrangements between the traditional, centralized and unified civil service, 'where ministers ought not to have hands-on and day-to-day responsibility, but should still remain ultimately accountable to Parliament for their performance' (1993, p. 20) and where it is possible to leave provision entirely to the market. The question this volume seeks to address is whether this organizational device does deliver the benefits of customer/client relations while retaining the strengths of the civil service or whether they are an unhappy set of compromises that damage what exists while yielding little improvement.

In practice, the agencies have been retained as part of the government system, but more recent 'market testing' proposals open up the possibility of allowing private organizations to tender for activities currently carried out in the civil service. Each agency is headed by a chief executive, usually recruited by open competition, employed on a fixed term contract, and paid not according to traditional civil service scales but on the basis of an individually negotiated contract usually containing a clause on performance related pay. The chief executives are responsible for managing their agencies within policy and resources frameworks agreed between them and the sponsoring departments. Within the constraints of those frameworks the chief executives have, in theory, complete discretion to manage in ways which they believe appropriate for the delivery of the services for which they are responsible. The so-called framework documents which establish these constraints may be viewed as pseudo-contracts, and in this sense the agencies are 'contracted' by their parent departments to provide specified services. Performance targets are included in the framework documents and agencies and their chief executives are held accountable for the achievement of these targets. However, unlike normal contracts, they can not be enforced in the courts.

To ensure that the pace of change should be rapid the Efficiency Unit Report called for the appointment of a 'project manager', who would have full permanent secretary status and who would be responsible for 'planning and supervising the process of change' (Efficiency Unit, 1988, paras. 41 and 42). As noted above Mr (later Sir) Peter Kemp became the first project manager, with the status of second Permanent Secretary in the Cabinet Office. He left office in somewhat unusual circumstances in 1992, and was replaced by the current project manager, Richard Mottram. This event signalled the controversial nature of these changes.

Kemp's enthusiasm for the programme was to ensure a breathtaking pace of change though at first the reforms seemed cosmetic. The first *Annual Report* on the initiative, published in February 1989, indicated that there were only three agencies actually in place: the Vehicle Inspectorate, Companies House and HMSO. All three were already outside of the departmental mainstream and terming them as 'agencies' was a relatively simple matter. In the first half of 1989 five more agencies were created: National Weights and Measures Laboratory, Warren Spring Laboratory, the Civil Service College, the Queen Elizabeth II Conference Centre, and the Resettlement Unit of the Department of Social Security. Again, to turn these bodies into agencies may seem to have been a rather modest attainment. However, soon both the pace and the extent of change were to grow rapidly, and the belief of the Efficiency Unit that 95 per cent of civil servants could be working in Next Steps agencies by the end of the century does not now seem to be overly optimistic. Indeed, in 1994 considerably more than half of civil servants are working in such agencies, including nearly everybody in the Department of Social Security which has been split into the Benefits Agency on the one hand and the Contributions Agency on the other, as well as other smaller agencies. When the *Next Steps Review*, 1993, was published in December 1993 there were 92 agencies in place. Together with the 31 Executive Units of HM Customs and Excise and the 33 Executive Offices of the Inland Revenue (which are covered by an ill explained formula 'working fully on Next Steps lines') they employ more than 60% of the civil service. Most of these agencies represent new arrangements for work previously done within the older style service, but the Child Support Agency and the Northern Ireland Child Support Agency were set up as agencies to operate the administration system demanded by the Child Support Act, 1991.

The pace of change has been so rapid that uninformed observers might be forgiven for believing that the introduction of agencies has been unproblematic. Such an interpretation would be fallacious. There are problems associated with the Next Steps, and some of them are of great constitutional importance. It is with these problems that this book is partly concerned.

Conflicting Perspectives on Next Steps

A former senior civil servant, Sir Kenneth Stowe, observed in 1991 (1992) that one of Mrs Thatcher's beliefs was 'if it ain't broke, don't fix it'. It can be argued, however, that the maxim has not been applied to the British civil service. There seems to be a penchant for 'fixing' that organization, even though there is little consensus about whether it is 'broke'. Even those who see it as defective are unclear about the nature of its defects.

Instead of a rational critique of the civil service in Britain the detractors have taken to bestowing a retrospective justification for the changes they have set in flow by endorsing American critiques of their government. They are typified by Osborne and Gaebler who begin their attack by asserting that:

> ... We know that cynicism about government runs deep within the American soul. We all have our favorite epithets; 'It's close enough for government work', 'feeding at the public trough', 'My friend doesn't work; she has a job with the government.' Our public schools are the worst in the developed world. Our health care system is out of control. Our courts and prisons are so over crowded that convicted felons walk free (1992, p. 1).

They accept as new gospel any assertion about waste:

> Waste in government does not come tied up in neat packages. It is marbled throughout our bureaucracies ... it is employees on idle, working at half speed - or barely working at all ... It is the $100 billion that Bob Stone estimates that the Department of Defence wastes with its foolish overregulation. Waste in government is staggering (1992, p. 23).

It seems rather foolhardy to rely on such a superficial analysis when seeking to reform British government. It is not surprising that some observers of change in Whitehall are cynical of much of the associated rhetoric.

In addition, of course, the current reforms in the civil service are further to a whole series of previous reforms. The reformers may be disgruntled at the lack of academic enthusiasm for their activities, but there is a limit to the number of times that we can be told that the washing powder washes whiter, even whiter, ever more whiter. Academics have attended conferences in the University of York or at the Civil Service College or other venues for decades and been told that weaknesses were being addressed. We have had the FMI, Rayner Reviews, PAR, MINIS, Trading Funds, departmental agencies, performance pay - quite apart from dramatic reductions in numbers in the first half of the 1980s, and from the reforms associated with Fulton.

Since all of these moves have been declared successes by their advocates, those accepting these perspectives have seen a civil service working well but potentially at risk from ill thought out changes of the Next Steps and market testing type. While Kemp may concede that there is a degree of 'reform fatigue' inhibiting the Next Steps programme, what can he expect? It is not surprising then that he has concluded that what has been achieved is less than the revolution he might have hoped for:

> We can already see the beginnings of this process with the development of agencies and purchaser/provider relationships out in the field where much of the real work of the civil service is being done. There are welcome breakthroughs *but they do not add up to a revolution.* At the centre, in Whitehall, old attitudes and the old guard prevail. *The only heads that have rolled have been among the revolutionaries themselves* (emphasis added)(1993, p. 8).

Kemp is alluding to a struggle within Whitehall about how radical the Next Steps changes should be. In a series of lectures, Sir Robin Butler, Head of the Home Civil Service, has stressed the need to maintain a unified civil service. This would not be a priority for Kemp who portrays the existence of a monolithic civil service as a 'myth' (1993, p. 3). He asks that agencies be made 'genuinely independent' by cutting them off from their parent departments. All agencies, he says, should be in the position of the Ordnance Survey which is responsible to a minister who bids for their public expenditure provision. He argues that agencies should employ their own staff. Chief executives should be given an agency financial limit - negative or positive - and within that should be left to run the agency as they wish.

So while ministers and agency advocates paint the developments as remarkably successful and problem-free these assertions can be balanced by comments from Kemp about the limited impact of what has been achieved. His views follow on earlier analysis by Mr Graham Mather in *Public Money and Management* (1990, p. 6) and elsewhere, who advocated organizational change but seemed suspicious of the Next Steps developments, arguing that no real market was established to force down costs.

The neglect by Margaret Thatcher of Next Steps agencies in her memoirs perhaps shows that this was not an area free from controversy (1993, p. 49). Clearer signals that there is political disagreement includes the comments by Nigel Lawson in *The View From Number 11* (1993 edn, p. 390). He starts his discussion with the heading 'Stumbles on "Next Steps"'. He recounts how, in the first years in Office the Thatcher Governments had reduced civil service staffing by 20% and in 1982 created the FMI. He describes how, when Robin Ibbs took over the Efficiency Unit in 1983, a split emerged between the Unit and the Treasury. As described by Lawson, Ibbs was too ready to accept the argument that departments could attain savings by investment. Lawson argued that as long as public services existed, insulated from the market place, Treasury control was needed. His view was that as there was no price mechanism at work there had to be Treasury discipline or none at all. His argument that the chaotic consequences of the collapse of the Soviet Union showed what happened when market disciplines did not replace a command system, indicates that Lawson was out of sympathy.

Lawson's description of the introduction of Next Steps agencies was decidedly cool:

> With this background, I was inevitably suspicious when, towards the end of 1987, I and other Cabinet colleagues were informed by No 10, out of the blue, of a new Ibbs initiative, which apparently had Margaret's enthusiastic support ... the main burden of which was a recommendation that the executive functions of Government should be hived off into separate agencies, to be run like businesses by chief executives ... it was clear that Ibbs had not addressed either of the two principal problems involved in a change of this kind, however attractive the concept may have been. The first was the question of parliamentary accountability ... But even when this was solved there remained the second problem, that of maintaining effective control of the agencies' expenditure, in which Ibbs showed no interest ... a long battle ensued, resulting in a lengthy concordat negotiated by Peter Middleton on behalf of the Treasury and Robin Butler on behalf of Number 10 ... The main practical advantage I see is that by creating accounts, boards of directors and saleable assets, future privatization may prove less difficult (1993, edn, p. 393).

By November 1993 there was a public airing of the disputes at the centre of government when Kemp described the process of change as having degenerated into a battle among wayward barons, pulling in different directions. An interview with *The Independent* described him as arguing that the civil service was:

> unhappy, unsure of itself and becoming 'littered with policies that do not work'. The controversial market testing programme - the review process that can lead to contracting out - had, he claimed, gone 'hopelessly awry'.

Some have criticized the Next Steps as too radical; Mather and Kemp suggest to the contrary that the changes have been too limited and more is needed. In contrast to both perspectives former Treasury civil servant, Sir Leo Pliatzky, suggests the most significant feature of these bodies might be the modesty of the change that they represent (1992). He underlined the fact that, 'The agencies will generally be within the Civil Service, and their staff will continue to be civil servants'. (Pliatzky, 1992, p. 558) Pliatzky's argument is that Next Steps changes, despite the 'hype' by their supporters, were a quite minor re-organization within departments. As he points out the Next Steps agencies kept activities within the government and retained parliamentary scrutiny. For him this improved the political acceptability of the initiative:

> In the absence of fresh legislation, so it seems to me, ministers cannot abrogate responsibilities placed upon them by existing legislation. What they can do is delegate authority for operations, but without surrendering ultimate responsibility for them, and that is what is involved in the Next Steps agencies (1992, p. 559).

Organizational, Constitutional and Political Questions

No doubt it is naive to expect those in charge of change to underline weaknesses in their schemes, or the controversies which have surrounded them, both from within and outside the system. However the Next Steps programme has been presented in a particularly Panglossian manner. For example, a *Briefing Note* dated 31 October 1991 (and numerous subsequent Notes) briskly begins:

1. Next Steps is a programme which is delivering better quality central Government services, within available resources, for the benefits of taxpayers, customers and staff.
2. The Government machine is too big and its activities too diverse to be managed as one unit. The solution in most cases is to set up free standing agencies to carry out specific activities. Each agency is headed by a Chief Executive directly accountable to a Minister. Chief Executives are set tough financial and quality of service targets and have financial and management freedoms tailored to help them do the job better.

Such an account, or rather series of assertions, cannot be expected to be passed on to students without some reservations, qualifications and criticisms. Where is the evidence that services are better or that taxpayers or customers or staff all profit from these arrangements? Where is the evidence that the old style of management was 'too big'? Was government really as homogenous as implied, or was there not, in reality, a federal system in which there was already scope for differing management systems and styles? Which theory justifies the new units when the scale runs from thirty staff in the Wilton Park Conference Centre to the 65,000 in the Social Security Benefits Agency? How is the description 'free-standing' reconciled with conventions of ministerial accountability? Who judges the targets to be tough? Where is the proof that these new so-called 'freedoms' increase effectiveness?

One of the central questions is whether decentralization is indeed 'a good thing'. Again, this is an area which remains largely unexplored in the public presentation of the Next Steps proposals. Instead of allowing that there is an issue as to whether central control of the new agencies is too tight or too loose, we are led to believe that in all examples, under all circumstances, control is just right. Is a matter such as a 'take up' campaign by the Benefits Agency just an executive matter or is this a matter in which the parent department or perhaps even the Treasury might want a say? Will the chief executive of the Vehicles Inspectorate be able to close an expensive inspection station even though this will be unpopular with local business people? The usual response to putting this sort of dilemma is to suggest that chief executives will be politically sensitive and that they will consult and clear any important initiatives. However, this only solves easy cases. Consultation does not cover cases in which ministers and chief executives hold different views. The formula on offer is useful only in fair weather. It says that when things are straightforward the minister will give strategic direction and the chief executive will run the day-to-day operations. It must be conceded that it is impossible and unwise to create a set of conditions to meet every extraordinary contingency. To do that would be a recipe for strangulation. But such a relaxed 'play it by ear' approach cannot avoid the criticism that there is uncertainty over 'doomsday scenarios'.

The purpose of this book is to explore these sorts of issues, first by examining the context of change, secondly by examining particular aspects of the work of the new agencies and thirdly by analyzing some of the problems which have emerged. To achieve this purpose the book is split into three parts. Part one, of which this introduction is a part, contains a contribution by Chris Painter, in which he raises in general terms some of the questions dealt with in later sections of the book. For example, he is concerned with such matters as whether some agencies will be privatized; with implications of resourcing for the agencies; with questions about citizenship and the so-called 'customer orientation'. Some of these questions are explored in relationship to specific agencies in the second part of the book. Painter also raises queries about such matters as the future shape of the civil service, for example, whether we shall still be able to describe it as unified, what role will be left for the core departments and whether current constitutional arrangements need to be redefined. Again, these questions are dealt with in a more specific manner in a later part of the book.

The third chapter in the first part of the book is by Andrew Gray and Bill Jenkins. They deal with the implementation of the Next Steps programme. In itself this a vitally important question because most of the changes brought about in consequence of the programme have been carried out without specific legislative action. It is very probably the case that there is no other advanced democratic country in which such major constitutional changes would be allowed without considerable legislative debate or legislative action or without recourse to an administrative or constitutional court. Of course, this is one of the advantages of an unwritten constitution; but there must surely be some fears about the nature and extent of executive action in the field of public administration, especially in a society such as that in the United Kingdom in which the level of political awareness is abysmally low. Gray and Jenkins are primarily concerned with the mechanics of implementation, and set that against the background of the theory of organizational change and the (rather chequered) history of change in Whitehall.

Part two of the book is about agencies in action. There are three chapters. Christine Bellamy's is centred on the Department of Social Security (DSS), a department in which nearly 97 per cent of staff work in agencies. The focus of her chapter is on information agendas and information systems in DSS. As she notes, the DSS is highly 'informatized' and is heavily dependent on information and communication technology. She regards information as a strategic resource and her chapter explores the issues involved in developing and managing new kinds of information systems. Where such systems dominate there are all sorts of implications in terms of resources, resource allocation and the role of the market in influencing that allocation. The implications go beyond the DSS, and raise questions about 'outsourcing' and privatization, and the consequent worries about access to the information held by DSS agencies on individual citizens. Moreover, the very nature of government itself becomes an important issue.

Michael Hunt's chapter is about the Employment Services Agency. It is a more general exposition of the history of the agency since its foundation in 1991. The problems the agency encountered were basically in two areas, target setting and accountability to Parliament. The latter of these seems now not to be so much of an issue, but the question of target setting is more controversial.

The third chapter in the second section is by Neil Carter and Patricia Greer, and deals with this precise question. The use of Performance Indicators (PIs) is an operational matter right at the very heart of the Next Steps programme. The conclusions of this chapter indicate that PIs are highly political instruments mediating the delicate relationships between departments and agencies. The framework documents setting agencies up, and the other documentation associated with the creation of agencies, establish the performance criteria for each of the agencies, and these are negotiated between the minister responsible for each agency and his senior officials on the one hand and the chief executive on the other. As Carter and Greer point out, the 'PIs are the means of exercising "hands-off", control and holding agencies accountable'.

Part three of the book returns to the major controversies surrounding the Next Steps programme. Peter Barberis deals with the extremely important question of the role of the core departments. As more and more activities are being carried out by agencies, what role is left at the centre, both of the individual departments and of the Whitehall machine itself? This question can be extended to the question of what is the role of ministers and Parliament, and this is dealt with in the O'Toole-Chapman chapter on accountability. While ministers and others may proclaim that nothing has changed the traditional constitutional position, it is quite clear that the Next Steps programme fundamentally undermines traditional values and approaches. And this is the case too with the vexed question of the uniform and unified civil service. This question is addressed in the chapter by O'Toole on the role of trade unions and industrial relations in the civil service. The unions have been consistent in their belief that the new industrial relations regime in the civil service undermines all the benefits that the old system was able to bring without creating any new benefits. Is this the case?

Finally, where do we go from here? Jonathan Boston's chapter on the experience in New Zealand may provide us with some lessons. That country is much further down this path than the United Kingdom. What is the position there? What can the New Zealand experience teach the United Kingdom? Finally, there is the new emphasis on the Market Testing programme. This is dealt with in the final chapter.

Clearly this book cannot provide a definitive answer to any of the questions posed here. By the very nature of the Next Steps programme, which is constantly moving, it is impossible to deal in detail with the workings of any one of the agencies, let alone the numbers that have now proliferated. However, some tentative attempt can be made to illuminate some of the more important questions, and perhaps to raise others. The intention of this book has been to do precisely those two things.

Appendix
The Options - the Language of Reform

Several related terms need to be distinguished if agencies and market testing are to be placed in context of a range of reform options: privatization has in the past been used to describe all the trends discussed below, but as practices have developed specialization in the language has followed.

Termination is where the activity ceases. The Government decides that it is unnecessary.

Privatization is the transfer of an activity to the private sector so that the government no longer has a legal responsibility for the service or the delivery of the service. The assumption is that the activity can be more efficiently carried out in the market sector. Thus matters such as water supply and sewerage treatment continue to be required but (in England and Wales) are delivered through regulated markets.

Contracting out (or 'out sourcing') is where the Government wishes activities to continue but to be conducted by the market sector for the public sector. The function is delivered on behalf of government so that, it is claimed, government itself can concentrate on its core activities. For example, there is no reason to suppose that office cleaning needs to be done by government staff when there is demonstrably a capacity to perform this by non-governmental organizations. Examples are ground maintenance of work on the Royal Parks and contracts with private sector suppliers for major IT projects in the DSS.

It seems almost an accident of history that government has done some things itself (administered pensions), used other agencies (e.g. provision of public housing), or gone to the market to buy in delivery (e.g. construction of roads). Government could, for example, have been organized to employ its own staff on road construction. The benefit of *not* doing a job in house was indirectly signalled in the November 1993 budget. The Chancellor was able to point out that the fact that the roads programme was delivered by competitive tenders meant that the construction costs had fallen by 25% from the time the programme was announced in 1989 - because firms were bidding aggressively to get work in the recession.

The best elaboration of the contract approach has come from Graham Mather:

> This contract model separates the political process of determination of objectives and specification of services from their delivery, removing conflict of interest which occurs when those specifying a service are also its deliverers. It reduces the public choice phenomenon of lobbying for bureaucratic expansion by introducing built-in competitive pressures ... It strengthens opportunities for quality control and concentration of resources on supervision and compliance ... (Mather, 1989, cited in Stewart, 1993, p. 8).

'Agencyification' , the major tool that has been utilized in recent years to change the Civil Service has been the Next Steps agency programme. As noted above the agencies have been created as a compromise between market and traditional forms of organization.

At one time Next Steps agencies were seen as an alternative to privatization but increasingly they are presented as an incremental step towards privatization. Ministers, it is claimed, continue to keep under review the basis on which Government services are provided and, before a Next Steps agency is created, the feasibility of privatization is one of the options considered. The decision to privatize DVIOT (an IT service for the Department of Transport and its Agencies - set up on 1 April 1992) was announced by the Secretary of State for Transport on 19 October 1992. NEL has been identified for future privatization and ADAS is another candidate.

At the review of agency framework documents (usually after three years) there is a formal opportunity to consider whether privatization, or abolition or contracting out may be appropriate. By August 1993 it was reported that Companies House was being seen as a privatization candidate and that the future management of all the DTI laboratories was being investigated for privatization or rationalization.

Market testing is sometimes used interchangeably with contracting out but in a technical sense it is less 'extreme'. The activity in question is not seen as being better performed in the private sector but it is claimed is subject to decision on a value for money basis. Government has no prior preference whether or not the activity is carried out in the public or private sectors. It tests whether it should contract out because it has no other basis for decision other than value for money.

In practice market testing need not be such a neutral and compromise concept as this form of words suggests. Like Next Steps agencies, market testing is seen by some critics as a means to preserve the public sector (who will win the 'tests') and by others as a back door means to change. It may be a more politically acceptable way to arrive at contracting out or privatization. It may have significant consequences for the public sector even if the activity remains in house.

As noted above it *may* be that market testing is the logical extension of the agency approach. The agency premise was that there should be a customer/client relationship between the Department and the unit delivering the work. The market testing idea is that the customer should 'shop around' among competing service delivery organisations. But, for better or worse, the original drive towards the Next Steps agencies did not feature these ideas. In the agency model improvement was to come about by a planning approach of imposing on the agencies stiffer and stiffer targets - with a turnover of chief executives if performance was judged to be inadequate.

The Next Steps Reforms and Current Orthodoxies

CHRIS PAINTER

Introduction: Agency Reform in Context

What precisely has happened to the public sector during the last decade or so? Has it been systematically dismantled, progressively squeezed, fundamentally restructured and transformed, or has it been the victim of ill-considered 'flavour of the month' experiments? This seemingly elementary but in fact complex and problematic question was explored in general terms in an article in *The Political Quarterly* (Painter, 1991). This account has as its particular focus the Next Steps Agency Management Initiative (AMI). With in excess of 300,000 civil servants transferred to some 92 executive agencies the bandwagon rolls on as further candidates for such status continue to emerge, including the courts service and a highways agency to take over the management and maintenance of roads. There are even suggestions that the NHS too should be re-organized along agency lines. What follows therefore is a critical overview enabling one management landmark to be seen in the wider public sector reform context. That now means taking on board subsequent developments. The Citizen's Charter, unveiled in July 1991, is in many respects a natural extension of changes that the AMI has helped to bring about. Indeed, departmental agencies are to be 'important vehicles for carrying forward the principles and the improvements to public services set out in the Citizen's Charter' (Prime Minister, 1991a, p. 1). But the *Competing For Quality* initiative launched in

November 1991 appears to mark a significant new phase, moving on the Whitehall reform agenda by a new emphasis on Market Testing.

What is regarded as good administrative practice at any historical juncture, so determining prevailing doctrines, is likely to be contingent on a wider political and social context (Hood and Jackson, 1991). Clearly, ideologically 'Thatcherism' had much to do with the (re)construction of a liberal political economy. This political project has also been identified with the restructuring of the state for a 'post-Fordist' society, signifying paradigmatic change in the form of post-bureaucratic organizational techniques of regulation and control (Hoggett, 1991). Nonetheless, administrative reform post-1979 exhibited interesting parallels with the Government's privatization programme, essentially a pragmatic policy developing its own dynamic rather than a carefully conceived plan:

> the Conservatives in 1979 did not set out with the benefit of a coherent civil service reform strategy, or with anything approaching a blueprint for action, as distinct from an obsession with cuts and profound mistrust of the Whitehall establishment. (Painter, 1989, p. 474).

It was from this platform that the managerial reform programme evolved. Moreover, the immediate context for the Next Steps initiative had been the disappointing achievements notched up by 1986 and therefore growing frustration at the lack of momentum behind the change process, Mrs (now Baroness) Thatcher only belatedly travelling down the road of Whitehall structural reform in an endeavour to overcome barriers to further progress. Even then, affinities with earlier Fulton recommendations (Fulton Report, 1968) were striking, Next Steps arguably breathing life into the managerial philosophy espoused in the late 1960s. Also, the more revolutionary options for Whitehall re-organization - notably those that might fundamentally affect the mandarin elite and central policy making core of departments - largely continued to be eschewed, something emphasized not least by Sir Peter Kemp (Bevins, 1993).

Nonetheless, Next Steps does exemplify contrasting appreciations of the change process, something applying to public sector reform more generally, with no necessarily agreed definition of the situation. Did the programme of departmental agency creation, by aborting some of the more radical options for change, represent yet another triumph for the civil service culture, or is it accelerating the demise of that established ethos? However, despite these alternative perceptions of the nature, implications, and particularly significance of the Next Steps reforms, they are in many respects symptomatic of changes taking place throughout the public sector, and with hindsight constituting something of a pattern, albeit - as already emphasized - not the result of implementing some grand design with a coherent theoretical underpinning, but more the outcome of a cumulative and evolutionary process as one thing led to another.

These change characteristics include the decentralization of managerial responsibilities to designated service delivery units; contractual (if not necessarily in the strict legal sense) rather than hierarchical relationships (separating purchaser and provider roles); a greater customer service orientation; improvements to service standards within given resource limitations and therefore value for money; and more emphasis on a performance culture. These dimensions of public sector reform are accordingly examined below with specific reference to Next Steps. This lays the foundation for a critique of what were to become the newly-established orthodoxies, namely:

- preference for disaggregated rather than unified structures, with associated institutional fragmentation and greater organizational differentiation;
- the predominantly operational (service delivery) focus of public management reform, as opposed to issues of strategic policy analysis;
- a tendency to use business analogues and to adopt private corporations as the appropriate role model for public sector institutions (importing 'good' business practice);
- the implied precedence to be given to individual utilities rather than collective community interests, indicating how public sector management reform has also become essentially consumerist in inspiration;
- hence the increasing dominance of a 'business-consumerist' as opposed to a 'governmental-citizenship' paradigm, therefore a preoccupation with customer not political rights, and with managerialism rather than constitutionalism.

These 'current orthodoxies' raise many fundamental issues, but the first characteristic identified in the above list particularly - the preference for small instead of large scale, for diversity rather than uniformity, and for uncoupling previously unified responsibilities - is a prime example of Hood and Jackson's contention that good administrative practice remains deeply contestable, more a matter of persuasive assertion than of incontrovertible demonstration of the superiority of chosen design principles, as well as of the rapid turnover of administrative doctrines (comparisons with the received wisdom of the early 1970s were very revealing). They also point out that, contrary to the implied novelty of the 'new' public management, many of the shifts in doctrine that this administrative philosophy represents - with its eclectic intellectual base - have a long history, as with the application of business efficiency principles to public management. Moreover, given 'the many private consultants now thronging the lobbies of government buildings ...' (Cellan-Jones, 1992), the dangers of becoming 'slaves to the meretricities of the administrative fashion trade of consultocracy and pop management' (Hood and Jackson, p. 24) are all too evident. One purpose of this contribution therefore is to evaluate the shortcomings of the administrative fashions exemplified by Next Steps.

Privatization and Resourcing

Parallels between the Government's privatization and managerial reform programmes were referred to in the introduction. But is the connection merely one of analogy? The announcement of the AMI in February 1988 stressed that Next Steps is principally about those activities destined to remain inside government, the idea being to make it clear at the outset where there was a firm intention of privatization: 'These agencies will generally be within the civil service, and their staff will continue to be civil servants' (Official Report, 1987-8, Col. 1157). Yet the Ibbs Report made interesting allusions in this respect:

> We recommend that 'agencies' should be established to carry out the executive functions of government ... An 'agency' of this kind may be part of government and the public service, or it may be more effective outside government ... Ultimately some agencies could be in a position where they are no longer inside the civil service in the sense they are today (Efficiency Unit, 1988, pp. 9-10).

Hence the suspicion that departmental agencies may be a first step en route to eventual privatization. The Commons Treasury and Civil Service Committee (TCSC) emphasized the importance of removing such doubts: '... it is vital when establishing an agency to avoid any uncertainty as to whether its future lies in the public or the private sector' (1989, p. xxi). The Government proved more circumspect: '... it cannot be ruled out that after a period of years agencies ... may be suitable for privatization' (HM Treasury, 1989, p.7). So, what are the prospects of moving on from 'internal' decentralization (devolving operational management to units inside government organization) to 'external' decentralization (transferring responsibilities outside government)(Hoggett, 1991)? Agencies are likely to increasingly diversify as they develop, notably when comparing the 'self-funding' ones with those continuing to rely principally on exchequer funding. The distinct possibility does exist of some of those in the former category moving into the private sector (Greer, 1992). Moreover, pressure for a 'radicalization' of the programme, not least from the influential former director of the Institute of Economic Affairs, Graham Mather (Hencke, 1991a), may strike a chord as the search for fresh privatization candidates commences in earnest given the depletion of state-owned industries.

One favoured option of those advocating a 'core' civil service of no more than 10,000 policy advisers is a massive programme of contracting out. There has certainly been some response to such demands, given government policy of extending 'market testing' for civil service operations, in accordance with one of the themes central to the Citizen's Charter, that is the importance of competition and choice to service standards, and with £1.5 billion of work now in the process of being put out to tender. The intention was that every department and agency should devise plans for up to 25% of their activities to be subject to competition before the next general election. This 'contractorization' - as distinct from 'agencyification' - stems from the White Paper *Competing For Quality*. Depending on the vantage point, it represents a welcome and more fundamental cultural change for Whitehall than anything signified by the agency reforms themselves, or the real threat posed now to the whole concept of public service values (Phillips, 1992).

There are those respects in which the public sector is in any case being encouraged to adopt a private sector commercial ethos. The changeover to agency status certainly provides examples, the Meteorological Office turning itself into one of the nation's more profitable assets, seizing the opportunity presented by the new arm's length relationship with the MOD to develop commercial business and to increase income by selling its services (Hencke, 1991b). Generally, it is perhaps significant that the 'language of the new agencies, unlike that of many top mandarins, is unashamedly borrowed from the business school rather than the Oxbridge senior common room' (Hencke, 1991c).

Moreover, such developments have occurred against a background of tight resource constraints, changes post-1979 often motivated by the desire to curtail public expenditure. Trends have not always mirrored the political rhetoric, social investment in fact proving to be the main casualty. Nonetheless, commenting on 'the leper status of the public sector', the Economics Editor of *The Guardian* notes how 'public spending in Britain has been squeezed by more over the past 20 years than that of any other leading industrialized country. Of the 24 OECD countries, only Britain is spending no more as a percentage of GDP than it did in the late 1960s' (Hutton, 1991a). Agency reform had therefore been pursued in this financial climate: 'The main aim of the Next Steps initiative is to deliver government services more efficiently and effectively, within available resources ...' (Prime Minister, 1988, p. 7). The emphasis on finding ways of converting money that could be afforded into better services was also integral to the Citizen's Charter. Whilst some departmental agencies thrived in a more bracing commercial environment, others - the Warren Spring Laboratory an example - however were soon experiencing financial difficulties and therefore a cash crisis, searching for further cost-cutting measures (Hencke, 1991d), and indeed threatened with closure.

A Customer Orientation

Given the eventual transition from almost exclusive concern with expenditure restraint to a restructuring of public institutions, the changes can alternatively be construed as creating more sensitive service delivery mechanisms, based on a very different set of principles from traditional public bureaucracies. Hence disaggregation of structures and devolved managerial responsibilities, moves towards contractual rather than hierarchical relationships, and injection of commercial disciplines and extension of consumer choice, thereby rendering markets an increasing reality for many public organizations (whether real, administered, internal or simulated!). This 'post-bureaucratic' paradigm offered not only the prize of greater efficiency, but also more adaptable and responsive organizations, presenting major challenges to those managing in this new environment, not least the need to acquire financial management and marketing skills (Flynn, 1990). The effect of such structural and managerial changes, taken in conjunction with more flexible working practices and systems of remuneration, is that the old-style monolithic public services 'are withering fast' (Adonis, 1991).

In this context, the significance of the Ibbs Report is clearly evident. Despite the belief held in some quarters that - compared to the other organizational options available - agencies are too close to 'classic public sector arrangements' (Treasury and Civil Service Committee, 1988, p. xv), and some suspension of judgement in recognition of the fact that the real test would come once the larger, politically sensitive operations had been so converted, the restructuring of Whitehall that this entailed did herald more discrete organizational entities with greater flexibility. As Hennessy points out, the programme 'surprised most "Whitehall watchers", accustomed as they were to see the more ambitious civil service reforms gradually subside into the quicksands of inertia' (1991a, pp. 471-472).

Moreover, besides promoting value for money (VFM), the intention was to develop greater awareness of the needs of recipients of government services. The TCSC expected 'the success of the Next Steps programme to be judged in large measure by the extent to which it improves service to customers' (1989, p. xviii). The contention therefore is that it 'offers a prize to all future governments: an effective and adaptable civil service ... better attuned to deliver the high quality public services for which the citizen increasingly looks' (Prime Minister, 1991a, p. 13). Devolving responsibility to service delivery units, so enhancing managerial freedom, was regarded as the key to more responsive and flexible organizations, a customer focus, and operational effectiveness:

> The best results will be achieved if the staff can respond directly to the needs of their clients. It is one of the main aims of Next Steps that ... chief executives should have the authority and responsibility to manage their

agencies in the way best suited to their customers' needs ... (Prime Minister, 1991b, p. 36).

This called for attitudinal and behavioural changes, not least willingness to assume responsibility, but also to be more innovative than is customary in the public services. There are indeed examples of this developing customer ethos, the first agency established under Next Steps - the Vehicle Inspectorate - one such instance, reflected in changes made to the unwieldy bureaucratic system inherited (Hencke, 1991e). It is a development, moreover, to be seen in the context of greater recognition of the importance of quality in well-managed service provision. With seeds sown through the Next Steps reforms, the Citizen's Charter has elevated public service standards to the status of a central theme of the 1990s. However, 'quality' is an elusive concept with different connotations, often commercial in origin and therefore not necessarily appropriate for a modern welfare system (Coote & Pfeffer, 1991). In fact, its definition, let alone quality assurance, presents many more difficulties in the service - particularly public service - context than in the case of manufacturing goods because of their very different attributes (Walsh, 1991).

Moreover, the notion of a 'customer focus' itself raises delicate issues for public services, not least determining how consumer satisfaction should be evaluated. The Government claims that almost all agencies have now instituted arrangements for consulting customers, following initial complaints about failure to carry out market research (Prime Minister, 1990, p. 11). But there are inescapable dilemmas in being 'user-friendly' and at the same time containing expenditure (it often seems more a matter indeed of deterring rather than attracting custom because of resource rationing). Revealingly, the Benefit Agency's customer charter omitted targets for social security offices to improve the take-up of benefits! And generally there is the veritable minefield in applying a notion of customers to the public sector, analogous to that found in the conventional business model, when relationships between service providers and service users (including elements of dependency and compulsion) are so much more complex (Flynn, 1990).

A Performance Orientation

The idea of the 'well managed state' entered into currency during the 1980s. Moving from an administrative to managerial culture marked a changeover from bureaucratic to output controls, and therefore less obsession with procedural conformity as opposed to results achieved with available resources. At issue is a performance orientation and culture. Although concern about sub-optimal public sector performance is not unique to the 1980s, this was a period nonetheless characterized by mounting pressures from the highest level (Number Ten) to improve the management of Whitehall (and of the public sector more generally). But despite progress in the guise of the Rayner Scrutinies and later the Financial Management Initiative (FMI), for Ibbs much remained to be done to successfully implant such a performance-orientated culture: 'While the introduction of management systems has helped make civil servants cost conscious, there is less consciousness about results' (Efficiency Unit, 1988, p. 25). Determining internal accountability for this, with all the attendant paraphernalia of performance indicators and rewards for success, awaited satisfactory implementation: 'At present the freedom of an individual manager to manage effectively and responsibly in the civil service is severely circumscribed' (p. 5). Progress was especially imperative for Whitehall 'businesses' on the delivery side; hence the creation of agencies for operational management purposes.

In this respect, Next Steps can therefore be regarded as a significant landmark in the development of public management. Indeed, with their increased personal responsibility, calling agency chief executives to account for achievements is one of the hallmarks of the AMI. It is becoming ingrained in the culture, judged as these operations are on performance against published targets, the Government post-Ibbs anxious to highlight 'the way that emphasis has been shifting away from inputs and towards results' (Prime Minister, 1988, p. 3). It also became a prime feature of the Citizen's Charter, given explicit statements of service standards, related targets, and published information - including comparative league tables - on outcomes. This changing culture is being facilitated, moreover, by civil service pay reforms establishing linkages with performance and providing for greater flexibility, precedents for agencies moving to their own pay and grading systems (including performance bonuses) existing in the shape of the Vehicle Inspectorate and HMSO.

But there are grounds for apprehension about the appropriateness of what is being targeted, and therefore suitability of the performance indicators to which these targets relate. Although significant progress has been made, there remain formidable difficulties with performance measurement in the public services: hence 'lop-sided' approaches relying more on economy/efficiency criteria than on effectiveness/quality considerations (Pollitt, 1990a). The point was taken up by the TCSC, expressing concern that 'the systems for choosing and setting targets for agencies should be improved, that those targets should include measures of quality of service ...' (1991, p. x). Targetry, moreover, is a risky business, providing potential hostages to fortune! Witness the ensuing scramble to meet the pledge contained in the patient's charter, that no one should have to wait for more than two years for an operation from April 1992, in order to avert political embarrassment. The same example underlines some perverse effects, patients with relatively minor conditions given priority over more pressing cases so as to achieve the target.

As for performance-related pay, this rests on dubious theories of motivation (Lawton & Rose, 1991, ch. 8). Indeed, the search for measurable work indices as a basis for rewarding effort smacks of 'neo-Taylorism' (Pollitt, 1990b). The attendant control philosophies point to a management ideology with a narrowly-conceived approach to organizational performance, 'harder' efficiency measures taking precedence over the 'softer' management skills of communication, motivation and leadership.

Institutional Tinkering

In any case, was the radical rhetoric of Thatcherism as deceptive with regard to public institutions as in some other respects, even once a restructuring process had been embarked upon, especially taking account of the progress made with administrative reform in some other countries? As Hennessy observes, there is less scepticism than hitherto about the significance of Next Steps: 'When it was published in February 1988 it was an instant victim of the Whitehall 'disbelief system' ... it would ... take its place ... in the gallery of failed reforms ... it's now expected that Next Steps will turn out to be the most substantial reform of the civil service this century ...' (Treasury and Civil Service Committee, 1990, p. 60). Nonetheless, Dunleavy and Francis maintain that international comparisons should be selected carefully: '... the Next Steps programme is unlikely to produce a systematic or comprehensive pattern of non-executant central ministries such as that found in Sweden. Instead previous highly unified Whitehall departments may move towards the more segmented intra-departmental structure of bureaux characteristic of the US federal government' (Treasury and Civil Service Committee, 1990, p. 69).

Doubts moreover have been voiced, including by Hood and Jones, about the durability of the current messy 'half-way house arrangement' (agencies neither fully integrated with nor operating outside departmental boundaries), therefore questioning whether the reforms are likely 'to constitute a formula for a new stable system of public management' (Treasury and Civil Service Committee, 1990, p. 78; 81). Indeed, strictly speaking, the status of these agencies is not even quasi-governmental, despite repeated references to the 'hiving off' of civil service functions! Given the other organizational options available, the issue again raised is whether the adopted structural formula is too close to 'classic' public sector arrangements, and as such yet another exercise in superficial tinkering with the Whitehall machine, a cosmetic 'revolution' frustrating more fundamental reform. There are already some signs of destabilization.

The real test is how agencies will perform compared with what could have been expected from those same responsibilities being retained within the traditional structure, an on-going debate reflected in Parliament's regular monitoring of the AMI, the TCSC recommending that 'departments establish evaluation programmes ... to assess how far agency status has changed the effectiveness of their operations'

(1990, p. vii). Even the Cabinet Secretary acknowledged the danger of a 'scorecard' mentality, concentrating on getting agencies up and running irrespective of whether this promoted substantive changes (Butler, 1991). However, in the absence of systematic evaluative data, and therefore not unconnected with the contestable nature of administrative doctrines, here we are very much in the realm of alternative perceptions. At its most polarized, there is the stark contrast between the belief that Next Steps is contributing to public sector revitalization on the one hand and threatening the very future of valued public institutions on the other. First, the positive construction placed upon developments.

Transforming and Fragmenting Whitehall

The organizational differentiation promoted by Next Steps reflected growing disenchantment with large-scale orderly bureaucracies and centralized control. The freedom denied by traditional civil service hierarchical arrangements hampered good management practice, preventing the decentralization and accessibility fundamental to 'customer-driven' service delivery, as well as the flexibility in organizational design necessary so that structures could reflect functional and task requirements. It also underlines the growing trend towards a contract structure - in this case - internal contractual relationships, with the implied greater clarity in service specification and hence again of performance criteria. Thus, the TCSC regarded the policy and resource frameworks for departmental agencies as amounting to a contract between themselves as service suppliers and the 'parent' department acting as representatives of the customer (1989, p. xiii). Indeed, it was something the Government was eager to highlight:

> The objective is to move away from 'management by command' to 'management by contract' ... the intention is to move to a situation where controls are more strategic and rather less detailed than previously (Prime Minister, 1990, p.15).

A danger of contract-based management, however, is giving the impression that service specification is a purely technical issue, when in fact it is inherently political and contestable, affected by conflicting and changing social values (Walsh, 1991).

Nonetheless, the belief in some circles is that the Next Steps reforms were but one manifestation of the more dynamic and enterprising culture now permeating the public sector, displacing previously rigid organizational modes, in the process transforming an anachronistic administrative culture and counteracting bureaucratic obstacles to change. The associated 'wind of change' contained the ingredients of a 'new deal' for both users of public services and taxpayers. And the leadership qualities relevant to this new environment are quite unlike those hitherto required, demanding a more businesslike approach and capability to efficiently manage public operations and assets. But agency creation does raise the efficacy of structural change and whether it is the most important element organizationally in promoting changes of culture, attitude and behaviour, let alone the doubts about whether this is the appropriate structural solution (Flynn et al., 1990). Moreover, one person's innovatory disaggregation is another person's counter-productive fragmentation!

Further structural differentiation and complexity can be a recipe for narrow organizational loyalties, adding fuel to the conflicting interests permeating the administrative process itself (Gray & Jenkins, 1991). There are also potentially adverse consequences for public policy goals. Indeed, the importance to public sector management of multi-organizational approaches and concerted action (as opposed to the quashing of competitors so central to strategic success in the private commercial sector), given the nature of public policy problems and realities of organizational interdependence, has been emphasized often enough (Bozeman & Straussman, 1990). Far from diminishing barriers to co-ordination, the fragmented (and competitive) environment now being constructed in the public sector is likely to militate against the institutional collaboration widely acknowledged to be necessary, exacerbating the integrationary problems previously plaguing Whitehall, and compounding a perennial problem for the public services:

> Complex and multifaceted problems cry out for systematic and well ordered responses, yet the reality is all too often a jumble of services fractionalized by professional, cultural and organizational boundaries and by tiers of governance (Webb, 1991, p. 229).

Moreover, given the nature of administrative doctrines, judgements about the durability of institutional trends, whether developmental or cyclical, do depend on the time frame used as a point of reference. After all, it is only a matter of twenty years or so since the prevailing tendency was the opposite one of institutional aggregation, bureaucratic juggernauts at that time believed to provide optimal administrative arrangements!

Challenges and Threats to a Unified Civil Service

Institutionally, Next Steps obviously affects both the civil service and government departments. The latter are being reconstructed into more loosely coupled and discretely organized entities. But it is the civil service that particularly faces major challenges as a result of these reforms, the Ibbs Report maintaining that the disadvantages of uniform arrangements outweighed the advantages: '... the civil service is too big and too diverse to manage as a single entity' (Efficiency Unit, 1988, p.4). More autonomous units tailored to the needs of individual tasks would certainly seem to have implications for the continuation of a 'national' civil service. This indeed is a logical corollary of the greater managerial freedoms envisaged. But are we likely to witness the demise of a civil service as we have known it, or merely a move towards less monolithic arrangements?

The agency reforms are impacting upon some of this institution's long-standing traditions. The precedent established by open competition for agency chief executive posts is contrary to the notion of a career service, as is the practice of using fixed-term contracts. Standardization is also being progressively abandoned. Departments and agencies were given more freedom in April 1991 to conduct their own recruitment processes, if necessary turning to private sector facilities, leading to the irony of the newly-established civil service Recruitment Agency itself experiencing financial difficulties in competition for this departmental business (Hencke, 1992a)! And there are the previously mentioned departures from common grading and pay structures, therefore the emergence of varying terms and conditions of service, with attendant risks to staff mobility. The greater flexibility achieved by agencies in this respect is clearly a significant step towards the breaking up of centralized civil service pay bargaining.

Obviously, no institution should be sacrosanct. Yet as the TCSC observed: 'It would not be satisfactory if a major change in the structure of the civil service were to be introduced piecemeal, without proper opportunity for full public discussion'. Moreover, barriers to transferability would indeed be erected if agencies were allowed to build the equivalent of 'miniature Berlin walls' (1991, pp. xiii; xvii). The Government, despite accepting that Next Steps is 'radically altering the organization of the civil service', argued that there were limits to which its precise shape and structure could be 'planned or foreseen in advance' (Prime Minister, 1991a, p. 3), making it all seem something of a voyage of discovery! The TCSC had previously accepted that 'it should be possible to maintain the national character of the civil service while recognising the diversity of its functions' (1989, p. xix). However, two years later the Committee was critical that the future of this institution had not been adequately addressed: 'We are concerned that the important common characteristics of the civil service should not be lost sight of in the process of change' (1991, p. xiii). It was particularly essential to ensure that two classes of people did not emerge, those in agencies and those at the centre.

Related, of course, is the fear that we are seeing a reversion to the crude policy-administration dichotomy so discredited in the past, and the artificiality of which was again demonstrated for example by the Benefit Agency's apparently key role in controversial policy changes, including the tightening of rules relating to social security arrears - the agency actively campaigning for this change (Brindle, 1991).

But what particularly stood out was the need for more strategic thinking about the long-term direction of the civil service, including the respective demands made by the diversity that agency effectiveness called for and the minimum common standards essential to such a service. The Cabinet Secretary himself maintains that it is not only the management reforms that are important, but also familiar civil service qualities - integrity, safeguards against corruption, merit, impartiality, and concern to serve democratically elected governments - prescriptions as valuable today as they have ever been (Butler, 1991). Hence the case for balancing greater discretion in interpreting guidelines on civil service codes of conduct with the maintenance of certain key central principles. Nonetheless, if we do single out for attention the management aspect, what is it that is most striking about the approaches recently adopted?

Operational and Strategic Management

Accepted in principle by the Government in February 1988, Next Steps only slowly impinged on operations near to the 'heart' of the administrative system. But as an evolving initiative, applying the lessons of experience as part of a learning process, the programme gathered considerable momentum. After initial misgivings about progress, the TCSC applauded how it was being 'implemented with impressive speed' (1991, p. vii). Moreover, the Citizen's Charter contained a new target for completion of reform: 'The aim is that all the executive activities of government will, as far as practicable, be operating along these lines by the end of 1993' (Prime Minister, 1991b, p. 36).

Next Steps had much to commend it, promising to resolve contradictions between the devolved management responsibility central to the FMI philosophy and the career civil service as conventionally organized. The comments of the then project manager, Sir Peter Kemp, were instructive: 'The civil service might be perceived as one huge employer. In point of fact, the civil service is a large number of small businesses' (*Independent*, 1990). Hence the case for tailoring organization to the job in hand. Ranging from the HMSO to the Benefits Agency, one of the characteristics of the operations put on the new footing is their sheer variety, including with respect to proximity to mainstream departmental policies, which has 'meant that there could be no one pattern to which every agency would conform' (Treasury and Civil Service Committee, 1991, p. viii). Thus, relationships between the interested participants have to meet each agency's own circumstances, reflected in 'custom-built' framework documents (Treasury and Civil Service Committee, 1989, p. xii). The Ibbs Report also highlighted the tendency to be too preoccupied with inputs (economy) to the detriment of outputs, contrary to the demands of a performance-orientated culture. The proposed reforms, moreover, had a non-partisan appeal, operable by governments of any political persuasion, given the scope to change framework agreement objectives (Treasury and Civil Service Committee, 1990, pp. viii-ix).

But there were also drawbacks to the approach adopted. The risks to a unified career bureaucracy without thorough examination of the consequences have already been noted. And in one respect particularly Next Steps seemed very much a continuation of an established managerial paradigm, manifest in the desire to redress the low priority accorded to the delivery end of government, and to correct the precedence given in Whitehall to policy formulation rather than managing operations. A prime consideration therefore was 'to ensure that the organizational structure and the skills of the civil service are adapted to deliver government services as effectively as possible' (Efficiency Unit, 1988, p. 12). This reinforced what had become the predominantly operational concerns of public management reform, downgrading strategic issues such as the management of environmental change, effective networking in circumstances of organizational interdependence, and indeed constitutional re-design, management reform viewed in isolation from the broader institutional framework, and with attendant dangers of pouring new management wine into old accountability bottles (Metcalfe and Richards, 1990). It was indicative of a micro perspective, a preoccupation with the day-to-day management and 'production' of services.

There are benefits in releasing top management to concentrate more on policy development, and allowing William Waldegrave to claim - in deference to Osborne and Gaebler (1992) - that the Conservatives were 'reinventing' government (Hencke, 1992b). But in keeping with other post-1979 initiatives, the AMI still signified retreat from the strategic and analytical focus of Whitehall reforms during the early 1970s, reforms which themselves fell victim to the British style of government, with its characteristic departmentalism, defence of policy domains, and propensity of ministers to fight their corners (Radcliffe, 1991). This narrowing of focus reflected how Thatcherites, as conviction politicians, did not necessarily want policy advice from civil servants, whose role was to be cast in another mould. Next Steps accordingly provided additional impetus to this new-found emphasis on managerial efficiency and implementation, as opposed to on policy analysis and deliberation (Wilson, 1991). Yet, the ability of the Employment Service to meet job placement targets highlights the dilemma. Although it can assist the efficiency of the labour market, the key to success nonetheless is the quality and coherence of macroeconomic policy itself.

As agency creation gathered pace, debate certainly centred on the operational freedoms and flexibilities given to managers, with how departments could be induced to adopt a 'hands-off' approach and discouraged from unwarranted interference (Treasury and Civil Service Committee, 1989, p. xxi; 1990, p. xxii). The burning issue was that of effective delegated responsibility and empowerment of agency chief executives. But avoiding the 'neo-colonial syndrome', given departments' reluctance to let go (Hennessy, 1991b), involved more than just self-denying ordinances. At stake is how their functions should change as a result of Next Steps, so that strategy and planning supersede routine, detailed intervention (Treasury and Civil Service Committee, 1990, p. xvii). It was a matter addressed by the Efficiency Unit inter-departmental study, conducted under the supervision of Sir Angus Fraser, reviewing the Whitehall ministries themselves, and how they ought to adapt and redefine their role, reappraising their structures, size and methods of working in the light of agency formation (Efficiency Unit, 1991). Significantly, the relevant analogies were considered to be large private corporations, rather than arrangements in comparable governmental systems.

Hence the interviews conducted by the Efficiency Unit with senior business executives. It discovered that 'a chief executive of a subsidiary operation was given almost complete control over all resources ...', noting the experience of those companies 'where increased delegation to line management has frequently led to reductions in excess of 50% in the number of headquarters staff' (1991, pp. 14-19). In terms of the challenges facing Whitehall, this was a parallel that the Cabinet Secretary took to heart: 'We could all name major companies ... which have headquarters from which those running the companies set general strategies while the managers of subsidiaries and operating units have substantial freedom in running their operations within firm overall budgetary controls and are held responsible for the results' (Butler, p. 364). It provides yet another instance of the growing appeal of business analogues.

But it was not just the core functions of departments that demanded reappraisal. Similar strategic issues arose in redefining the role and size of the Treasury and Cabinet Office (Efficiency Unit, 1991, p. 9), which the TCSC felt had been relatively neglected: 'Much thought has been given to the proper relationship between agencies and their parent departments but the role of the central departments appears to have been less deeply considered' (1991, p. x). They should particularly play a stronger part in delineating the overarching frameworks within which managerial freedoms were exercised.

The TCSC, then, was beginning to express concern on a number of counts about the future direction of agency reform. It, at least, showed signs of grasping the strategic nettle, encouraging ministers to do likewise. Indeed, there would appear to be increasing scope for a radical streamlining of Whitehall as a result of agency creation, privatization, and contracting out. Yet, it remains curious that the strategic implications of operational delegation for sponsoring ministries, central departments and a unified civil service are only now coming to the fore. Change had to start somewhere, agencies providing a useful catalyst. Moreover, there is always an argument for proceeding with reform in manageable chunks (incrementalism in whatever guise!), given the risks of biting off more than can be chewed. But it still highlights the danger of vital strategic considerations being addressed almost incidentally.

An operational public management focus also developed at a time when there is growing appreciation of the importance of a 'strategic template' to clarify organizational purposes, inform what is done, and to provide pattern and coherence (bearing in mind the clarity of vision marking the more successful private companies). Yet, many difficulties are encountered in this connection in the public sector. There is the complexity of defining what is to be achieved and institutionalized conflict over what the objectives should be. This leads on to the whole issue of public sector management's distinctiveness. The debate about the extent to which a business ethos and public service values can mix continues to rage, and not only in the Whitehall context (it is manifest for example in the recent controversy over reform of the police service).

Business Corporations and Public Institutions

Given the pressures for improved management in government organizations, of which Next Steps is a prime example, undoubtedly there is much to learn from best practice elsewhere. However, the tendency has been to use business analogues as a role model, in line with the ascendant ideological belief in the 1980s that private is inherently superior to public. Yet, emulating the world of business has ended in grief before, borne out by the experiences of the early 1970s when government slavishly followed the then fashion for organizational mergers and amalgamations.

It raises the question of transferability, given the different demands, constraints and operating conditions faced by public management. This distinctive environment has manifested itself in the organizational culture of the public services, the risk-avoiding behaviour to minimize chances of ministerial embarrassment, and meticulous consultation to safeguard collective governmental interests. Such behavioural patterns have been reinforced by expectations of consistency and equity. Moreover, statutory obligations prevent withdrawal from unpromising markets. The very first Next Steps agency, the Vehicle Inspectorate - despite achieving significant efficiency improvements and savings - has been constrained by the commitment to maintain a network of large vehicle testing centres, many operating below capacity (Hencke, 1992c).

Of course, management reform is all about changing public service cultures, and in turbulent times it should come as no surprise that the established ethos has come under close scrutiny. But public authorities are not simply in the 'business' of service delivery; there are regulatory and policing responsibilities to be undertaken. There is also the governmental role itself to be performed, the essence of which is acting as guardian for collective community interests as distinct from the utilities of individual service users, and related concerns with citizen (as opposed to consumer) empowerment. Hence the makings of a very different agenda: political participation, democratic accountability, and rights to access official information. And although the political process, with its attendant instabilities, uncertainties and ambiguities, obviously has profound implications for public managers' freedom - enmeshed as they are in this process - the AMI was specifically designed to expand this autonomous sphere, threatening to give precedence to managerial over democratic values. The related notion that there is some kind of trade-off between these values, indeed, is hardly conducive to a climate encouraging public managers to cultivate their skills of political awareness and sensitivity.

Even in the narrower administrative context, the value base of 'managerialism' left something to be desired, placing frugal resource use centre stage at the expense of rectitude and resilience (Hood, 1991). But it is when change threatens to impinge on the very fabric of democratic structures, and on parliamentary accountability for the exercise of public power, that concern is particularly warranted (Plumptre, 1988). For example, the increasing separation of policy and management within the Department of Health threatens to foster contrary cultures, with all this entails for the running and public accountability of the NHS. Yet, the Next Steps Report identified what it regarded as positive political benefits in reconstructing Whitehall along agency lines, at least for ministers, addressing the problem of overload and enabling them 'to concentrate more on their main political task' (Efficiency Unit, 1988, p. 13). Curtailing the proliferation of detail referred upwards, political control would be strengthened by the explicitness of delegated responsibilities and agency accountability for performance.

But is it feasible for ministers to extricate themselves from such detail in the event of politically sensitive situations? Revealing is the saga of the unassigned civil service entrants inherited by the Benefits Agency, deciding they were surplus to requirements, only to reverse this position following expression of Prime Ministerial interest (Brindle, 1992)! Likewise Kenneth Baker's decision, then Home Secretary, to give the Prison Service greater operational independence from April 1993 - thus converting it to agency status - so making ministers responsible only for overall policy. Apart from associated concerns about accountability, doubts have been expressed that a Home Secretary can avoid intervening in day-to-day incidents, when the public are likely to demand a 'hands-on' rather than 'hands-off' approach (Carvel, 1992).

Managerialism and Constitutionalism

Clearly delineated responsibilities and delegation of executive powers to named civil servants is pivotal to the Next Steps reforms. Framework documents therefore 'publicly set out the respective roles of ministers ... and those of agencies ... they make transparent the resulting accountabilities within government and to Parliament' (HM Treasury, 1989a, p. 17). But apart from anything else, is the implied arm's length relationship compatible with established constitutional ground rules? The Ibbs Report did, in fact, raise the issue of changes in formal accountability arrangements to underpin managerial delegation:

> Clearly ministers have to be wholly responsible for policy, but it is unrealistic to suppose that they can actually have knowledge in depth about every operational question ... We believe it is possible for Parliament, through ministers, to regard managers as directly responsible for operational matters ... (Efficiency Unit, 1988, p. 10).

Some developments anticipated in Next Steps did materialize, notably the accounting officer position following the changes announced in November 1988. However, that there was to be no fundamental overhaul of formal public accountabilities became abundantly clear from the outset: 'The Government does not envisage that setting up executive agencies within departments will result in changes to the existing constitutional arrangements' (Prime Minister, 1988, p. 9). Thus, chief executives continued to give parliamentary evidence on behalf of and under instructions from the minister, to whom they are answerable and from whom they derived their authority. Nonetheless, the TCSC took the view that because their responsibilities are clearly laid down in a framework document 'they are unlikely to be able to decline to answer questions on matters which are within those delegated responsibilities' (1991, p. xxiii).

Indeed, ministerial responsibility has been undergoing revision almost by stealth. Accepting that ministers should be challengeable in Parliament for any action of the civil service is very different from insisting that they should accept the blame for every wrong decision of subordinates, especially those of which they know nothing, nor reasonably could be expected to (Hennessy, 1991c). There has, it seems, been an increasing divergence between actual practice and formal constitutional prescription, with distinctions being drawn between the policy and operational spheres, establishment of executive agencies involving further 'developments in the way in which external accountability is discharged' (Prime Minister, 1988, p. 9). Therefore, both in the case of select committee investigations and Parliamentary Questions, sources of information now normally follow the allocation of responsibilities in framework documents.

Yet, ambiguity remains when the Government insists it continues to attach 'great importance to the ... full accountability of ministers to Parliament for the whole of their departments, including agencies' (Prime Minister, 1991a, p. 11). Thus, we have the classic dilemma posed when administrative reforms of the kind represented by the AMI are unaccompanied by wider constitutional review. But this constitutional debate has become significant for a much broader citizenship agenda. Indeed, recent obsession with managerialist values is in stark contrast to the lack of vitality of our democratic institutions. Nonetheless, it was the Government's contention that Next Steps has had beneficial effects in exposing government operations to greater scrutiny: 'publication of framework documents and agency annual reports and accounts are a real step forward in openness and accountability' (Prime Minister, 1990, p. 3).

Also contributing to a 'small explosion of information' (Hencke, 1991f) - notably performance information for users of public services, including comparative statistics and league tables - the Citizen's Charter was nonetheless revealing in this broader constitutional context, the absence of freedom of information legislation, and which the Government continued to resist in its white paper on open government in July 1993, signifying the lack of any new political rights or fundamental changes in the relationship between state and citizen. Indeed, its customer focus is very much consistent with the 'business-consumerist' rather than 'governmental-citizenship' paradigm, so carrying a distinctly Thatcherite pedigree. However, questions of citizens' rights and constitutional reform are likely to grow in significance in the UK as long as 'the institutions of "democracy" are so palpably abusable and abused ... Mr Major's government has shown itself to be the equal of its predecessor in bending the unwritten constitution so that the state can serve party' (Hutton, 1991b). Indeed, there is a particular irony in that at the same time as the decentralizing managerialist ethic of the FMI and AMI was being espoused, concern mounted about the increasing concentration of political and governmental power (Gray & Jenkins, 1991)!

Transcending Current Orthodoxies: A Changing Agenda?

Mrs Thatcher's preoccupation with cost-consciousness erected some necessary financial disciplines, but its limitations as a dominant public sector management paradigm had become increasingly apparent. At least Next Steps signified some broadening of horizons, continuing the search for VFM but also laying greater emphasis upon the customer responsiveness in service delivery that was to become even more pronounced as part of the Citizen's Charter. In contrast with inherited public service cultures and behavioural norms, a corollary of these changes is willingness by those in designated service delivery units to exercise managerial responsibility and to be held accountable for performance. This 'user-orientation' facilitated by decentralized management structures is widely viewed as a positive development. Yet, apart from the potentially deleterious effects of structural fragmentation, management reforms in the UK have continued with an essentially operational focus, delivering services within a largely predetermined framework. Belatedly addressed, there has been a distinct danger of the larger strategic issues - including the future of the civil service as a national institution, the appropriate role for the central departments, and changing relationships between agencies and their sponsoring ministries - being eclipsed.

And although the AMI creates new possibilities in organizationally disentangling policy from detailed operations, is the long-standing lack of a convincing strategic capability in British government any nearer to resolution? As Sir Robin Butler comments: 'Good government is about well-considered, well-designed policies as well as the efficient delivery of services ...' (1991, p. 369). This enhanced strategic analysis had been a recurring theme of the Heath government, albeit falling victim to continuing departmentalism, which proved inimical to those broader strategic aims (Radcliffe, 1991). Moreover, the consumerist inspiration behind public sector management reform reflects the pervasive influence of business analogues, this willingness to settle for imitations inhibiting the breaking of new ground more appropriate to the distinctive terrain of public management (Metcalfe & Richards, 1990). Also, by giving 'customers' precedence despite so-called 'citizens' charters, an impoverished concept of rights is in danger of taking its place alongside an impoverished concept of management. In fact, increasing unease about problems on the real citizenship front, as well as the public accountability dilemmas posed by developments such as Next Steps, is imposing strains on the constitutional status quo. And whereas recent changes have aspired to make public agencies more like private corporations, improved government performance is critical precisely because of market limitations and the intrinsic importance of the public mission in promoting society's welfare (Cohen, 1988).

As for the future, much obviously depends on whether the ascendant business-consumerist paradigm of the 1980s continues to be the principal reference point in government circles. The extent to which a 'post-Thatcherite' agenda has emerged under Mr Major remains shrouded in some ambiguity, with signs of a more positive stance towards public services, but other developments pointing to even greater fiscal and market pressures. Nonetheless, despite continuing resistance to legally enforceable rights, whereas the 1980s were preoccupied with micro issues to do with how public services are managed, there are indications that the 1990s in contrast may eventually move on to the constitutional high ground of how we are governed, a prospect hardly diminished by the policy and political traumas so far characteristic of John Major's second administration.

Implementing the Next Steps: A Choreography of Management Change

ANDREW GRAY AND BILL JENKINS

When the Government announced in 1988 that it was to embark on a programme to transform the delivery of the vast majority of central government services by establishing departmental executive agencies (Efficiency Unit, 1988), it was received as the latest, no better, no worse, of a series of reforms attempted by the Conservative Government of the 1980s to remodel the management of the civil service. Five years later, in the autumn of 1993, there were 90 agencies and a further 63 units managed on agency principles in the Inland Revenue and Customs and Excise. In all, 350,000 officials had been embraced by the agency programme, with tens of thousands more in activities identified as potential agencies. When William Waldegrave, Chancellor of the Duchy of Lancaster and minister responsible for the newly formed Office of Public Service and Science, spoke in July 1992 to the Institute of Directors about the 'genuine revolution in Whitehall' and praised the project director, Sir Peter Kemp, for his management of this revolution, it was one of those rarer occasions when a minister was justified in his language (Waldegrave, 1992). The twist, however, came with his sacking of Kemp, two days later. It was a remarkable event in a remarkable implementation story.

Not surprisingly these reforms have attracted the attention of a variety of observers in the UK and overseas (Price Waterhouse, 1992; Optimum, 1991-92; Royal Institute of Public Administration, 1992), not to mention investigations by the Treasury and Civil Service Committee (1988, 1989, 1990, 1991, 1993) and the

National Audit Office (1992). All these enquiries have sought to assess the role on the Next Steps as an enabler, catalyst or stimulus in the wider programmes of change within the public sector. In central government, there have been implications for the way the centre relates to departments and departments relate to the management of their programmes. In fact, in the eyes of many, the very nature of the UK civil service is becoming more federated as there develops a network of semi-autonomous agencies around a central core (Davies & Willman, 1992; Treasury and Civil Service Committee, 1990-1, para. 415).

As a programme of change, therefore, the Next Steps initiative appears to have made a significant impact where previous efforts have faltered. Thus, it is worth asking whether the agency programme is different from previous approaches to the management of change in government, if so how, and what the experience suggests about the nature of implementation of management reform. The interest is thus less in the programme's macro-political effects, such as public accountability, as in what it tells us about the management of change in government, especially inter-organizational relationships (e.g. between the centre and departments) and intra-organizational relationships (e.g. within departments and agencies themselves).

This chapter seeks to examine these issues, first by placing the Next Steps programme in context, then briefly discussing some theoretical issues in organizational change and management, and describing specific aspects of the implementation of the Next Steps programme itself. The chapter concludes with an attempt to analyze and assess these developments.

Whitehall and the Management of Change

The track record of attempts to reform the structures and processes of UK central government since 1945 has been at best patchy. It can be argued that politicians have generally shown only a superficial interest in machinery of government problems (Pollitt, 1984), and the higher civil service has proved a serious obstacle to attempts at change (Kellner & Crowther-Hunt, 1980). Both arguments may have some validity, although the second is more difficult to determine. However, there have been persistent, if not consistent, attempts to reform the structures and processes of central government.

Some of these efforts owe their origins to outside thinkers, such as Fabians on the political left and, more recently, the Centre for Policy Studies and others of the New Right. Other pressures for change have come from within central government, initially from those who wished to develop a more rational approach to government and later from those who saw management as the key to administrative salvation (Hennessy, 1989). These efforts have rarely been orchestrated and have met with varying and variable degrees of success. They do, however, represent different approaches to the management of government that coincide closely with different periods of recent administrative history, in particular the periods 1960-79 and 1979-90.

We do not intend here to offer a detailed analysis of the attempts by the Plowden Committee to reform public expenditure planning, by the Fulton Committee to revamp the civil service, or by the Heath Government to rationalize it on business lines. It is worth remembering, however, that the 1960s and 1970s saw sustained (if disconnected) efforts to install a planning capacity into British central government (the Central Policy Review Staff) and raise the status and profile of management in general and personnel management in particular (Civil Service Department). To these can be added the search for efficiency and effectiveness through institutionalized policy analysis and evaluation (Programme Analysis and Review).

Within five to ten years most of these efforts had run into difficulties. Some continued but only by adopting a more modest role and by diluting the grander objectives that they had been created to serve. So why did this occur? One reason was undoubtedly that the political and economic environment changed. In economic turbulence, for example, control rather than planning becomes the political priority. Secondly, some argue that attempts to change the structure and processes of both the centre of Whitehall and the departments themselves were 'sabotaged' by powerful interest groups and a dominant traditionalist culture (e.g. Kellner & Crowther Hunt, 1980). Our own thesis, based on the experiences of PAR, is less conspiratorial; the reforms failed to meet the technical, organizational and political preconditions of engineering change in administrative structures (Gray & Jenkins, 1982). It may be that public management in the 1980s, including the Next Steps, learnt something of this lesson.

Writers, such as Pollitt (1990) and Hood (1991), demonstrate that it is far too simple to attribute the New Public Management to the arrival of Mrs Thatcher as Prime Minister. However, the political drive behind reform should not be minimized. There was more that just a rhetorical commitment to restrain public expenditure and, perhaps more tellingly, there was a clear policy to cut the numbers of public sector employees. This reflected a shift in the reforms of the 1980s both in their focus and style of implementation. This can be seen most notably in the Efficiency Strategy's programme of scrutinies and the Financial Management Initiative (FMI).

The reform designers of the early Thatcher years came from both within and outside government and included management consultants, political advisors, businessmen and senior civil servants. This was a diverse group, but it shared a view that previous reform efforts had been too ambitious, wrongly targeted and offered few incentives to make them stick. What was required was a focus on management in general and resource management in particular. This would devolve responsibility for the management of resources and install a sense of individual responsibility. This involved not only a set of new procedures, however, but also a change in civil service culture (Metcalfe and Richards, 1987; Hennessy, 1989).

To develop this new focus, a different implementation strategy was sought. Although previous efforts were top-down in conception and implementation, many thought they were poorly co-ordinated, suffered from a weak incentive to produce results (especially in the departments) and were insufficiently supported politically. Hence, the programme of efficiency scrutinies developed after 1979 was small scale, tightly focused and driven by a small committed team with high level political access. Its achievements can be judged as modest or significant (depending on one's perceptions), but the programme demonstrated that reform was sustainable and that attitude change was possible within traditional departmental cultures.

As we have noted elsewhere, the FMI was altogether a more broadly based programme than the efficiency strategy, having a departmental wide scope and focusing on improving financial management throughout the civil service (Gray & Jenkins et al., 1991). In implementation terms, its guidance and management at the centre of government followed at least something of the efficiency scrutiny model. For example, the management of the initiative was placed in the hands of a small central team, the Financial Management Unit (FMU), whose tasks included promoting what it saw as good practice in and across departments and protecting those in departments responsible for establishing the systems and making them work. As one official said to us, the unit was 'six against six thousand'. Yet, by a policy of active promotion, enforcing deadlines for submissions and leadership, it sought 'to counter internal opposition in Whitehall and to establish a legitimacy that would be difficult to oppose' (ibid, p. 48).

The FMI changed significantly the way various management levels in departments conceptualized their activities, especially the management of resources, as well as the practices of dealing with the Treasury and other parts of the centre. There can be little doubt also that, at least in terms of implementation, the FMI was more successful than any effort that preceded it. This can be attributed to the way those guiding it, both at the centre and within departments, paid conscious attention to a strategy for its implementation. In technical and organizational terms, departments made varying but generally significant efforts to identify and manage the implementation demands. Further, in terms of internal politics, many senior officials clearly committed themselves managerially at the same time as a strong political commitment to the reform emanated from Downing Street and filtered down to ministers and departments via the FMU and senior Treasury officials. This, of itself, was often enough to make even the laggards in departments keen to demonstrate progress.

As the agency programme was designed as the Next Steps for civil service management after the FMI, it is natural to ask whether the FMI was a model for implementation. Sadly the answer to this question is far from clear. There was not one but many FMIs, with variations reflecting the differentiated character of Whitehall (and its outposts), and the systems were narrowly targeted (principally on running costs) and offered only limited freedoms and rewards (Gray & Jenkins et al., 1991). Moreover, it is perhaps rather naive to assume that there is a universal model of change appropriate for public and private sectors or that success in the management of change is easily defined. These and other factors involved in the management of change merit closer consideration. This is the task of the next section.

Organizational Change: Myths and Problems

The management and organizational literature is full of references to success and failure in the management of change (e.g. Pettigrew & Whipp, 1991). In the last decade, this literature has taken a new twist as it has pursued the criteria of 'excellent' organizations. Invigorated by the work of Peters & Waterman (1982), this search was extended by writers such as Kanter (1990), while Peters himself has redefined his position and now seeks to promote different types of organizational forms (1989). In the meantime, much of the debate's vocabulary has passed into popular management mythology with much talk of 'bias for action', 'close to the customer', and 'loose-tight' systems of control.

The popular use (and frequently misuse) of Peters and Waterman's terminology by public sector managers and consultants reflects the search for panaceas of organizational success since the dawn of scientific management and classical management theory. This is a symptom both of an effort to simplify the study of organizational design and to reinforce assumptions, made particularly by the New Right, on the form and shape of management change required to enhance public sector performance (see Hood, 1991; Pollitt, 1990). At least three of the assumptions often made in this area require questioning:

a) public sector organizations are inherently inefficient and that the models to be emulated are those of successful private sector enterprises;
b) there are universal secrets to organizational success;
c) bureaucracies naturally resist innovation and implementation has to impose change driven by a strong authority.

The first of these points arises primarily from the claims of public choice economists and others that public sector organizations, especially bureaucracies, are by definition inefficient and ineffective. As a consequence, market or quasi-market models are often advocated as a mechanism for changing organizations. The difficulty with this analysis, aside from the general lack of evidence to sustain it as a universal truth (Dunleavy, 1991), is that it assumes that public sector organizations are homogeneous. It also misrepresents bureaucracy and bureaucratization which, in a classical Weberian sense may have a number of strengths such as efficient organizational control, well defined personnel systems and a focus on task achievement. Indeed, bureaucracy is to be found in both public and private sectors and in a variety of forms. Thus the myth of 'public is bad' and 'private is good' in organizational terms needs to be rejected and replaced by attention on what organizational form is efficient and effective in particular sets of circumstances.

The purpose of change is to achieve organizational success or to design the structure that will ensure an organization is successful. But what is success in organizational terms? The answer to this is not always clear, as was illustrated by the encounter of the well known industrial trouble shooter, John Harvey-Jones (formerly of ICI), and those who run the Morgan Car Company (Harvey-Jones, 1991, Ch. 4). For Harvey-Jones, Morgan Cars was an anachronism sustained by its reputation but constrained by a limited view of company success. It was long term failure. For Morgan's owners, their tradition was their strength, their client group well defined with values which coincided with the company. Thus the seven year order book! They saw a different reality and assessed it in different terms. For them, success was to stay as they were with only marginal adjustment. To change, for example, to more mass production, would jeopardize the values they wished to secure.

The point of the above story (now much used a management training case study) is to caution against easy retreat to universalisms. What is a successful organization or not depends on what value systems are applied to it. It can also be argued strongly that not only may these differ from one situation to another but that they certainly often differ across the public - private sector divide (Stewart & Ranson, 1988). Thus, prescriptions for change, strategies for their implementation, and their assessment need careful consideration.

This argument clearly applies equally to the assumption that those who work within public bureaucracies are resistant to change and lacking in any innovative capacity. There may be no dispute that some organizations can change (or can cope with change) more rapidly than others, yet the cause may lie less in an inherent resistance to change as a failure by implementers to appreciate that different conditions require different change strategies.

The difficulty with change and reform is that it is often initiated by ideologues who not only know what is wrong and what is right but also that the only way to make others see the light is to impose change as quickly as possible using a strong authoritarian structure. Such a mission is frequently driven by a zeal to convert the unbelievers or put them to the sword. To question the assumptions or the message itself is a sign of weakness. This is the implementation strategy of command.

Others, however, argue that effective organizational change requires a more analytical and conditional model that takes account of the differing tasks of organizations and the circumstances in which they operate. Business historians, such as Chandler (1962), and other observers of organizations, such as Mintzberg (1979, 1983) and Williamson (1975), illustrate the variety of organizational structures that may be successful in differing circumstances and the capacity of such structures to embrace change. Thus, the transition from policy as formulated to policy as implemented demands the identification of the conditions for perfect implementation and their explicit management (Hood, 1976, Hogwood & Gunn, 1984). The implication of this approach is that implementation requires a systematic and rational analysis of implementation conditions with an explicit strategy to alter individual and group inducement-contribution ratios in favour of change.

A third approach to the implementation of change takes this line of thinking a stage further by holding that it is the complexity of joint action (Pressman & Wildavsky, 1973) which renders implementation so difficult and that this interactive nature has to be recognized and exploited to work in the direction of change. This was pointed out by Burns (1966), who argued that individuals in organizations frequently have a variety of sub-goals related separately to the organization itself, to the internal political system of the organization and to the career system of which they are a part. If such systems are not in harmony (N.B., not necessarily identical) then action to maximize one may well jeopardize success elsewhere. In some circumstances, therefore, resistance to change is logical and rational. If this analysis is accurate, those who seek to design organizational change should seek to reconcile organizational goals, internal political systems and career systems.

This requires providing a climate in which managers and others come to think logically that the way to pursue their own managerial success is to think in terms of innovation and experiment. For some, this can lead to a logical incremental strategy for change (e.g. see Quinn, 1980) in which consistent innovation emerges from a climate in which a coherent but generalized mission is facilitated through differentiated responses to local conditions. The emphasis is on experiment and adjustment, keeping change feasible and manageable. Thus the directive for implementing change is to recognize in the implementation strategy the significance of leadership, mission, culture and internal structures of incentives and motivation in relation to both individual and group goals.

None of this assumes the inferiority of particular structures (e.g. bureaucracies) and the superiority of others (e.g. markets) in all circumstances and for all tasks (Rose, 1985). Rather, it seeks to place activities in context and to assess the arrangements for achieving objectives under systems of constraint. It also seeks to assess what mechanisms are suitable or otherwise for achieving and sustaining change and hence to recognising the importance of 'enabling', 'facilitating', and 'encouraging', rather than 'imposing'. Organizational change is not a simple subject and to treat it so is a serious mistake. As the next section demonstrates, those who managed the Next Steps appear instinctively at least to have learnt something of all this.

Implementing the Next Steps

Improving the Management of Government: the Next Steps was published in 1988. For Davies and Willman, the specification for the project manager was 'awesome', i.e., 'to make certain that obstacles to change are removed and that the totality of the centre is helpful to the management of change' (1991, p. 13). Nevertheless, despite the lack of detail on how this task was to be achieved, progress has been rapid and wide ranging. This section will examine more closely three aspects of this: first the inter-organizational changes involving the centre and departments leading up to agency creation, second the intra-organizational changes relating to departments and agencies themselves, and third the possible limits to these changes.

Inter-Organizational Change: The Centre, Departments and Agencies

Fundamental to the development of Next Steps has been the designation of agencies and elaboration of frameworks for them to work within. At the centre, the major players in these processes have been the Next Steps Project Team (headed until July 1992 by the Project manager, Peter Kemp), the Treasury (in several different guises) and individuals in the Cabinet Office including the Cabinet Secretary, Sir Robin Butler.

As was noted above, the Next Steps Report argued for the programme to be steered by an independent unit with both political and administrative clout. For the Government the Project Team's task was 'to promote a management environment in which Next Steps can flourish' (Prime Minister, 1991a, p. 3). This gave it not only a clear role in relation to the creation of agencies and managing the process of change but also in sustaining the momentum of the reform and preventing inertia and back sliding. This has been expressed by the Project Manager as throwing grit into the civil service machine or taking a Socratic stance that forces departments to justify their activities. 'If we are to achieve permanent change we must question, question, question what we are doing and continually seek for ways of improving it' (Kemp, 1990, p. 31).

For all at the centre the major task therefore has been to select, launch and sustain individual agencies while developing and maintaining the momentum of the total programme. Looking back, a Treasury spokesman has described the initial three year period of the Initiative as a phase of 'positioning', i.e., setting up agencies, clarifying roles and objectives and developing delegated pay and personnel systems. This will now be followed by a performance phase: assessing what actually happens (Treasury and Civil Service Committee, 1991, p.57).

It is clear that two issues have been central to the first phase: the actual inter-organizational relationships developed between the centre and specific departments and a broader marketing exercise where the centre has sought to promote the initiative. While this discussion concentrates on the first of these issues the second cannot be ignored. Unlike any previous initiative, the benefits and the political neutrality of the Next Steps have been sold to journalists and academics, as well as politicians and civil servants, by a variety of means. The success of this tactic can be gauged from the broadly favourable reception given to it by such bodies such as the Treasury and Civil Service Committee (1991 - 'a piece of transferable technology') and even spokesmen for the Opposition (Smith, 1991).

Negotiations with departments over agency designation and frameworks have not always been smooth. As with the FMI, departments have taken different stances, ranging from the enthusiasts and the converted through the sceptics to those who were covertly hostile to change. Some departments, already organized on federal lines (e.g. Employment), have found little difficulty in adapting to agency status. Others have welcomed the initiative as taking them down a road that powerful interest groups within departments have wished to move (e.g. Social Security in the aftermath of the Moodie report). Further, at the level of individual candidates, some were already almost in agency form (e.g. Her Majesty's Stationary Office as a Trading Fund) or moving in that direction (e.g. the Vehicle Inspectorate).

If this observation suggests that the speed of implementation has been conditioned by the self-interests of the departments and organizations involved and their calculation of advantages and disadvantages relating to agency status, it should not be surprising. The pattern follows closely that predicted by classical studies of innovation diffusion where the take-up is led by a small number with the greatest self-interest (and the least internal opposition), to be followed by a larger number where the advantage is less clear cut and leaving behind a small number of laggards (the classical 'S' curve noted by Rogers (1983)). Yet, if this is the case it is also worth noting Rogers' later findings relating specifically to innovation diffusion in public sector organizations. In this he draws attention to how innovations are shaped by those who adopt them. Hence, organizations are not simply passive recipients of new ideas introduced from external sources but 'are active shapers of innovations as they are adapted and modified *to fit an organization's circumstances*' (Rogers & Kim, 1985, p. 105, emphasis added).

If the implementation of the Next Steps has, therefore, been crucially dependent on the perceived interests of departments and potential agencies, this should not detract from the force and impetus of the Next Steps team as change-agent. Yet, it is a matter of debate whether its own interests have always been in accord with those of the rest of the centre as represented by the Treasury. In public the Treasury and the Project Manager have presented a united front. However, as Davies and Willman point out rather sharply, this hides potential and serious differences of interest:

> The fundamental paradox of Next Steps is that it seeks to develop an enterprise culture in the public services, and to focus on outputs and the delivery of services within the input dominated, cash limited public expenditure system. This problem was familiar to managers in the nationalized industries ... In the context of its over-riding concern to keep public expenditure down the Treasury has an interest in withholding from Agency managers the independence and delegated authority that Next Steps aims to give them (1991, p. 43).

Treasury spokesmen would no doubt see this as conspiracy theory run riot. While never denying their commitment to public expenditure policy, they would point out the freedoms that departments have in financial matters if they would only take advantage of them (HM Treasury, 1991a), the promotion of trading fund status for agencies who merit it (Treasury and Civil Service Committee, 1991, Appendix 10), and a willingness to negotiate financial and personnel freedoms within tough systems of targets. In reply, critics would emphasize the restricted nature of what has occurred to date, together with the paucity of quality (or non-financial) targets in the frameworks negotiated (Treasury and Civil Service Committee, 1991, pp. 59-60), a deficiency acknowledged by the former project manager who committed himself to press for more 'proper, robust, non-financial targets' (Treasury and Civil Service Committee, 1991, p.110).

To some extent, then, the progress of Next Steps has taken advantage of a prevailing wind of change blowing through the civil service. It is thus a matter of debate how many changes would have taken place even if Next Steps did not exist. However, the initiative has also been carried forward by the strong political drive that characterized previous initiatives and has built on changes they have promoted (e.g. by the FMI in Customs and Excise). This suggests that the Project Team and others have learnt some of the lessons of change management.

Intra-Organizational Change

The Efficiency Unit's report, *Making the Most of Next Steps* (1991), also known as the Fraser Report, took a hard look at departmental-agency relationships. It concluded that, although there was much to be praised, there was serious room for improvement if the Next Steps ideals were to be realized. Hence, there were recommendations for the development of a 'shared vision' of what an agency is for and a more hands-off regime to be practised both by sponsoring departments and by the centre (especially the Treasury) to allow further progress in delegating freedoms. The Government's response was favourable although the economic constraints were, as ever, re-emphasized: 'The Government believes that Agencies' delegations and flexibilities can be enlarged as their track record of performance is established, provided that essential controls on public expenditure are not jeopardized' (Prime Minister, 1991a, p. 5).

Whether Fraser's analysis is correct (and it is not hard to discredit it (Treasury and Civil Service Committee, 1991, pp. 48-51)), it is useful in pointing out that the implementation of Next Steps has been strongly influenced by departmental interests. The report also emphasizes importantly that, not only do departments differ, but also organization differs within departments. These perhaps obvious points are of crucial importance in identifying different patterns of department - agency relationship and, perhaps *ipso facto*, of helping to explain the rate and nature of implementation.

Throughout, the Project Managers (Kemp was replaced by Richard Mottram in July 1992) have emphasized that the civil service is a heterogeneous rather than a homogenous entity. Thus, there is no single agency model. Rather, Next Steps is a scheme for the better management of government that seeks to promote tangible improvements and benefits for taxpayers, staff and customers. This can be achieved through an organizational system that may have common elements across agencies but also has significant differences in each particular case. As a consequence, agencies are not fixed but represent negotiated arrangements in which the specific interests of the centre, the department and the activity (and those who operate it) contribute to the organizational design. Further, this design is open to re-negotiation as circumstances demand or at least in the triennial reviews.

The question of 'what is an agency' is therefore not always easy to answer (Davies & Willman, 1991; Flynn et al., 1990). What is clearer is that there are types of agency and that these reflect different patterns of relationships with departments both prior to agency creation and after agency launch. The Fraser Report (Efficiency Unit, 1991, Appendix A) identified four such types:

a) those fundamental to mainstream policy (e.g. the Employment Service, the Social Security Benefits Agency);

b) those exercising statutory (usually) regulatory functions (Companies House, the Vehicle Inspectorate);

c) those providing services to departments (or other agencies) (Government Research Establishments);

d) agencies not linked to any of the main objectives of the department (HMSO, Historic Royal Palaces).

The logic of this typology is of less interest than the issues that flow from it, particularly the political and financial salience of agencies with regard to departmental and ministerial interests and the extent to which agency tasks can in practice be isolated from other departmental activities. Such factors affect both the selection (and non selection) of agency candidates and the regime of controls that departments seek to develop. Moreover, the development of agencies transforms a department into a more federated structure. How far this coincides with how the department (and its ministers) see its objectives is therefore an important issue. In the words of business historian Alfred Chandler (1962), 'strategy' comes before 'structure', and to a great extent the creation of agencies will (or perhaps should) be driven by political and administrative strategy. Thus, if agencies are (as their advocates often stress) not an end in themselves but a means to an end, a major question to be addressed is what ends they are intended to serve. In this way the selection of agencies indirectly questions the function of departments (and their ministers) and their relationships with the centre, and their creation shapes the machinery of government itself. As such, it is far from a neutral piece of technology, especially in areas where policy and administration are not easily separable.

However, what of agencies themselves? How far will they carry the philosophy of Next Steps forward? Is agency status itself a guarantee that the programme of change will be continued? Studies by the NAO (National Audit Office, 1992) and by Mellon (1991) on five of the early agencies indicate that the value of Next Steps may be primarily as a catalyst for changes already underway, acting as a focal point for concentrating management interest and energies. Mellon's work also suggests that success in achieving targets, empowering staff and relating more closely to customers varies between agencies. This is attributed to leadership styles of chief executives, to policies regarding delegation, and to efforts to relate to customers and clients. Here Companies House is held out as a model while others (unnamed) are found wanting. The conclusion is that structural change of itself is not enough. Rather, the successful implementation of Next Steps needs management and organizational development which focuses on motivation and other human relations issues.

The Limits to Change

Are there limits to the implementation of change? Commenting on the successes and difficulties of the Vehicle Inspectorate in its first few years as an executive agency, the NAO noted that '*without policy changes* the scope for radical improvements will become exhausted and management may find further gains more difficult' (National Audit Office, 1992, p.5, emphasis added). Although this observation relates to a set of issues specific to the Vehicle Inspectorate (e.g. its capacity to act in a commercial way and expand its business), the wider point on political constraints is important. It emerges forcefully in the discussions of the Treasury and Civil Service Committee on the indicators of the Social Security Benefits Agency. In its investigations, the Committee asked agency officials why the take-up of benefits was not an agency target. When pressed on this, the chief executive replied that targets were not a matter for him but for the Secretary of State (Treasury and Civil Service Committee, 1991, pp. 32-4). This position was later confirmed by the Project Manager:

> At the end of the day these Chief Executives are operating under discipline and they actually have the choice of doing one of two things. They can buckle down and do what the Minister has asked them to do; or they can resign (Treasury and Civil Service Committee, 1991, p.106).

In constitutional terms there can be little quarrel with the Project Manager's reply. Agencies are part of departments and chief executives are answerable to ministers. Targets are a ministerial responsibility in the light of advice given by the chief executive (Prime Minister, 1991a, p. 9). However, there is also a tension between policy and administration and a problem of conflicting goals, delegated responsibilities and accountabilities within a political framework. The same point also clearly applies to the Vehicle Inspectorate: on the one hand urged to act innovatively, effectively and quasi-independently and on the other prevented for policy reasons from offering services available in the private sector (National Audit Office, 1992, p. 4).

As a consequence, change in the Next Steps appears to be limited as a result of conflicting goals. While there can be little doubt of the importance of macro-economic criteria in establishing financial regimes and targets, and of the political importance of many issues that impinge on agencies, these frequently constrain the management systems that can be developed and applied. This, in turn, affects a number of crucial issues such as the definition and measurement of quality (agency effectiveness), the relations developed with client groups and the internal incentives.

One of the changes clearly in train, however, is a federated system of political and departmental management. Whether a strength or a weakness, the 'F' word is rejected in the wider reaches of government for its loss of sovereignty, financial control and even ability to keep the unwashed from crossing the borders, while (ironically) it is being championed in Whitehall as a means to facilitate a new world of public service delivery. It undoubtedly has the potential to do this but, like all federal models, its implementation requires a redistribution of power and resources not only at the departmental level and between departments and the centre, but at the political level as well. This is an issue recognized by Davies and Willman who, with an eye on developments in New Zealand, call for a legislative framework to define the scope of framework documents, i.e., to give a legislative basis to the devolution and hence to strengthen agency powers and accountability (1991, pp. 65-75).

Commenting on the development of Next Steps, Sir Angus Fraser told the Treasury and Civil Service Committee that there was a need to change the environment in which agencies operated from a 'restrictive' to an 'enabling' one (Treasury and Civil Service Committee, 1991). In terms of implementation it is clearly crucial to identify what the latter means and to harmonize systems (strategic, financial, human resources) accordingly. In all this the key term is strategic. In many ways Next Steps may have been a success so far exactly because it has avoided areas of strategy and side-stepped difficult and potentially damaging issues. Whether this is also a weakness is a question that will be dealt with in the conclusion.

Conclusion

In evidence given to the Treasury and Civil Service Committee in 1991 a Treasury representative described the Next Steps as 'a progressive programme of change' and stressed the need to adapt to new issues as they came along. In reply the Chairman of the Sub-Committee, Giles Radice retorted that this strategy seemed to be 'English pragmatism gone mad' (Treasury and Civil Service Committee, 1991, pp. 57-8). His comment may be unfair. In terms of the implementation of change, one of the strengths of those directing the Next Steps may be that they have pursued an incremental strategy 'preferring to get successive batches of agencies up and running and dealing with problems progressively as they arise rather than formulating a blueprint organization which all government functions would be tailored to fit' (Davies and Willman, 1991, pp. 13-14).

That this is an appropriate strategy for change appears confirmed by work on the FMI. Tomkins and Colville, for example, argue in their work on Customs and Excise, that success comes when a department moves incrementally away from the 'safe pair of hands' approach and keeps risks within acceptable bounds at each stage. Incremental improvement can thus accumulate marked change while all-in-one approaches are likely to result both in 'successive unease by those affected and in confrontation preventing change' (1989, p. 19). Similarly, Bryman (1989) argues for the adoption of an iterative approach to change that may have special applicability to the public sector. This is linked to a model of leadership based on continual experimentation and feedback, task fragmentation and an approach that avoids pushing people into a stampede for change. However, if risk taking and enhanced performance are to be installed, new sources of status and rewards may be required backed up by new incentive systems.

Our own work on the FMI confirms much of the above both with regard to the style and approach of change agents in Whitehall and to the frameworks necessary to sustain change. First and foremost, top-level support at both the political and administrative level is required, less to back up a regime of threats as to develop a system of incentives where rewards can be made clear and opportunities offered. In particular, links must be established between efforts exerted and results, not simply in terms of pay but also in terms of the goals that organizational members seek to achieve. Identity is especially important for staff motivation.

Yet, as with the FMI, motivation and identity can cause problems. The thrust of decentralized management systems, if carried to their logical conclusions, should 'empower' not only managers but also staff in the true sense of the word. As Hambleton (1988, 1992) has noted, decentralization (like participation) can range in meaning from the symbolic to the substantive in terms of freedoms and discretion granted to organizational members and their involvement in target setting and decision making. Hence, while the theory of decentralized management does not yield all control from above, it does encourage the ownership of problems and significant trade-offs of freedoms. If this promotes quality and consumer satisfaction then serious control difficulties can arise.

In the case of the FMI, for example, a common problem for middle level managers was that they saw few results for their efforts. Similarly, Tomkins and Colville found that in Customs & Excise the FMI was often viewed as part of efforts to exert greater central control and consequently judged as more 'evaluative than enabling' (1989, p. 16). With regard to Next Steps there are indications that similar tensions may be in evidence both in terms of limits to empowerment and of subsequent staff motivation (Mellon, 1991).

As noted above, the limits to implementing Next Steps may lie with the underlying conflict between a political model of public sector organizations and a market driven consumer model devoted to hands-off management with a real rather than a symbolic commitment to empowerment. Further, if such a decentralized model is to be effective, then it needs to be diffused throughout the organization rather than be isolated at the top (Tomkins & Colville, 1989; Mellon, 1991). Moreover, if organizations are to respond successfully to change, the systems of strategic management need to be harmonized with internal politics and career development. This is difficult enough in private sector organizations making well defined products in a non-turbulent market (Burns, 1966). However, as Tyson has pointed out, the civil service is attempting to develop managers in diverse organizational cultures to achieve different objectives:

Most of these objectives are political and change as priorities change. An ideology of managerialism based on efficiency is not enough in motivational terms. There must also be a commitment to the public good, because unless there is a moral purpose to public policy it has no intrinsic worth (Tyson, 1990, p. 30).

Such a moral purpose may be provided of course in the Citizen's Charter (Office of Public Service and Science, 1991). This identifies agencies (all of which will have been established by April 1995) as valuable vehicles for achieving many of the improvements to public services set out in the Charter. This is recognized by the Next Steps Unit (Prime Minister, 1991a, p. 1). As such, in addition to the traditional use of 'command' and the more recently developed 'contract', the Government may be adding 'communion', i.e., shared public service values, as an instrument of implementation.

Indeed, the Next Steps does confirm that implementation is interactive and provides its own issues (separate from the underlying policy) which have to be recognized and managed. The success of its implementation can be attributed to a form of logical incrementalism, in which a clear but generalized mission has been promulgated by a coherent leadership unit (the Project Team) and developed by differentiated arrangements designed to accommodate local environments and managements. If there has not yet been enough recognition (or is it Treasury nerve?) of the need to create climates in which innovations will follow inherently from genuine managerial freedoms in pursuing targets (rather than from imposed regimes such as market testing), this reflects the continuing adherence by some of the 'command' type of implementation strategy and a remaining constraint on its progress.

An old Taoist story describes how the philosopher, K'ung Fu-tse, was walking towards a waterfall when, although still some way off, he saw an old man in danger of drowning in the violent and turbulent waters. However, by the time he and his followers had reached the water's edge, the old man had climbed out and was sitting on the bank. Not surprisingly, the philosopher expressed surprise at the escape. 'Ah', said the man, 'I have learnt not to fight the forces: I go down with the water and I come up with the water, avoiding the forces that are against me and using those that are with me. By those means I live on.' Certainly, the waters of civil service management change are turbulent. If the Next Steps have achieved a measure of implementation success, it may be due to an ability to work with forces consistent with their mission, and at least to avoid the hostile forces that dragged earlier reforms down. Yet, at least in the sense that implementation may also have to create climates in which these favourable forces can hold sway, much remains to be learnt.

PART TWO
AGENCIES IN ACTION

Managing Strategic Resources in a Next Steps Department: Information Agendas and Information Systems in the DSS

CHRISTINE BELLAMY

A common - but relatively unnoticed - dimension of recent initiatives to improve management in government is that they amount to a new information agenda for public administration. None can be successfully or fully delivered without new kinds of information and new information flows. For example, the Next Steps project, Citizen's Charter and market testing all assume that technologies and methodologies are, or can quickly be put in place, to capture and process information about managers' performance. The creation of new kinds of relationships - between agencies and customers, between agencies and ministers, between purchasers and providers, and between contractors - are all predicated on new ways of defining, measuring, recording and accounting for transactions which have acquired new patterns and new significance. Similarly, the increasing emphasis on customer satisfaction is stimulating new ways of exploiting information technology to deliver public services. This chapter explores the issues involved in developing and managing new kinds of information systems (IS) in a large government department, the Department of Social Security. The focus is on institutional changes associated with Next Steps, and the information agendas implied by them. Compared to many departments, DSS is highly 'informatized'. Since the early 1980s it has invested massively in new technology, and has in consequence become heavily dependent on information and communication technology (ICT). It is also one of the most thoroughly 'agencified' departments.

Over ninety-seven percent of DSS staff work, or will soon work, in Next Steps agencies. Nevertheless, even in DSS, IS to support management reform is underdeveloped compared with other uses of IS. A central theme of this chapter is that the development of IS to support management reform is hindered by lack of clarity about the institutional forms which are being established. Computerization is intolerant of ambiguity, but Next Steps is inherently ambiguous. The specification of new, comprehensive, technologically-based IS exposes the conflict between the demands of external accountabilities and financial regimes (which reflect the integrity of a government department) and the logic of management reforms (which increasingly fragment departments and subject agencies to internal and external markets). That is, there is a tension between the extent to which a government department should be regarded as a holism, and the extent to which agencies should be regarded as free standing business units. IS points up this tension because its development requires agreed conceptualizations of the basis on which the parts of an organization relate and transact. It follows that a focus on information issues is helpful to the study of Next Steps in two ways. First, information systems are a resource of increasingly important strategic significance. Moreover, in DSS they are a resource in which all business units (that is core department and agencies) have a major stake. IS in DSS provides, therefore, a revealing case study of the issues involved in managing strategic, department-wide resources in a thoroughly agencified department. But, secondly and more importantly, the design of IS exposes the issues attached to the development of new institutional forms and business regimes in government. This will become clearer if the impact of Next Steps and informatization on DSS is outlined.

Next Steps in DSS

DSS is undergoing a particularly thoroughgoing process of agencyification, taking the project, as Peter Kemp said, to the very 'heartlands' of the civil service (Treasury and Civil Service Committee, 1989, Q4). With the creation of the Child Support Agency in April 1993, over 97% of civil servants in DSS now work in executive agencies. The structure of the 'DSS Group' is shown in Figure 1.

In addition to the five agencies listed in this table, it is envisaged that a War Pensions Agency will be created. The War Pensions Unit currently spends about 1% of the administration budget. The total manpower employed by DSS is planned in 1993-4 to be 98,268 person years (DSS & HM Treasury, 1993).

The 'core' department of DSS is organized into three groups: Policy; Resource Management and Planning (which includes the Finance and Corporate Management Divisions); and Legal Services. Their functions are to support ministers, to support the corporate management of the Group as a whole, and to provide specialist services (particularly legal and analytic/research services).

DSS agencies have been created according to no consistent principle. ITSA is a 'common service' organization; Contributions Agency (paying-in) and Benefits Agency (paying-out) are functional organizations, and the newest agencies, Child Support and War Pensions, are organized by the client group principle.

All DSS agencies are 'on-vote' agencies. The whole of DSS budget is negotiated by the core department through the public expenditure survey (PES) process: agency budgets are delegated from the core department. DSS departmental votes and the National Insurance Fund remain unitary funds for which the Permanent Secretary as Departmental Accounting Officer remains ultimately responsible. The designation of agencies as separate 'businesses' is, therefore, a matter of internal administrative arrangement: Next Steps carries no implications that the statutory or financial basis of social security has been formally disaggregated. In 1993-4, departmental administration costs are planned to be £4,197m and are now arranged in sub-heads by agency (DSS & H. M. Treasury, 1993). Departmental programme costs of £66,400m are not apportioned by agency but by benefit or policy programme.

Agency	date of establishment	% of DSS staff (planned totals 93-4)	% admin costs (planned totals 93-4)
Resettlement Agency	1989	0.6	1
ITSA	1990	5.0	14
Benefits Agency	1991	78.1	53
Contributions Agency	1991	10.7	5
Child Support Agency	1993	2.7	3
Core department		1.6	3
Corporate expenditure			19

Figure 1 (derived from DSS & HM Treasury, 1993)

IT and IS in DSS

DSS employs IT for a wide range of purposes. A central problem in developing IS for management is that there have been, and will continue to be, enormous competing demands for IS to be developed for operational purposes. In an environment where resources are constrained, this crowds out the development of management information systems (MIS).

Since the early 1980s, the major IS effort in DSS has been devoted to the Operational Strategy (Bellamy & Henderson, 1992; Dyerson & Roper, 1991a,

1991b; Margetts, 1991; Margetts & Willcocks, 1992). The Strategy was developed to modernize and to increase the efficiency of benefits administration, by means of a national network connecting all DSS local offices, DSS central offices and (eventually) employment offices to massive mainframe computing power. It provides on-line processing and automatic payment of claims for Income Support, Retirement and Widows Pensions, Family Credit, Social Fund, the new Disability Working and Living Allowances and Unemployment Benefit. In addition, the Operational Strategy network provides access to the Departmental Central Index, which is a national index to the computerized records of every person in the social security system.

Operational Strategy systems will continue to require further development, probably for the rest of the century. The Strategy is crucial to administering social security in the post Next Steps civil service. It supports the achievement of more rigorous efficiency targets. In 1991-2, some £124m of the £196m efficiency savings achieved by Benefits Agency were attributed to the Operational Strategy (DSS & H. M. Treasury, 1993, p. 29). It also supports more ambitious accuracy and clearance rate targets. More importantly, however, the Strategy also offers radical options for service delivery improvements, and is seen to be essential for developing a more customer-oriented social security administration. For example, it permits a 'footloose' approach to organizing local offices, because for the first time front-office functions can be relocated away from back-office processing. Thus it is possible to provide accessible and user-friendly offices in high streets or shopping malls. ICTs also permit the lateral integration of customer accounts, which are currently held in separate benefits systems. This could make possible 'one stop shopping' for social security, whereby a single telephone call or visit to a caller office would open the gateway to the whole of the social security system. One ramification of this might well be the provision of specialist services or outlets for different client groups, the long term sick, the elderly or single parents (Benefits Agency, 1992a). Another might be the reorientation of social security administration from benefits processing towards advice giving, supported by the use of smart machines for self assessment.

For options such as these to be fully developed, DSS will, however, require not only massive investment in systems, but also cross-agency co-operation. Operational Strategy was developed pre-Next Steps for a unitary department. In consequence, five agencies have direct stakeholdings in Strategy systems or DCI: Benefits Agency, CSA, War Pensions and Contributions, as users, and ITSA as the supplier. But post-Next Steps, agencies have divergent priorities, and they also have competing requirements for non-Strategy IS. For example, Contributions Agency badly needs a replacement for the ageing and fragile national insurance records system, NIRS. Contributions and Child Support Agencies (which are in effect debt collection agencies) need to develop appropriate financial control systems. That is, it is in the context of growing demands for IS, stimulated by the new emphasis on service delivery, that the management information systems needed to support Next Steps are being developed. To this extent there is a trade-off between these two aspects of Next Steps.

MIS go back a long way in DSS. The present financial information system has its origin in the early 1970s, in Management by Objectives, and in the Central Accounting System (CAS) established in 1979 (Matthews, 1979). Together, they established the principle of financial contracts between tiers of management. The FMI stimulated further development of CAS, and cost centres were established in 1983-4. By the mid 1980s DSS had in place many important building blocks for a devolved financial regime. Nevertheless, the development of MIS has been difficult, for reasons that have yet to be fully resolved. MIS has not only been obliged to compete for development resources against operational demands for IS, but it has also suffered from the turbulence created by successive change programmes in government. Moreover, the creation under the Next Steps project of separate 'businesses' focuses the attention of agency managements on their own needs, their own performance criteria, and their own time horizons. The very process of agencyification creates competing requirements for management information. The history of MIS in DSS is a classic example of organizational structures defining interests.

Following the Treasury-led multi-departmental review of budgeting in 1986 (HM Treasury, 1986), DSS commissioned a feasibility study for a resource management system to control administrative costs. The result was ARMS: the Administrative and Resource Management System. A number of factors intervened, however, in its development. First, there were technical problems. ARMS was a new venture for ITSA, whose experience lay in high volume operational and payroll systems. A pilot version developed by ITSA was not a success, and the work is now contracted out to consultants. Secondly, Next Steps changed the planning environment by fragmenting the user constituency, and by causing Treasury financial and accounting rules to be respecified (HM Treasury, 1989a; 1989b). User requirements therefore moved on, and the specifications of ARMS were superseded. Eventually, the changing business environment in DSS, particularly the growing emphasis on performance measurement, led to the view that personnel, finance and resource management systems should be integrated. The result, in April 1991, was the establishment of a new project in BA's Finance Directorate, to be known as FAMIS: Financial and Management Information System. The long term aim of FAMIS was to develop a resource management information system to meet the needs of top management, core department and agencies, by integrating information on finance, staffing complements, workloads and performance for management at all levels down to district offices. No less. FAMIS inherited from ARMS the assumption that it would be a department-wide system. It would require a formal decision at top management level to reverse this assumption. All the signals are that DSS top management wants to emphasize the corporate unity of DSS group (for example, DSS & H. M. Treasury, 1993, p. 24). As we have noted, the social security system has a financial unity, of which core department is the guardian. Furthermore, if the agency structure is to be mutable in future, the department needs flexibility and connectivity in MIS across agency boundaries. This has implications not only for the technical design of the electronic network, but it also requires congruity throughout DSS in the data which will be carried on it. The political point is that this implies a limit on agencies' freedom to customize information and information systems. This is easy to specify, but less easy to achieve. Hence, the pace of change, the priorities for systems development and the scope of the FAMIS project are all at issue within DSS.

A resource management system necessarily serves a number of functional stakeholders. In DSS they include customers for departmental statistics for policy-making; for top management information; for staff complementing data; for business planning data; for PES bidding data; for financial accounting data; and for data to support field management in local offices. This plurality is compounded by the creation of six agencies, each with their own priorities. For example, Benefits Agency needs to move quickly to develop its resource management processes, to support devolved management. BA is massively larger than the rest of DSS, including core department, put together. The *Agency Study* report of 1989 outlined the advantages of Next Steps for DSS, and considered whether a larger number of smaller agencies should be created (DSS, 1989). But analysis yielded no clear principle by which the administration of benefits could be subdivided - hence the creation of Benefits Agency with over 60,000 staff. Nevertheless, the wisdom of establishing such a monolithic agency has been questioned (Treasury and Civil Service Committee, 1989).

BA accepts, therefore, that the rebuilding of the old DSS in another name must be avoided by an overt change of management culture, and has invested considerable top management time in a programme of change (Benefits Agency, 1992b, p. 19). An important strand of the change programme is the substantial devolution of management freedom and budgetary responsibility to the district office level. The agency is, therefore, developing a bottom-up business planning process which links the management of resources to the PES process. Managements at all levels are required to establish a contract for the level of service to be delivered against specified resources. The whole process depends, however, on timely, accurate, management information on performance and resources being available right down the management line. This remains problematic without comprehensive, sensitive, reliable data, which DSS has failed so far to provide.

BA has, therefore, a particularly urgent need to develop automatically-generated on-line performance data. At the outset of planning the Operation Strategy, it was intended that the computerization of social security transactions would yield important operational data, providing management with timely, reliable statistics on, for example, clearance rates and error rates throughout the country. However, this facility was jettisoned because there were problems in meeting the deadline for roll-out and thus in achieving the promised staff savings. Thus, efficiency and operational objectives crowded out the exploitation of the systems for managerial or policy purposes. Therefore management data has continued to be captured manually in local offices. The data which has been gathered is that which interrupts benefits processing least: there is a trade off between maximising the value of data and the diversion from operations of the resources necessary to produce it. DSS statistics have been crude, because the department has found it impossible to justify the manpower, the time and the intrusion into local office administration required by more sophisticated demands. In consequence DSS statistical data has been rudimentary and of questionable accuracy. A statistical facility is being added to the Strategy systems so that performance data can be generated automatically. Only then will it be possible to improve the methodology of service quality assessment, and refine the quality and utility of the agency's targets.

Despite its informational shortfall, BA has, however, a legacy of accounting, complementing and performance methodology on which to build: it understands its needs. In contrast, the newer agencies are developing their business from a standing start, and core department is coming to grips with its own new role. These parts of DSS may, therefore, need longer to develop a clear view of their information requirements. ITSA, in contrast, has well-established responses to its business pressures. For example, in contrast to BA, which has to account for a large number of small revenue transactions, ITSA manages a relatively small number of large scale, capital intensive systems and projects. Over 80% of its budget is subcontracted, and of all DSS agencies it is most open to the threat of external competition. Its management has, therefore, clearly perceived the need for its accounts to be placed on a commercial basis: this includes the establishment of an accurate assets register, accurate costings of its business activities and accruals accounting (ITSA, 1993, p. 20). Assessed against current Treasury guidelines for Next Steps agencies, ITSA has been the 'only boy in the band in step', and is, understandably, reluctant to adjust its pace to the other agencies.

To compound conflicts between agencies about MIS, messages coming from the top of DSS and from the Treasury have been ambiguous, because there are tensions between the demands of external accountabilities and those of new management doctrines. For example, whilst Treasury formally prescribes accruals accounting (1989a; 1989b), its expenditure divisions, backed up by core department Finance Division, have been less than happy about departing from cash based accounts which were easily reconciled with Parliamentary votes. Treasury and Finance Division have similar doubts about introducing hardcharging between agencies, because they fear that it also undermines the integrity of the departmental vote. These are not simply technical issues about accounting conventions: they reveal fundamental tensions about the institutional regime which should be established within departments, post-Next Steps.

It may be that the demands of market testing will bring the accounting requirements of the other agencies swiftly into line with ITSA, and force the hand of FD. They may also force Treasury to be less ambivalent and hesitant about the transition to financial regimes that are more congruent with a competitive business environment. But for the present, conflicts about FAMIS reflect an uneven vision of the logic of Next Steps.

Managing a Cross-Agency Strategic Resource

It follows from the discussion above that information issues are strategic for DSS, in three ways. First, in DSS, IS/IT development is large scale, and long term: Operational Strategy may take two decades to come to full fruition, and the demands of FAMIS would seem huge in any organization which had not experienced Operational Strategy. Secondly, many systems and projects are common to more than one agency: indeed all DSS business units have a stake, yet their priorities diverge. Thirdly, IS is seen to hold the key to fundamental shifts in the way DSS plans to deliver its services and manage its business. IS/IT therefore expose the many important issues involved in co-ordinating strategic resources in an environment where those resources are managed, owned and supplied through a range of semi-autonomous business units. This will be further complicated if market testing leads to substantially increased direct outsourcing of IS.

So what thinking is there about strategic management in a post Next Steps department? Many discussions have focused on accountability and performance measurement. That is, they have concentrated on vertical relations between agencies and core departments, and external relations with Parliament. Moreover, such discussions have been largely conducted as though 'management by contract' were simply a more hands-off, explicated, formalized version of the 'management by command' (e.g. Chapman, 1988; Flynn, 1990; Kemp, 1990; Greer, 1992; Jordan, 1992; Pliatzky, 1992). That is, much of the debate about changing institutional forms in government has been restricted by a dominant hierarchical paradigm, and little effort has been made either to apply alternative institutional models or to consider their behavioural and organizational dynamics. For example, scant attention has been paid to the increasing importance of lateral relationships between business units, suppliers, contractors and partners. The exceptions to this are undeveloped attempts to evoke the notion that government departments are becoming more like commercial 'groups' or conglomerates. Thus, Hood & Jones have observed that Next Steps represents an unstable compromise between 'corporatization' - 'the unbundling of a formerly unitary organization into units with separate identity and ... management practices' - and the demands of traditional external accountabilities and civil service management practices which have been predicated on an integrated, centralized department (Treasury and Civil Service Committee, 1990, Appendix 6). On the same lines, the Efficiency Unit's 1991 Report, *Making the Most of Next Steps* (the Fraser Report), employed the analogy of a business group consisting of a parent company and subsidiaries, in an attempt to shift thinking away from the hierarchical paradigm (Efficiency Unit, 1991).

The tenor of both the Fraser Report and Hood & Jones's evidence is to establish a dichotomy between 'corporatization', on the one hand, and the hierarchical, unitary department on the other. This dichotomy is suggestive, but unless it is substantially developed it is oversimplistic and misleading. In practice commercial groups embrace a range of institutional forms. For example, there is the pure 'holding company', where subsidiaries are discrete, autonomous and self-sufficient, and where the main interest for the parent is their bottom-line performance. In such a group the role of the parent company will be confined mainly to buying and selling subsidiaries and hiring and firing their managers. In contrast, there is the 'strong corporate' group, where subsidiaries are interdependent and where there is a clear, strong and effective group strategy determined and enforced by a dominant parent company. In such a case, group policy may be enforced by the centralization of strategically important functions, including human resource management, marketing, R & D, and IS/IT.

The tendentious purpose of the Fraser Report is shown by the fact that the business models it cites - GEC, P&O, RTZ and Hansons plc - are all much nearer to the holding company than to the strong corporate group. The purpose of the Report was to persuade HM Treasury and core departments that agencies should be much more loosely tied to centralized financial and personnel regimes, and to top-down direction by core departments. For this reason, Fraser found it rhetorically convenient to assume a department where agencies have a relatively high degree of operational independence, both from each other and from the core. That is, it assumed congruence between the degree of interdependence (low) within the group, and the degree of centralized hierarchical control (also low). However, the interesting questions for strategic management in a 'group' is where there is a disjunction, for example where there is high interdependence and weak hierarchical control. DSS is such a case.

In many respects, DSS continues to be highly centralized: there are strong pressures for retaining a strong corporate identity and these have been clearly signalled by its core department. Historically, DSS was a unitary department which has been disaggregated into units, mainly for extraneous reasons. In contrast to many holding companies, it is not a set of hitherto independent companies which have been bought out. Some of its agencies do not even coincide with pre-existing business divisions. In consequence, DSS's agencies are operationally interdependent, and their structure may well prove mutable in response to changing political priorities (viz. the recent establishment of Child Support Agency). We have already seen that Next Steps does not involve the formal disaggregation of DSS's financial framework, and the Secretary of State retains ultimate political responsibility for all its parts.

However, core department's control and grasp of strategic business issues are relatively weak, because the management of strategically important information resources and systems has been defined as a task for agencies. Cross departmental IS is recognized to be a common function, and it is increasingly recognized to be a core function, but it is not owned and managed directly by core department. Core department's role is primarily to manage the framework of inter-agency relations.

IS strategy has been, and will continue to be, formally determined by the Departmental Information Systems Strategy Committee (DISSC) and its sub committees. DISSC was established in the mid 1980s to provide steerage for the Operational Strategy. It is essentially a representative forum in which the various stakeholders in departmental IS/IT meet to prioritize the proposals for expenditure which emanate from DSS's various business units. In turn, these proposals result from negotiations undertaken between project managers in user agencies and ITSA. DISSC has evolved criteria against which projects are evaluated and these are derived from agencies' 'key values'. Within the parameters set by these criteria, outcomes inevitably reflect accommodations between agencies. Strategy-building is, therefore, best understood as a consensual process of partisan mutual adjustment between competing interests within a framework supplied by agencies' framework documents.

Core department's Corporate Management Division has a formal role in steering department-wide IS policy. There are however major reasons why, at least in the short term, this role does not imply strong top-down direction of IS/IT. Core department is itself a stakeholder in MIS, but it is one which is coming from the back of the field in defining its own IS needs (which stem mainly from its new role monitoring agencies' performance against targets). This reflects the crucial fact that core department has not seen itself as a prime customer of departmental IS. This in turn is a historical legacy of the perception that IS is a technical, operational function, concerned with implementation but not with policy making. Hence, it has been the responsibility of senior officials rather than top management, and this responsibility has been located in functional commands (which are now in agencies) rather than in the strategic divisions or policy group which form core department. Core department therefore has the authority that comes from access to ministers but it has little autonomous understanding of IS.

IS know-how is distributed between agencies, particularly ITSA and Benefits

Agency, and the internal politics of IS reflect the tensions in their roles and relationships. BA is the dominant agency within DSS, not only by reason of its overwhelming size and budget share but also because it owns much of the practical management expertise on which post Next Steps initiatives rest. For example, BA's Benefits Support and Business Development Branches 'own' the Operational Strategy systems and the strategic development of benefits administration. BA's Finance Directorate is responsible for the DSS's accounting system, and is managing FAMIS. Clearly a central issue for DSS as a whole is the extent to which BA's needs and expertise, and its inevitable dominance of the mathematics of business planning, will crowd out the interests of smaller agencies.

There is also a clear tension between the formal responsibility of user agencies (particularly BA) for information projects and systems, and their dependence on ITSA to manage the technological infrastructure. This tension is exacerbated by the widespread resentment of 'techies' which is a legacy from the early years of the Operational Strategy when users had but a naive understanding of technological issues. Most of DSS's technical IS expertise is now in ITSA. ITSA also controls access to external suppliers and consultants. It therefore defines the limits of technical feasibility and provides costings of projects. Much of the hard information around which negotiations take place is, therefore, supplied by ITSA and in this way ITSA clearly shapes outcomes. The relationship between ITSA and user agencies in relation to IS/IT has, therefore, been a major issue in the implementation of Next Steps. Core department's contribution has been to define the 'rules of the game'. The mutual dependence of agencies on operational systems, together with the dominant mainframe environment, would in many organizations indicate a centralized IS function. However, in deference to the stakeholdings of user agencies, a recent IT/IS Strategy Study commissioned by a core department plumped for a 'federal' IS framework. This study formally recognizes that 'the responsibility for IT management activities is shared between ITSA, the Department's HQ and the other agencies of the DSS group' (ITSA, 1993, p.13).

Internal Markets and Open Markets in DSS

In practice, DSS is clearly moving towards an internal market model, in which the supplier/producer power of ITSA will be more obviously balanced by that of user agencies as 'customers'. Internal markets are closely related to total quality management: the aim of both is to control the power of producers by creating surrogates for the consumer sovereignty which supposedly characterizes markets. Unlike 'real' markets, internal markets do not necessarily imply competition or hard financial transactions. They are therefore compatible with appropriation accounting and the ultimate integrity of a department's vote. Under internal markets, however, the organization is divided into 'purchasers' and 'providers', sellers and buyers, in such a way that the prioritization of activities, and hence the allocation of resources, is determined by purchasers. This is most simply achieved by arranging for the purchaser or customer to bear the budgetary consequence of his purchases rather than for the costs to fall on the supplier's budget. That is, internal markets tend to support a shift from functional or divisional budget heads to output budget heads.

In 1989 an IT Services Directorate was established to take responsibility for departmental IS/IT. At that time, DSS's expenditure on IT was consolidated into a distinct accounting head under the control of ITSD which in 1990 became ITSA. That is, the IT budget was given to the supplying agency not to the user agencies. This ran counter to the recommendations of the DSS's *Agency Study Report* (DSS, 1989). The DSS report proposed that there should be no distinct IT subhead once agencies were established. Instead, IT would be financed from agencies' running costs, and ITSA's services would be hardcharged to agency budgets. This proposal has remained firmly on the agenda within DSS, because it would suit both user agencies and ITSA (Cant, 1992). IT users complain that they feel themselves to be less than customers, because they are forced to bid for IT, they are forced to accept ITSA's costings, and they have no choice but to use ITSA's services. ITSA argues that a bidding regime causes user agencies to treat IT as a free good: the fact that users bear no direct costs stimulates a level of demand which cannot be met. There are no incentives for agencies to consider non-IT solutions to their problems, or to find ways of using IT more efficiently.

Despite this apparent unanimity, the establishment of a hardcharging regime has been delayed for a number of reasons. First, Treasury expenditure divisions have questioned whether it is in principle compatible with the integrity of the DSS's vote. Secondly, DSS was the first department to apply hardcharging to capital finance under an accruals accounting regime, and there have been many technical accounting problems for which no Treasury guidance existed. Thirdly, hardcharging depends on accounting techniques, particularly the introduction of accruals accounting, which FAMIS is only now beginning to deliver. Fourthly, and most importantly, it has raised sensitive questions about the way agencies will relate to each other in future. In particular, it raises the question how far IS supply is to be subjected to the test of an open market.

There are three possible motives for introducing a hardcharging regime between agencies. One is simply to expose costs, and thus to make users more cost-conscious. This has utility in promoting economy, though it is often derided as 'playing at shops'. It is alleged that it spawns bureaucracy and creates jobs for accountants with little concrete return to the organization. A second motive might be to develop a pricing policy to secure more efficient management of a scarce resource. For example, just as a bus operator might price peak services at a premium while discounting fares for off-peak travel, so ITSA might place a premium on the usage of the Operational Strategy network during the twin-peaks that occur in mid-morning and mid-afternoon. This would help to spread the load on Departmental Central Index, and postpone its extension or replacement. It has obvious advantages for the management of IT, but the process by which prices are set needs to be considered. If the supplying agency is allowed to set prices unilaterally, whilst user agencies are still tied to using its services, then this would tilt the balance of power strongly in favour of the supplier. In other words, either prices must be set by cross-agency negotiation, or the introduction of a price mechanism implies the introduction of external competition.

Thus, proposals to introduce hardcharging lead inexorably to discussions about 'real' markets involving open competition. This raises two issues for the Next Steps project and for DSS management. The first is that, once exposed to the test of the external market, the supplying agency would balk at disclosing its costs for fear of giving advantage to an external competitor. Thus there are issues concerned with the disclosure and withholding of financial information within a departmental 'group', and problems about accounting for what would still remain an integral vote. Secondly, it raises the question whether ITSA should be a tied supplier of IT services to DSS. Put simply, if agencies are 'buying' IT with their 'own' money, why should they be forced to buy from or through the departmental IT agency? The response to this question is complex. Not only are there some three thousand civil service jobs in ITSA, but ITSA represents an important reservoir of expertise and experience within DSS. DSS knows itself to be dependent on IS, and believes itself, therefore, to be dependent on ITSA.

The logic of this argument brings us full square to the role of the market. Should markets be regarded prima facie as the preferred instrument of resource allocation, the first-choice alternative to hierarchical control once government bureaucracies have been disaggregated? This question is one which relates to the renewed theoretical interest in institutional forms in social science, for example in the 'new institutional economics'. Beginning in the 1970s, Williamson and others have called for more attention to be paid to the relative economic efficiency of different ways of institutionalising economic relationships, and have argued that, under certain conditions, the market is not the most efficient way of conducting transactions (Aoki, Gustafsson & Williamson, 1990; Clarke & McGuinness, 1987; Francis, Turk & Willman, 1983; Williamson, 1975 and 1985) . To take an example relevant to IS: where the number of firms able to compete is low, where the capital and human assets developed to deliver contracts are highly specific, or where the obligations on contractors cannot be anticipated or easily specified (for example in an environment of technological innovation), a firm may become unacceptably vulnerable to opportunistic, short term advantage seeking by contractors. That is, a combination of low numbers, high technical lock-in and narrowly bounded rationality may indicate that market transactions are not optimal for the business. In such a case it may be more efficient to 'make' rather than 'buy', by substituting the costs of internal production and management for the risks of the market place.

Contracting In and Contracting Out IS/IT

It is on such grounds that it has been argued that government departments should be wary about contracting out IS (CCTA, 1992a, CCTA, 1992b), though it is interesting to note the Citizens Charter *First Report* indicates that IT is one of the most frequently mentioned functions in departments' market testing plans (Prime Minister, 1992). For example, there are worries that in relation to IS, government departments are not yet sufficiently 'mature'. That is, it is argued that their relative lack of experience, especially in relation to IS strategy and to the IS commercial market, means that they cannot act as intelligent or powerful customers. Likewise, it is argued that the continuing turbulence of departments' business environment, coupled with rapid technological change, makes management by contract an insufficiently flexible option (Earl, 1991; Lacity and Hirscheim, 1993).

In this vein, Willcocks has drawn attention to the 'very mixed record that significant contracting out of IT already has in many public sector organizations' (Willcocks, 1993). He draws a useful distinction between 'insourcing', where an organization buys in resources to be deployed under its own management, and 'outsourcing', where management is transferred to the contractor. His work suggests that in conditions of high business uncertainty, low technological stability, and low IS maturity, strategic IS, or IS that is highly integral to the business, should be managed in-house. The use of contractors should be limited to 'insourcing' (Feeny, Willcocks, Rands & Fitzgerald, 1993). In DSS, for example, the management of Operational Strategy area computing centres has been outsourced, but most of ITSA's budget has been spent on insourcing. The debate on market testing in DSS is, therefore, how far to shift from insourcing to outsourcing, and whether user agencies should be permitted to go direct to the market, bypassing ITSA.

In contrast to the arguments above, it is often said that the very rapidity of technological change and the growing turbulence of markets and macro-economies, mean that the inflexibilities and high overheads associated with mass production in large scale, capital intensive, highly integrated organizations are becoming too risky to be permanently sustained in a growing number of companies (Aglietta, 1979; Lipeitz, 1987; Piore and Sabel, 1984). In the case of IT, an argument relevant to many government departments is that the costs of technology refreshment and the risks of innovation are best borne by specialist, commercial contractors (Child, 1987). The case for downsizing bureaucracies so that only core functions remain in-house is reinforced by the impact of new kinds of information and information flows, supported by new information and communication technologies, on the costs of information processing and communications relative to other costs of organizations (Madnick, 1987; Scott Morton, 1991). In turn, this is alleged to have major repercussions for organizational configurations. Space and time shrink: physical proximity is no longer at a premium in the location of organizational functions (Hepworth, 1989). In both the spatial and logical sense, the organization of the future can not only get 'closer to the customer' but can also get closer to markets, contractors and partners.

Competition, Networks and Partnerships

The literature suggests that there are three major trends in the ways in which economic relationships are institutionalized. Co-ordination by means of hierarchy gives way to transactions based on exchange; emphasis on vertical integration gives way to emphasis on lateral relationships; and management by command gives way to the management of contracts. Increasingly the M-form organization, the loosely coupled, compartmentalized, multi-divisional organization, replaces the top-down, bureaucratic hierarchy (Thompson, Frances, Levacic & Mitchell, 1991).

The shift towards hands-off management also supports the downsizing of organizations by means of greater use of outsourcing. Once suitable information flows are established to govern intra-organizational contractual relationships then they can be applied also to the government of relationships with external contractors and collaborators. Increasingly the line between the organization and its environment becomes fluid, blurred and, perhaps, irrelevant. Production and service delivery are organized flexibly by means of alliances between partners rather than exclusively through the monolithic organization. The ideas postulated in this literature are self-evidently in tune with the rhetoric of Next Steps and market testing. But the literature parts company with the ideology of managerialism in government in the way it treats competition and markets. Competition is an efficient device for allocating resources where it is relatively easy for significant number of competitors to enter and remain in the market; where there is low asset specificity; where the cash nexus provides sufficient connection between contractors; when contracts can be clearly specified; and when the market can be appropriately retested at short intervals. Where these conditions do not hold, it is argued that networks and partnerships will become an increasingly important medium for transactions (e.g. Johnstone and Lawrence, 1988). A case in point might well be the management of strategic IS (OECD, 1992).

By the term 'network' is meant the creation of multiple, cross cutting relationships of exchange, persisting over time, between peers. Networks arise when two conditions exist. First, networks are the consequence of mutual resource dependency: they are the product of exchanges which occurs when a number of actors severally control resources which are necessary to achieve their objectives. Secondly, exchange relationships become institutionalized into networks when it is efficient for actors to invest in creating and maintaining them. That is, the partners must be prepared to forgo short term gains, and to devote resources to establish goodwill, loyalty and trust. Thus actors gain the advantages of co-operation whilst minimising the risks involved in exposing themselves to opportunistic behaviour by partners.

Clearly the vulnerability of both user agencies and suppliers is high for large scale IS. Where IS is supplied internally between agencies, there is an incentive to act co-operatively for, willy-nilly, users and suppliers are locked into a long term relationship. The risks are, however, compounded when supply is externalized. Moreover, the risks exist on both sides. Particularly for large-scale government information systems, IS suppliers would be required to undertake large investments in expertise and equipment, and to develop know-how which is not easily transferable to other contracts. These costs and risks may be particularly unsustainable if the contract period is short. On the other side, if the user agency divests itself of hands-on IS competence it will weaken its capacity to act as an intelligent, self-protecting customer (CCTA, 1992b).

One response to market testing in a mainframe dominated, large-scale IT environment is that being pursued by Inland Revenue. Inland Revenue, like DSS, knows that there are few commercial companies which can realistically tender for IS on the huge scale it employs. In going to the market at all, IR is inevitably into small numbers competition. IR has therefore decided to let a single contract for the whole of its IT function (currently performed by its IT Office and IT installations) for ten years, and aims thereby to establish a long-term, 'strategic partnership' with a commercial contractor (Inland Revenue, 1992, 1993). There are obvious, high risks on both sides, not least because the contractor will be committed to enormous, specific investment and IR will inevitably be denuded of practical know-how. Hence there is maximum incentive on both sides for the development of mutual commitment, loyalty and co-operation.

DSS has chosen an alternative route. As noted above, the questions of using competition to enhance user power relative to producer power and using pricing to management resources efficiently, were on the internal agenda, even before *Competing for Quality* was published. ITSA's response has been to invest heavily in winning the trust of user agencies, to promote a sense of partnership and common interest. For example, ITSA has appointed customer account managers to build long term, personal relationships with user agency managers, and to demonstrate its responsiveness to customer needs. Personnel have also been recruited from Benefits Agency, to promote inter-agency understanding and goodwill.

Nevertheless, the competition agenda in DSS has not gone away. It has been stimulated by problems in reconciling the several, and probably incompatible, roles of ITSA. ITSA manages IT procurement for DSS and the extensive network of DSS's sub contractors and consultants. But ITSA is itself also a direct provider of services. At the same time, ITSA is a major repository of IS know-how: it therefore performs a strategic advisory function which in a commercial group might well be performed by a division within core department. Therefore, even if IS supply is market tested, DSS is determined to protect ITSA's experience and expertise as a departmental resource.

Henceforth, a small group within ITSA, to be known as the Departmental IT Agency (DITA), will act as the DSS's principal advisers on IT/IS. DITA will be located in London, whereas the rest of ITSA will continue to be located in Lytham St. Annes. DITA's brief will be to maintain and develop IS strategy, to regulate IT standards, technical architecture and policies, and to regulate IT procurement within the group. Thus DSS aims to maintain sufficient know-how and hierarchical control to protect the integrity of the systems, secure value for money, and guarantee fair procurement practices (ITSA, 1993). From 1993-4, the rest of ITSA's services, which amount in value to over 95% of its budget, will be provided under a hardcharging regime involving the notional transfer of the IT budget to ITSA's internal 'customers' (The transfer is notional because it will not involve the re-organization of subheads in the DSS vote: it is, at least in the first instance, an internal arrangement). That is, DSS is institutionalising the distinction between IS direction (deciding what to do, and where to go) from its development and operation (Earl, 1989).

The designation of DITA clearly raises questions about the long term future of the rest of ITSA: separated from the functional core of DITA it could easily be privatized, either *en bloc* or through extensive market testing of discrete functions. The stated intention is that, within three years, ITSA will become the 'first choice' supplier of IT services for the DSS group (ITSA, 1993). This formula leaves open the volume and range of IT services which will eventually be externally supplied, though it reflects a preference for maintaining ITSA as a major departmental resource.

Strategic Management of IS/IT

What then of the question: how will IS strategy be managed in the DSS group? In the short term, the creation of DITA does not necessarily imply a stronger corporate IS line. The 'federal' IS framework leaves BA in charge of major IS projects, including Strategy systems and FAMIS, and this limits DITA's strategic grasp. At the same time, neither BA nor DITA can be seen to neglect the interests and priorities of the smaller agencies. The odds are that IS strategy-making in DSS will continue to be pluralist and consensual, conducted by partisan mutual adjustment within the framework of DISSC.

In the longer term, however, there are alternative scenarios. A statement that is often made about IS is that as it moves to the strategic core of the business, so it acquires the impress of mainstream organizational politics. For example, senior management acquired more power over IS at the point, in the late 1980s, when IS began visibly to impinge on the management of benefits. As IS continues to expose the interdependencies between agencies, then core department top management might expect to be drawn further into the internal politics of IS.

A shift in the balance of power in favour of core department could be reinforced by substantially increased outsourcing. If a considerable part of ITSA's work were to be privatized, then its continued existence as a separate agency might be in doubt. DITA might then be absorbed into core DSS. In such a scenario, core department's control of IS strategy would be much enhanced by the know-how and synoptic grasp provided by DITA.

It is a paradox that a decisive shift in DSS towards a 'strong corporate' model or a decisive shift towards widening the scope of market exchanges would both require a clear IS strategy. A condition of establishing a more thoroughgoing competitive regime is that a market has to be established, maintained and regulated. Hence, the imminence of market testing in DSS has stimulated the creation of DITA to regulate IS contracts and to define IS standards.

Conclusion

This chapter suggests that the 'corporatization' of government departments under Next Steps could take a number of forms. At one extreme there is a strong corporate model which would re-establish a high degree of top-down control, and could imply minimal changes from the conventional government department. It could also be compatible with minimal changes in accounting regimes. On the other hand, market testing is pushing departments towards widening the scope of market transactions, and this requires decisive changes in the financial regimes under which on-vote agencies operate in the direction of commercial practices.

DSS has clearly decided that more extensive open competition is compatible with strategic control of IS, so long as the department retains sufficient technical know-how and authority to establish and maintain a regulatory framework. In effect, by creating DITA, DSS is creating a centralized, strategic IS function, even though it is one which is not located in core HQ. That is, departments will need to develop and retain the capacity to steer IS and manage and regulate suppliers, even if project development and IT operations are contracted out. However, the establishment of open competition through frequent market testing may not be appropriate for all kinds of IT functions. The risks and costs which would fall on both sides indicate that, especially where large-scale capital investment or the development of specific know-how is involved, a longer term partnership may be more effective. What we have also seen is that the notion of 'corporatization' is useful, but that, unless it is substantially developed and specified, it will be a blanket thrown over the new institutional forms which are emerging under Next Steps. It needs urgently to be unpacked, and the range and variety of institutional forms emerging in 'groups' categorized and analyzed. In DSS, there is an evolving set of relationships, characterized partly by hierarchical authority, partly by market exchanges, and partly by the emergence of networks: these relationships indicate the institutional complexity which is contained within the new departmental 'groups'. There are a number of ways in which these institutional modes might be identified and revealed. In this chapter, for example, the nature of interdependencies within the group, the grasp and scope of the core, the distribution of technical expertise, the process by which strategic decisions are taken, the changing principles by which lateral transactions are conducted, the criteria by which departments engage in (internal or external) competition or partnerships have been examined. These are, therefore, just some of the variables which determine the institutional forms which are being adopted. It would also be fruitful to speculate on the contingencies involved: whether and how far, for example, the dominant institutional forms are the product of organization's history, business, technology, and cultures. What is clear, is that this case study points to the need for comparative institutional analysis of post Next Steps departments across government. That is, it is both the value and the limitation of a single case to indicate both the need for and direction of further research.

The Employment Service as an Agency: the First Three Years

MICHAEL HUNT

The Employment Service was an obvious and early candidate for agency status. It had been established in October 1987 as a separate organization within the Department of Employment Group, with its own chief executive, in order to merge the Unemployment Benefit service and the employment arm of the Manpower Services Commission. (Treasury and Civil Service Committee, Minutes of Evidence, 5 June 1991, p. 1). Its structure, purposes and senior personnel were therefore already in place before the publication of the Ibbs report in 1988, enabling the creation of one of the biggest agencies at a relatively early stage. Norman Fowler's announcement in December 1989 that the Service would be formally designated as a Next Steps agency with effect from April 1990 therefore came as little surprise.

The early establishment of the agency makes it worth studying for three reasons. As one of the largest of the new agencies its experience of the problems of transition is both more extensive and on a greater scale than most other agencies. It has already encountered many of the general problems that are likely to face other new agencies. Secondly, its sheer size means that it is a different kind of agency to many of its much smaller contemporaries. It cannot be regarded simply as an executive agency; it also has policy making responsibilities and this added complexity both to the task of drawing up the framework document and also to the practical implementation of the principles enshrined in it. Finally, the sensitivity of the issues for which it has responsibility means that it is always likely to be in the forefront of political attention.

There are important differences between the operating style of the new agency and that of its predecessor. The more 'arms length' proposals of the Ibbs report required the introduction of specific agreements about the relationship between the new agency and its 'parent' Department and more formal expression of the differing roles to be performed by the Secretary of State, Permanent Secretary, and Chief Executive. In turn, this has necessitated the creation of specific measures which allow the Department to monitor the performance and activities of its distant offspring. These are set out in the Framework document and in the annual performance agreement. The agency's Chief Executive, Mike Fogden, giving evidence to the Treasury and Civil Service Committee, suggested that the value of agency status lay in the increased managerial flexibility which it allowed in the areas of finance and personnel which in turn had allowed the agency to obtain better value from the money allocated to it. This, he argued, enabled the agency to provide a better quality of service to clients and to improve job satisfaction for employees by developing an individual corporate identity (Treasury and Civil Service Committee, Minutes of Evidence, 5 June 1991, p. 2). This 'corporate identity' is an important feature of the new agency and is specifically referred to in an internal publication for employees produced in the year after designation (Employment Service, 1991b). It reflects the managerial bias of the Ibbs report and suggests that the key features of the new culture will be first, an emphasis on outputs and service (i.e. that the service will be 'performance driven'), secondly, that there will be a more 'enabling' style of management, and thirdly, that 'managers will be encouraged to be innovative in the way in which they achieve results' implying a reduction in the constraints imposed by previous reliance on detailed rules and procedures. Finally, the document suggests that there will be a more open and trusting, two way, style of communications in the organization and that the culture will be positive and supportive. Such objectives undoubtedly fit the style of the 'new managerialism' although it is difficult to measure the extent to which they have been achieved. There is nothing in this document, nor in the Framework Document, to explain how the new culture will be attained.

At the time of its designation as an agency, in April 1990, the Employment Service comprised 37,000 members of staff largely located in 2,000 Job Centres and Unemployment Benefit Offices. The continuing rise in the level of unemployment, accompanied by a process of planned rationalization, meant that by September 1992 the number of staff had risen to 49,000 operating in 1,300 Centres and Offices. These are organized into fifty-nine areas in seven English regions with separate regions for Scotland and Wales. At the apex of the organization is an Executive Board of six members. This is headed by the Chief Executive who reports directly to the Secretary of State. He is joined on the Board by a Deputy

Chief Executive, other members having functional responsibility for Field Services, Human Resources, Business Development and Finance and Resources. The Chief Executive was appointed from within the Department, having had previous experience in the DHSS. This is particularly valuable since the Employment Service pays some benefits to unemployed people on behalf of the Department of Social Security; the agreement that it should do so forms a separate Annex within the framework document. In line with practice in other agencies Mr Fogden's appointment as Chief Executive in 1990 was for a period of three years, after which time the post would again fall vacant; after open competition Mr Fogden was re-appointed for a further three year period.

The framework document sets out the aims and objectives of the agency, the delineation of responsibilities for the agency between the Chief Executive, Permanent Secretary and Secretary of State, the ways in which it will (broadly) be accountable to Parliament, and the role of the Chief Executive in relation to personnel and financial matters and the provision of services. In addition, there are brief details of planning arrangements, the role of performance agreements and the function of the Operational Plan. It is not an extensive document (ten pages) and many of the details of its operation will clearly be determined in the light of experience (see, for example, the subsequent reference to discussions between the Chief Executive, ministers and MPs about the latter's right to have questions answered by a minister). As originally intended, the agreement lasted for three years before being reviewed in October 1993; it was subsequently re-adopted for a further three years following minor amendments suggested both by experience and by changes in government policies. It can, however, be amended before the end of the three year period if the Secretary of State, Permanent Secretary, or Chief Executive deem this to be necessary. In that event, an extensive consultation exercise takes place involving the principal actors already identified together with trade unions, the Treasury and the Next Steps team in the Cabinet Office. Presumably Parliament would only have the opportunity to comment on any changes if there was a debate on the Employment Service (unlikely on past evidence) or if the Employment Select Committee raised the matter during an inquiry into the work of the agency.

Aims, Objectives and Performance

The aims and objectives of the agency are set out in the framework document. The aims, not surprisingly, are fairly general and indicate the agency's commitment to providing assistance to unemployed people via its job placement service and its role in the payment of benefits.

The objectives are expressed in operational terms and can, therefore, be directly linked to performance targets which are decided annually. There are five objectives combining both pro-active and regulatory intentions, for example dealing with both the provision of benefit and also with the prevention of fraud. Each objective is broken down into a number of targets. In conventional fashion, the targets have been designed to measure output as a means of identifying the efficiency and effectiveness of the organization. The first objective, for example, concerns the placement of unemployed people into jobs, placements on the Enterprise Allowance Scheme, and placements into Employment Training. For 1990/91 the targets were the greater of placing 1.65 million unemployed people into jobs or 80% of placings of unemployed people among total number of placings; having 65,000 entrants to the Enterprise Allowance Scheme; and having 335,000 Employment Training starts with Training Managers (Employment Service, 1990b). These targets, together with some others, were not met in the year ending in March 1991. Only 1.4 million people were placed in jobs, entrants to the Enterprise Allowance Scheme numbered 38,700, and there were 254,300 entrants to Employment Training. The *Annual Report* for the year spends little time exploring the reasons for this other than noting that the number of people placed in jobs was affected by a 17% drop in notified vacancies (the fall in the number of placings of unemployed people into jobs was only about 6%). The failure to reach the other two targets was recognized during the year but agreement was reached with the Secretary of State that this lack of performance would not be taken into account when assessing the agency's overall performance. (This may well have been the correct decision although it may also raise questions in some people's minds about the value of utilising targets as a form of public accountability). The agreement with the Secretary of State was not publicized at the time which, whilst unsurprising, led to some adverse comment by the Employment Select Committee.

Any criticism of the failure to achieve the targets needs to be tempered, for at least four reasons. First, the difficulty of setting meaningful targets at the first attempt, a problem which (not surprisingly) the agency had recognized at a very early stage. (Employment Committee, Minutes of Evidence, 8 November 1989). Secondly, the nature of the targets themselves, which, in the main, were output rather than quality based. Failure to attain targets may not mean, therefore, that the service is inefficient or ineffective - only that it has proved difficult to measure this. John Major suggested (written reply, 16 May 1991, col. 1247) that indicators should deal with quality of service. These are in the process of being developed but it will be some time before they are in use. Thirdly, the influence of external factors (such as a deepening recession) on the attempt to achieve targets. Any inaccuracy in economic forecasting (a science which some have compared to completing the football pools) is likely to affect the realism of the targets set. Finally, developing a culture where targets are accepted as a part of organizational activity is a process which inevitably takes some time. The fact that targets are recognized and accepted within the organization may be regarded, therefore, as an achievement in itself.

Other targets were reached. For example, the guarantee that all claimants aged between 18 and 24 who had been unemployed for between 6 and 12 months be offered a place on Employment Training, on the Enterprise Allowance Scheme or in a Job-Club was met. Further, the target of paying 95% of Benefits correctly was met. In addition, efficiency savings of £13.6 million were made (representing 2.3% of running costs)(Employment Service, 1991a, p. 10). Finally, progress was made on the first stage of developing a unit costing system to improve the agency's capacity to measure its performance (for example, the cost of paying a benefit) and also allow it to deploy its resources where they were most needed (Employment Service, 1991b, p. 20).

By 1993 the agency was able to demonstrate that it was achieving most of its targets. For example, the target of placing 1,425,000 unemployed people into jobs was almost achieved with the placing of 1,420,000 into work. The target of ensuring that 19% of those placed in work came from the long term unemployed was surpassed; 24.3% of those placed were long term claimants. The target of paying 92% of payments promptly met with a response of 94.2%. To the extent that these targets are a measure of performance the agency has clearly improved its performance over the first three years of its life. Inevitably, the achievement of targets in one year has resulted in more demanding targets in subsequent years (Employment Service, 1993a).

To support its collection of indicators the agency has also conducted its own customer satisfaction surveys. In 1990/91 this involved a survey of 1,400 clients in 48 different areas; the results seemed to indicate that the standard of service was improving and that the quality of service in those offices which had been integrated was higher than in those offices where the two strands of the agency's work were separate (Treasury and Civil Service Committee, Minutes of Evidence, 5 June 1991, p. 2). Targets for the year 1991/92 were, in most cases, lower than those for the preceding year reflecting, perhaps, a greater realism in the light of experience and the pressures caused by the continuing recession.

Selecting an appropriate indicator is clearly difficult, as others have discussed elsewhere (e.g. Carter, 1989, p. 133). Whilst the agency has made clear its preference for challenging targets related to output there is always a risk that this puts a premium on activities rather than quality of service. There is no information for example about the appropriate matching of people into jobs, or whether the jobs last for a long time or whether, in effect, they turn out to be merely temporary. If the latter, there is no information on whether this is the fault of the company or the job seeker and (if the latter) what the Employment Service might do to make him or her more acceptable to potential employers. In short, some of the indicators might be regarded as measuring processes rather than the success of particular policies. Whilst it may be argued that this is sufficient and satisfactory for an executive agency which needs to have the success of its processes measured in order to allow effective control by its parent department, there must be a concern that the targets are seen as measures of efficiency within constrained limits rather than measures of effectiveness. This also raises questions about responsibility for the effectiveness of policy and the possibility that this responsibility may be blurred between a Department and an 'operational' agency.

A further difficulty with such indicators can occur when it is difficult for individual employees to directly affect the agency's performance. Whilst the indicators may be useful for managers in a broad sense, it may also be difficult for employees to 'own' them. This is particularly important because one of the functions of the indicators is to help change the culture of the organization (Employment Select Committee, Minutes of Evidence, 8 November 1989, p. 6). A feeling of frustration with the targets and a practical inability to identify with them would clearly have an adverse effect on the development of a new culture. On the other hand, the agency's own concern with the achievement of targets, and continuing government preoccupation with measures of efficiency is likely to enhance the capacity of staff to identify with the targets.

Responsibilities and Accountability

The framework document makes clear that the minister is ultimately responsible for the policies of the agency and is therefore answerable to Parliament for its activities. He agrees with the agency the output targets which it is expected to achieve, approves the annual operational plan, and then allocates resources to the agency. Once his approval has been given to the targets and to the plan the document makes clear that the Chief Executive is 'free to deliver programmes and services in accordance with them' (Employment Service, 1990a, para. 3.6). Further, whilst the Secretary of State may seek advice or information from the agency, 'he does not normally issue further directions to the Chief Executive ...'. The document envisages that this is only likely to happen 'if exceptionally, major changes in direction are necessary or circumstances arise which were unforeseen' (Employment Service, 1990a, para. 3.7).

Whilst the framework document can only outline the relationship between the major participants (and to some extent only states the obvious), its lack of precision carries a number of dangers. The cynic might suggest that it merely repeats the old and arguably discredited attempt to distinguish between policy and administration. Concern has already been expressed by some MPs over the minister's responsibility for answering Parliamentary Questions (see below) and this problem has been glossed over rather than solved. Further, the somewhat generalized nature of some of the document's statements do not allow for the possibility that different secretaries of state will interpret their role differently or, at least, have a different understanding of the term 'strategic' from that of their predecessors. In addition, the framework document states that the Secretary of State may call for a revision of the operational plan at any point during the course of the year. Such a revision, whilst obviously within the powers of a minister ultimately responsible to Parliament, could cause considerable disruption to the efficient management of the agency.

The policy making role of the Chief Executive is acknowledged in the document which refers to his membership of senior committees in the Employment Department Group. In addition, it makes clear his right to put forward suggestions to the Minister for changes in the policies and programmes of the agency. Not surprisingly, he is required to consult with the Permanent Secretary on any such proposals. More importantly, the document specifies his right to be consulted on any proposals submitted by the Department. Whilst, in one sense, this is no more than a statement of sensible practice, the fact that the document actually describes the rights of the Chief Executive gives a clear public indication of his independence and status within the DE Group. The importance of this has certainly not been lost on the Chief Executive (Treasury and Civil Service Committee, 1991, p. 3).

The document also describes the role of the Permanent Secretary, noting his position as the chief policy adviser of the Secretary of State with principal responsibility for advising the minister on 'the Agency's objectives, on the policies it is to implement and on its performance against targets'. More generally, he (rather than the Chief Executive) has responsibility for ensuring that the agency's policies are compatible with the wider policies and activities of the DE Group (Employment Service, 1990a, para. 3.2). In essence, this is also merely a description of sensible practice. The ability of senior officials to work in harmony is vital to the success of agencies and in normal circumstances it should not be necessary to refer to these terms of reference. The Chief Executive is certain to have frequent discussions with ministers on matters of policy; common sense suggests that he will keep the Permanent Secretary informed of matters that affect the exercise of his departmental responsibilities.

The ways in which the Employment Service is to be held accountable to Parliament for its activities are also set out in the framework document. This draws attention to the Chief Executive's role as an accounting officer for the agency vote, the possibility of review of the agency's activities by the Parliamentary Commissioner for Administration and the arrangements for dealing with correspondence from MPs (Employment Service, 1990a, section 4).

It is the last of these which seems, so far, to be the most contentious since the achievement of agency status has reduced the opportunities for MPs to question ministers about the work of the Employment Service. Although the framework document blandly notes that 'The Secretary of State is answerable to Parliament for the Agency's activities' (para 4.1) it also says that the Secretary of State 'will encourage (MPs) to contact the Chief Executive or other appropriate Agency managers direct on individual cases or operational issues' (Employment Service, 1990a, para. 4.3). This has meant, in practice, that questions on 'operational matters' no longer receive a reply in the House but are automatically referred to the Chief Executive. Copies of the answer are placed in the House of Commons Library. However, there does not appear to be an agreed definition of the phrase 'operational matters' and this has clearly been a cause of concern to a number of MPs. The evidence suggests that whilst ministers will not answer questions on matters such as the reasons for the closure of an office in a particular constituency, they will answer a question about the representations received for the closure of that office (Hansard, 12 February 1991, col. 462). Whilst there may be advantages to be derived from not overloading ministers with the necessity of answering questions that may more relevantly be addressed elsewhere, such an approach clearly challenges the normal assumptions of executive accountability to Parliament. Further, the lack of publicity given to replies may make it harder to identify those problems on which concern is being expressed from a number of quarters. Putting a copy of an answer in the Commons Library does not help those who do not have access to this resource and there was some doubt as to whether such answers would be covered by Parliamentary Privilege in the same way as answers published in the Official Report (Treasury and Civil Service Committee, 1990, p. xix). Concern about the matter led to an Adjournment Debate in May 1990 and an undertaking by the Minister of State that ultimately the Minister would reply in the House on an operational issue if a Member felt that his reply from the agency was unsatisfactory (Hansard, 21 May 1990, col. 151). The suggestion that questions referred by a Minister should also have an answer published in the Official Report has now been adopted. There seems to be widespread acknowledgement that there have been difficulties in explaining precise arrangements in framework documents and a recognition that arrangements which satisfy all parties will of necessity take some time to evolve.

The House of Commons Select Committee on Employment provides another means by which Parliament is able to hold the agency to account. The Committee usually meets the senior executives of the Employment Service once a year for what appears to be a relatively constructive exchange of views about the detailed work of the agency. Although the minutes of evidence of these meetings are available for public inspection they have not yet led to a formal report nor, of course, have they provided the basis for a Parliamentary debate on the work of the agency. Nevertheless, the information obtained may be useful as background material for other Reports. In addition, the Committee usually meets the Secretary of State once a year for a formal meeting where matters relating to the agency could, of course, be discussed. In addition, the Chief Executive has given evidence to the Treasury and Civil Service Select Committee on a number of occasions and this has been valuable as a contribution to a wider analysis of the work of agencies.

The Chief Executive himself makes a quarterly (private) report to the Secretary of State which, inter alia, indicates progress in achieving performance targets. In addition, the Employment Service publishes its own Annual Report which comments upon its activities during the year, its success (or otherwise) in achieving performance targets and its proposals for further development.

Personnel Changes

Although the Ibbs proposals envisaged agencies exercising a greater degree of independence in respect of personnel matters, it is a little difficult to separate the changes that have taken place in the Employment Service as a result of agency status from those that might have occurred anyway. The establishment of the Recruitment and Assessment Service, for example, increases the delegated powers of both agencies and departments in regard to the recruitment of staff. Within the Employment Service the Chief Executive has the power to create new posts up to Grade 6. At EO level the agency has produced a set of eight competences, specific to the agency, against which candidates for posts can be compared. Line managers may now be involved in recruitment for posts at this level. Additionally (and with the approval of the Permanent Secretary) the agency has developed a system of promotion by vacancy advertising which replaces the previous system of General Promotion Panels. These panels, common to the civil service, were regarded by some senior officials as time-consuming and frequently ineffective. The system of placing new recruits on a twelve month probation has also been reduced to six months. Agency status has not increased the recruitment of people into senior grades from outside the Service except for a few, specialized, functions. (In any case, the need to reduce the numbers of staff in other parts of the DE Group means that re-deployment of staff to the agency somewhat limits the need for external recruitment).

A potentially important change concerns the power to amend the *Personnel Handbook*. This Handbook, produced with the agreement of the Treasury, is a full compendium of the personnel policies and practices of all sections of the DE Group. However, with the agreement of the Permanent Secretary, the agency took responsibility for its own handbook with effect from April 1992. This did not mean that the agency's personnel policies immediately changed; it merely acknowledged that it has the power to develop, over time, policies which more specifically meet its own needs rather than those of other parts of the Group. An examination of those areas where changes might be made is currently being undertaken. Certain matters will remain common to all parts of the DE Group including re-deployment, redundancy and retirement. Others will be delegated but with the expectation that developments will be in line with 'Group-wide statements of principle'. These include equal opportunities, promotion and appraisal. All other matters, including recruitment, pay and general conditions of service become the sole responsibility of the service after, of course, discussion with relevant trade unions. This delegated power is important, not only because of the specific areas where responsibility is now delegated to the agency, but also because it reflects the developing confidence of the agency in its ability to take responsibility for its own affairs. As one senior official pointed out, the freedoms that followed agency status were not likely to be embraced immediately after years of conforming to codes of employment that affected all personnel throughout the civil service. Nor could it be expected that the Treasury would easily divest itself of the powers that it had held. Nonetheless, further delegation means that significant changes to the *Personnel Handbook* and to the pay structure of the agency will come into effect in April 1994.

Financial Changes

These are set out in the financial agreement which forms an appendix to the framework document. This establishes, in some detail, the individual responsibilities of the Chief Executive, Permanent Secretary and Secretary of State regarding accountability for the agency's spending. For example, it notes that the Chief Executive is the accounting officer for the agency which has its own Vote. Concomitant with this, he has control over the allocation of resources to different heads within the agency's budget. He has authority to switch expenditure between particular blocks, in accordance with guidelines agreed with the Treasury (Employment Service, 1993b, Memorandum of Financial Arrangements, Appendix 2) and to authorize the carrying forward of an agreed percentage of unspent running costs into a subsequent year. Further, he has authority to switch money, in-year, between capital, running costs and programme provision within agreed limits and, in 1990/91, used this power to transfer £850,000 from programme provision to meet its requirements for extra capital (Employment Service, 1991a, p. 24). In addition, 5% of capital funds can be carried forward from one year to another. There is also flexibility to generate revenue from activities approved by the Secretary of State (Employment Service, 1993b, Appendix 3). The 1990/91 *Annual Report and Accounts* notes that ten activities were approved in that year, eight of which involved work for the Training and Enterprise Councils. The projects generated £125,000 in income, of which £13,600 was retained by the agency. Where the Chief Executive does not have discretion is in the allocation of money to a new service or to expand the work of the agency in a way that would create additional expenditure commitments in the future (Employment Service, 1990a, Financial Agreement, para. 24). This is not surprising since expenditure in these areas clearly raises issues of policy that are properly the responsibility of the minister. Nonetheless, agency status has delegated a considerable degree of financial discretion to the Chief Executive and this might well be expanded in the future.

The budget for the agency still forms part of the PES and Estimates bids submitted by the Employment Group and the agency therefore bargains within the DE Group for resources rather than having its own connections with the Treasury. The agency appoints its own internal auditor (in conjunction with the Permanent Secretary and the DE Group's Principal Finance Officer). Although the latter may comment on the agency's audit plans and reports he has no managerial responsibility for the agency's auditor who reports to the Chief Executive (Employment Service, 1990a, Financial Agreement, 1990, Annexe 2).

Cultural Change

There is frequent reference in the agency's published documents, and in evidence to Parliamentary Committees, to the need for cultural change in the organization in order that the new freedoms can be fully utilized (see, for example, Employment Committee, 1990, p. 6). Such a change is particularly necessary since the process of combining the Job Centres and the Unemployment Benefit Offices involved the amalgamation of two services with distinct histories and traditions. Job Centres had previously formed part of the Manpower Services Commission and staff were accustomed to both a relatively independent existence and also to being pro-active and sympathetic in their approach. Within the centres, a senior official noted, the management style was generally participative. The more traditional Unemployment Benefit Offices were accustomed to working to detailed rules and procedures with little opportunity to exercise discretion. The two areas of work offered a different public image; going from Job Centres to some Benefit Offices was, as Fogden put it to the Employment Committee, 'like going from carpets to Colditz' (Employment Committee, 8 November 1989, p. 2). The task of combining these two traditions was therefore considerable. Many of the 'old style' managers had been appointed to equivalent positions in the agency and it was therefore important to set and encourage an appropriate culture as soon as possible. The nature of the new culture has been described on a number of occasions (see, for example, Employment Service, 1991b). It was clearly derived from the Job Centre arm of the agency and the process of achieving it was approached by establishing six 'work streams', one of which specifically looked at management style. From this, networks of 'innovative' managers were established to discuss good practice in participative management. The networks were organized in hierarchies, thus Grade 7 managers formed one network who then formed networks of SEOs in their areas. Other 'work streams' looked at Support Arrangements, Managing External Relationships, and Individual Performance. This process is continuing; the development and reinforcement of a culture is inevitably lengthy and it is difficult to come to any conclusion about the effects of the networks in the longer term.

Past and Future

The experience of the Employment Service during the past three years must surely meet the expectations of the authors of the Ibbs report. Its response to the opportunities afforded by the powers delegated to it has clearly been very positive and its work in both personnel and in the development of performance targets, not to mention the encouragement of a distinct culture, is entirely synonymous with the ambitions of the report. There has been little serious criticism of either its activities or of the way in which it is accountable to ministers and to Parliament. Ministers have, so far, resisted the temptation to try to intervene in the work of the agency; one of the more interesting aspects of its future development will be to see how long they are able to resist that temptation.

Next Steps and Performance Measurement

PATRICIA GREER AND NEIL CARTER

The formation of agencies represents the Next Steps in both the broad sweep of British public sector managerial reform (transcending the Financial Management Initiative) and, more narrowly, in the continuing development of public sector performance evaluation. The FMI encouraged the mass development of performance indicators (PIs) throughout the public sector but, because the objective of increasing decentralization was largely unfulfilled, PIs were used only cosmetically in most organizations. Under Next Steps central departments need to exercise 'hands-off' control over executive agencies: it is this structural reform of government, reinforced by the formal linking of performance indicators and targets to objectives and (ultimately) resources, which should provide a major incentive to improve and employ PI systems. Consequently, one yardstick by which to evaluate the impact of Next Steps is by the robustness of PIs and the extent to which they are being used by departments and agencies. If PIs are being utilized, much may be learnt about Next Steps by observing which dimensions of performance Whitehall is most concerned to control.

This chapter examines the important role played by performance indicators in the Next Steps initiative. Models developed in earlier work (Carter, 1991; Carter et al., 1992) are used to analyze the PIs found in the business plans of the five agencies formed by the Department of Social Security. Despite a decade of managerialist reform, departments and agencies have still found it necessary to allocate significant resources to improving the design of PIs - a response that suggests that Next Steps is forcing PIs to be taken more seriously than before.

Establishing the Links: Agencies and Indicators

The Next Steps initiative continues the public sector managerial revolution which Hood has called the 'New Public Management' (Hood, 1991). The overall objective of this revolution has been to transform the culture of the civil service through the introduction of managerial doctrines and techniques; in particular, a central concern has been to improve the monitoring, control and evaluation of performance. Yet Next Steps was born out of the frustration felt by Rayner and his colleagues that by 1986-7, despite several years of reform, the civil service still showed little sign of real cultural change. There had been some positive achievements: the efficiency scrutiny programme and the FMI had undoubtedly inculcated civil servants with a greater consciousness about costs and resource use, while MINIS and the FMI had improved the quality and acceptability of information systems in Whitehall (Metcalfe and Richards, 1990; Gray and Jenkins et al., 1991). However, it was clear that the substance had not really changed: the Whitehall culture of caution remained intact; a safe pair of hands was still preferable to an innovator; proven management skills did not necessarily improve individual promotion prospects (Hennessy, 1989). Despite the FMI there was still very little devolution of financial and managerial responsibility down the line. Worse, there was evidence of demoralization and demotivation, particularly at middle and junior levels of management (National Audit Office, 1986; Colville and Tompkins, 1989).

The same was true for the specific issue of performance evaluation. The FMI was the catalyst for the proliferation of performance indicators throughout the public sector: the number of output and performance measures included in the Public Expenditure White Paper rose from around 500 in 1986 to 2,302 in 1989, although there was considerable variation between departments in the 'coverage, amount, quality and detail of the published performance information' (National Audit Office, 1991a, p. 7). Departments discovered serious constraints on both the design and the use of PIs. The conceptual complexities facing the design of reliable PIs - particularly of effectiveness and the associated aspects of quality and consumer satisfaction - have been widely chronicled (See Carter, 1991; Carter et al., 1992; Cave et al., 1990; Pollitt, 1986). Yet, despite a growing consensus about the characteristics and looks of a 'good' PI system (Carter, 1991; Cave et al., 1988; Flynn et al., 1988; Jackson, 1988), progress continued to be hampered by technical obstacles, notably the availability of reliable data. Thus the Treasury and Civil Service Committee recently complained that 'We are disappointed that the lack of suitable management information systems should still be seen as an impediment to the comprehensive presentation of performance measures after more than a decade of seemingly radical civil service management reform' (1991, p. xi). Even when design problems are overcome, there remains the problem of integrating PIs into strategic and operational management: i.e. in actually using PIs. While there is evidence of a gradual increase, albeit limited and variable, in the use of PIs (Carter et al., 1992; Cave et al., 1990; Jenkins et al., 1987), when Next Steps was launched PIs could not be described as a central and irreplaceable tool of civil service management.

Hence the significance of the Next Steps initiative for the future development of performance evaluation and, vice versa, the crucial role that PIs must play in the agency experiment. At the heart of the Next Steps programme is the objective of devolving financial and managerial responsibility for service delivery away from the central department. But this creates the flexibility/accountability tension - the free-standing, flexible agency must still be accountable to its sponsoring department - and the paradox: that to decentralize it is necessary to centralize (Perrow, 1977; see also Carter, 1989; Metcalfe and Richards, 1990). In theory, a reliable system of performance indicators allows a department to maintain effective 'hands-off' control over an agency which retains its flexibility. In practice, because the department holds ultimate responsibility for performance it may not want to 'let go'; it may seek to obtain as much information as possible to allow it to exercise virtual 'hands-on' control (Greer, 1992).

The monitoring and control system is made explicit by the formalized performance target-setting which is built into the agency business plans. These plans include a number of PIs and targets agreed between the responsible minister, central department and agencies. In effect, the business plans are the agencies' 'contracts' by which they agree to deliver a specified performance within a given level of resources, taking account of Treasury forecasts regarding areas of uncertainty such as inflation, growth, unemployment. Such forecasts will generally be more significant for non-trading, service-providing agencies than for the more business-oriented agencies which raise all or part of their revenue from receipts. If there are marked variations between forecasts and events then agencies can submit supplementary bids for additional resources to meet unplanned demand. There is, however, uncertainty regarding the point at which it is appropriate for a Chief Executive to bid for supplementary resources rather than attempting to meet additional demands (and the set targets) within existing resources.

The expanding role of PIs has already had an impact on the relationship between the Treasury, departments and agencies. The increasing use of PIs by departments in exercising hands-off control over agencies provides the Treasury with more information about the use of resources in various aspects of departmental activity. This is a double-edged sword: on the one hand, there is less scope for departments to disguise inefficiencies; on the other hand, when bids are not fully met departments and agencies can ask ministers to be explicit about which areas of service should be cut.

A wide range of other interested bodies may also be watching PIs closely. PIs could be exploited by parliamentary committees and individual politicians to hold ministers and chief executives responsible for service delivery in the political arena. Interested professional and consumer groups are likely to pay PIs increasing regard particularly as a means of monitoring the quality of service delivery. This last trend is likely to gain impetus from the Citizens Charter initiative which requires service organizations to display publicly details of individual branch or unit performance against targets.

Thus Next Steps is the successor to the FMI in continuing the forward march of performance evaluation. At the end of the 1980s, it appeared that departments had introduced many of the basic requirements of performance evaluation - new information systems, a selection of performance indicators and a limited degree of target-setting. It seemed to some observers that the task of constructing PIs for the new agencies would involve little more than some fine tuning of existing PIs, with the possible exception of continuing the ongoing efforts to design better effectiveness and quality of service PIs (Lewis and Jones, 1990). We now turn to the early experiences of the DSS agencies to investigate whether the FMI enabled the Next Steps initiative to develop robust systems of performance evaluation.

The Department of Social Security Agencies

The Department of Social Security provides an informative study because it incorporates several 'types' of agency (Greer, 1992). The DSS has five agencies which employ over 97 per cent of the Department's staff: the Resettlement Agency, one of the first agencies (established in April 1988); the Information Technology Services Agency (ITSA; April 1990); the Contributions Agency (April 1991); the Benefits Agency, by far the largest of all the agencies with some 70,000 staff (April 1991); and the Child Support Agency (April 1993).

The Child Support Agency is an extreme example of an agency starting almost from scratch; it has inherited an Act of Parliament but few extant organizational structures. Less extreme was the starting point for the Contributions Agency which possessed no management structure as staff were previously integrated into the organizational structure of the Benefits buildings and areas in which they worked. The main tasks in developing the Contributions Agency have therefore been to establish a management structure, to distinguish its objectives and information systems from those of the Benefits Agency and of the department, and to develop appropriate indicators and targets for measuring the performance of the new agency. With this in mind, the Contributions Agency operated as a unit for one year to allow some time for structures to be developed prior to its launch as an agency. Similarly, the Information Technology Services Agency ran as a district departmental section for one year before becoming an agency. Prior to this, however, computer services had already been brought together in one division (the information technology services division) which allowed time for it to develop organizational structures and information systems. Although the Benefits Agency has also had to develop its own management structures, it had established information systems for the payment of benefits back in the early 1970s. The Resettlement Agency is unique because one of its primary aims is to close down all resettlement units to a planned timetable and hand over responsibility for its functions to local authorities. The agency was formed from a distinct division within the DSS, albeit a small and relatively unimportant section of the department as a whole. At the outset, its performance information was limited to one PI of 'cost per bed'. It had no effectiveness measures even for assessing the extent to which resettlement units were achieving the main objective of resettling homeless people into stable lives.

The Role of Performance Information in the Relationship between DSS Head Quarters and its Agencies

Reliable information is vital if central departments are to monitor and control agency performance. There is, however, a tension concerning the nature and extent of information about the agency that is kept by the centre. Departments have to balance the need for strategic information on the overall performance of an agency against any tendency to demand an excessive volume of information at such frequent intervals that the new autonomy and flexibility of the agency is curtailed. The relationship between the DSS and its agencies suggests that this balance of 'hands-off' control and 'backseat driving' has yet to be satisfactorily achieved. During the initial stages of an agency's existence there is a degree of ambiguity in its relationship with the department because the agency objectives, management structures and information systems are in a process of constant evolution. It seems that the departmental finance divisions and the Treasury have exploited this uncertainty to justify repeated requests for more information than is perhaps necessary for strategic control.

Agency framework documents state that departments are responsible for selecting performance indicators and targets in consultation with their agencies. This choice effectively establishes the framework for legitimate departmental interest in agency activities. There is no blueprint on the precise form that these consultations and negotiations should take. The DSS experience suggests that departmental headquarters very much took the lead in deciding the initial PIs and targets. However, with experience in the application of these PIs and targets, it seems likely that the agency will be able to play an increasingly informed and persuasive role in these negotiations.

Analysis of Initial Agency Performance Indicators

An analysis of the initial DSS performance indicators as they appeared in the agency business plans is contained in Table 1.

Table 1 Performance indicators in the first four DSS agencies

	Process	Efficiency Quant./Qual.		Effectiveness Quant./Qual.		Total
Resettlement Agency	4	2	0	1	0	7
Benefits Agency	0	6	0	0	1	7
ITSA	0	4	0	3	0	7
Contributions Agency	2	6	0	1	0	9
Totals	6	18	0	5	1	30

Source: Initial business plans of the four agencies.

Note: Quant. = quantitative indicators
Qual. = qualitative indicators

The analysis raises three main issues. Senior management at the DSS told us that there was a conscious decision to limit the number of 'high level' Secretary of State targets in order to retain room for management flexibility. However, there are some agency objectives for which there are no performance indicators - a feature which, according to the Treasury and Civil Service Committee review of departmental reports, reflects what continues to be a general weakness in published performance information: 'the welter of performance measures and indicators provided are often poorly related to departmental aims and objectives ... Key policies frequently have no indicators relating to them included in departmental reports' (Treasury and Civil

Service Committee, 1991, pp. x-xi). One omission relates to the provision of policy advice which is an objective common to all the DSS agencies; indeed, the agencies frequently offer advice on policy initiatives and policy implementation. The main reason for the lack of PIs in this area is the difficulty of measurement which has continuously plagued earlier attempts to evaluate government policy advice (Financial Management Unit, 1985; though see National Audit Office, 1991a). A second gap concerns the objective of the Contributions Agency to maintain 'comprehensive and accurate' national insurance records. There is, however, no explicit indicator for the accuracy of the records, although there are other less overt indicators such as the number of surveys undertaken. A recent National Audit Office (1991b) report shows that there may be many inaccuracies in the figures. Again this might be explained by the difficulty of constructing a suitable measure, but even if it were technically possible to devise a suitable measure revealing these inaccuracies, it may still be politically unacceptable to do so.

Second, there are a number of 'process' performance indicators measuring throughputs rather than outcomes. The Resettlement Agency has four 'process' indicators and the Contributions Agency has two. Two of the Resettlement Agency process indicators relate to establishing standards of quality of service and to developing a methodology for defining and measuring resettlement; areas which are central to its function but for which performance information had not previously been developed, possibly because of this work being given a low priority.

The Information Technology Services Agency technically also has process indicators such as 'to complete the work programme within cash allocation', but as the objectives to which these indicators relate are process objectives, then these can be regarded as efficiency and effectiveness PIs of how those process objectives are met.

Third, there is an overall emphasis on quantitative efficiency indicators and few effectiveness and, in particular, qualitative effectiveness indicators (although it is possible to categorize as effectiveness measures some of the throughput PIs - such as clearance times - categorized in Table 1 as efficiency measures). This reflects a general weakness in the PI systems that sprang up in the wake of the FMI: the paucity of effectiveness PIs, particularly regarding any measures of quality and consumer satisfaction. Indeed, the NAO recorded just 110 indicators of 'quality of service' - the extent to which the nature and delivery of the outputs meet objectives and, where appropriate, user needs - in the 1989 public expenditure white paper (National Audit Office, 1991a). Most of these, as in the Benefits Agency, were measures of timeliness or accuracy. Moving beyond this to measure quality in terms of outcomes, i.e. the nature of the final product, has proven technically very difficult (Carter, 1991). It can also be complicated and costly to measure customer (or claimant) satisfaction with the service.

Developments since Establishment of Initial Performance Indicators

The DSS agencies have put considerable effort into further developing objectives, performance indicators and targets. In part, recent progress has been made possible by technological advances that offer new potential for developing and using information systems. However, agencies have been returning to first principles by examining what should be measured and how this should be achieved. These efforts can be explained by the vested interest shared by the central department and the agencies in ensuring that the measures used in the contractual frameworks are relevant and robust.

This process of re-examination is particularly true for the Benefits Agency which, on the face of it, having had a set of PIs for some twenty years (Carter et al., 1992) should have less work to do than the other newly-formed agencies. Yet the Benefits Agency has taken a fresh look at the way in which it measures and reports clearance times and accuracy rates - its long-established core PIs. For example, the agency was forced to accept that its previous sample-based error rate PI was unreliable, thereby revealing that to improve these measures, it will have to concede that its performance was poorer than had previously been admitted. The most significant change is reflected in the 1992/93 Benefits Agency performance indicators which, in most cases, replace average clearance times with measured actual end-to-end clearance times; i.e. a move away from average clearance times to statements about the percentage cleared in a specified number of days (for example, the 1992-93 target for Disability Working Allowance is 95 per cent of claims cleared in five days). These new measures will allow the Benefits Agency to develop a more contractual relationship with its customers. Eventually it may be possible to move from measures of, say, 95 per cent in five days to 99 per cent in five days (though this may be some while off!). Compensation could then be made to those claimants whose claim is not cleared within the specified time. However, the aim of moving to 100 per cent or close to 100 per cent has implications for resources, diminishing returns and incentives: the extra costs involved in reaching the target may not be justified by the returns and, as failure in just one case may result in a missed target there is no longer the incentive to pull out the stops on the remainder.

The recent Treasury guide on setting targets and measuring performance of executive agencies states that measures such as those recently developed by the DSS 'should be avoided', as those people whose claims are not dealt with in the specified period will find little comfort from knowing that 90 per cent of all other claims were processed in that time (HM Treasury, 1992). Instead, the guide suggests that targets applying to the whole output are preferable (e.g. all correctly completed applications will be dealt with in four days and 80 per cent in two days).

It is therefore likely that the Benefits Agency will need to develop further its latest measures. Another change stemming from both Next Steps and the Citizens Charter is the attempt to develop more measures of customer satisfaction. At present this dimension is measured as part of the 'National Customer Survey' which provides a snapshot of the degree of satisfaction of a sample of claimants at a certain point in the year. The Benefits Agency has delegated responsibility for assessing customer satisfaction to local areas, possibly through the use of continuous surveys. Districts are actively encouraged to conduct customer surveys specifically designed to meet their local needs.

The other DSS agencies are reviewing their PIs as the development of their agencies throws up demands for different types of performance information. An example of this is that ITSA may soon be charging, at least notionally, for the services it provides. This will enable customers to consider the complete unit costs of their outputs, including the IT resource costs involved. Similarly, as ITSA may also be able to expand into other markets, it could produce a PI measuring its success in penetrating new markets.

A further reason why performance information may change arises from the limited potential for indefinite efficiency savings. For example, the Contributions Agency had the ever-tightening target of collecting outstanding National Insurance contributions, including those paid by the self-employed. Clearly, the size of the pot of outstanding contributions will reduce over time until there comes a point at which either the target will also have to be re-negotiated or it may be decided that such a measure is no longer appropriate. Nevertheless, departments are required to make efficiency gains of at least 1.5 per cent annually and cumulatively on the whole of their running costs provision. Agencies are expected to achieve a higher saving (HM Treasury, 1992). In this climate, the more successful agencies are in achieving targets, the more likely it is that targets will become increasingly stringent. If targets become too tight then the effectiveness of the growing number of performance related pay systems may be impaired. The salary of the chief executive is closely linked to the achievement of agency targets; excessively tough targets will have a direct impact on financial rewards. Moreover, although a group performance bonus is available in many agencies when targets are met, the sum paid to individuals is marginal compared to their overall salary. As targets become tougher staff will be less likely to respond: as one manager put it 'what's the point in working flat out all year for only £100 and then being squeezed even more the next year?' Thus it may be that the limited availability of financial rewards in the public sector will result in the paradox that new performance related pay systems designed to motivate individuals end up de-motivating many staff.

Conclusions

It is clear that the DSS agencies have responded to the requirement of Next Steps that they develop reliable and usable performance indicator systems. Although apparently 'neutral', PIs become highly political instruments mediating the delicate relationship between department and agency. For PIs are the means of exercising 'hands-off' control and holding agencies accountable. They are central to the target-setting mechanism and act as the conduit for resource allocation. Moreover, the current enthusiasm for 'market testing', requiring the department or agency to hold contractor organizations responsible for performance, should reinforce the pressure to develop and improve PIs.

The FMI played a key enabling role. It initiated significant advances in developing information systems (particularly financial) and persuaded many civil servants to become more aware of costs and to accept the use of managerial techniques like performance indicators. Yet it is interesting to observe the extent to which an organization like the Benefits Agency, with its long record of using PIs, has still returned to first principles. Despite the changes brought about by the FMI, it would appear that many fundamental design issues remain unresolved.

This observation points to a critical difference between FMI and Next Steps. The FMI ordered departments to manufacture PIs but the promised devolution of authority never happened; so PIs proliferated but remained of marginal importance. Under Next Steps there are stronger financial and managerial incentives to use PIs: now that the crucial link to resources has been made it is vital that PI systems be sound. Thus the Benefits Agency recognized certain shortcomings in its existing clearance time and accuracy PIs and has taken some action to improve them. Ironically, improvements in information systems allow departments to become more ambitious and, in so doing, reveal the weaknesses in existing PIs. Technology has not, so far, enabled equivalent improvements in other measures such as accuracy and customer satisfaction.

Nevertheless the general direction of developments is in line with the findings of earlier research. The design of the emerging systems is parsimonious rather than profligate in focusing on a small core of PIs; timely in the recording and publication of indicators; and, by returning to first principles, increasingly custom-built rather than data-driven (Carter, 1991). These characteristics are not definitive; it would be dangerous to prescribe the form a 'good' PI system should take. Moreover, it is too early to say whether the systems now in place are effective. However, the DSS agencies seem to have accepted the prevailing view that a system characterized by the above features will probably be more comprehensible and therefore more likely to be used.

The use of PIs is also changing. The majority of agency PIs are still 'tin-openers' in that they ask questions rather than provide definitive answers (Carter, 1989), but by setting formal targets linked to objectives many PIs are looking more and more like dials. One enabling factor behind this development is the general improvement in the quality and reliability of financial information and performance indicator systems which, as noted, is also changing the nature of the relationship between the Treasury, departments and agencies. The political momentum comes from the emphasis on targeting that is integral to Next Steps but given new urgency by the Citizen's Charter initiative with its exhortation to publish targets and league tables. It should be pointed out, however, that this focus on PIs represents a very narrow understanding of performance evaluation. Nowhere in Next Steps or Citizen's Charter is there any attempt to develop alternative mechanisms of performance evaluation. For example, despite the well rehearsed limitations of programme and policy evaluation, at least these more ambitious mechanisms are capable of probing issues such as quality and impact that PI systems tend to cover only partially.

A central aim of Next Steps (and the Citizen's Charter) is to improve the managerial competence of government, but the increased visibility of performance standards and achievement may bring new demands for greater accountability. It should be a broader form of accountability: not just to the department and to Parliament but also to consumers and service users. Of course, whether pressure groups or individual consumers will be able to wield the new information unleashed by the implementation of the Citizen's Charter to secure improvements in service delivery is another question. But it does appear that the prevailing political climate, with a senior Cabinet minister responsible for implementing the Charter, will at least encourage departments and agencies to continue their efforts to develop more and better PIs of the quality and effectiveness of service delivery.

PART THREE
QUESTIONS AND
CONTROVERSIES

Next Steps: Consequences for the Core and Central Departments

PETER BARBERIS

Introduction

The Ibbs Report acknowledged from the outset in 1988 that the Next Steps programme had 'substantial implications' for the core and central departments in Whitehall (Efficiency Unit, 1988, para. 25). The Treasury and Civil Service Committee (TCSC) noted that there would be radical changes in their character and functions (Treasury and Civil Service Committee, 1989, paras. 67 and 72). The Government agreed that relationships between agencies and their respective core departments would be one of the most 'important and difficult areas' (Office of the Minister of the Civil Service, 1990, p. 11). Similar sentiments have been expressed by the former Next Steps Project Team Manager (Treasury and Civil Service Committee, 1990, Q. 40).

On the whole, however, the implications for core departments have been slow to come to the forefront. Metcalfe and Richards (1990, p. 235) have noted the conspicuous absence of any sustained attempt to change the way core departments work. There are some obvious reasons for this. First, the very creation of agencies has naturally placed them rather than the core departments at the centre of attention. The moving parts of a system, so to speak, are more noticeable than those which seem to remain fixed. Second, debate has been dominated by operational rather than strategic management concerns (Painter, 1991, p. 83). Thus the emphasis has been upon questions of micro-management with which agencies are more closely identified. Third, inasmuch as discussion has transcended operational matters the primary focus has been on constitutional issues such as public accountability and ministerial responsibility. Core departments have therefore been somewhat overshadowed by the twin towers of agencies and ministers. Finally, the broad direction in which reform will unfold is itself as yet uncertain. According to one commentator, Next Steps is the antithesis of the reforms instituted by Sir Warren Fisher during the 1920s - reforms which (with notable embellishments) were predicated upon the Northcote-Trevelyan Report of the mid-nineteenth century (Hennessy, 1989, p. 618). On the other hand Timothy Renton, as Minister for the Civil Service, told the House of Commons in May 1991 that Next Steps could be seen as the culmination of the reform movement unleashed by Northcote-Trevelyan (Official Report, 1990-91, Col. 668). Much depends upon the particular aspect under examination but most would incline towards the Hennessy interpretation.

Nowhere are these uncertainties more apparent than in their consequences for the core. Yet there are few issues arising from Next Steps which do not have a bearing upon core departments, directly or indirectly. To some extent these bearings have been brought into focus by the Fraser Report of May 1991 - a report that is more prescriptive and speculative than it is empirical and analytical. This is perhaps inevitable. For there is quite simply little firm evidence about the impact of Next Steps upon the core. Yet, as Sir Angus Fraser and others have pointed out, the recent waves of reform did not begin with Next Steps, or even with the Financial Management Initiative (FMI) of the early 1980s, much as these developments have hastened the pace of change. On the contrary subterranean stirrings were already giving forth gentle tremors within the Whitehall core in the years following Fulton - more so than was perhaps evident at the time.

In examining and assessing the consequences for the core departments this chapter makes two analytical distinctions. First, to separate out, insofar as present evidence permits, the manifest impact of Next Steps to date from the potential implications, likely and possible. Second, where the consequences of Next Steps appear problematical, to distinguish between those which are inherent to Next Steps and those which have arisen, or seem likely to arise, from the particular mode of implementation. These perspectives will, where appropriate, inform discussion under six headings: core-agency relationships and the departmental hierarchy; the size, shape and structure of the core; the role of senior officials within the core; their career patterns; implications for the central departments; and the integrity of the core in terms of essential values and characteristics. Questions of public accountability are touched upon here only inasmuch as they pertain to the changing roles and relationships of those within the core.

Core-Agency Relationships and the Departmental Hierarchy

It is easy to picture the Ibbs Report as a programme for dynamic reform pitched against a background of top-heavy, policy-orientated, neo-classical hierarchies of the traditional ministerial department. This would be as misleading as it is an overstatement. Long before Ibbs the pattern of central government was already much more varied, relationships more complex, systems 'inherently less hierarchical in their operations' (Dunleavy, 1989, p. 252) than is often assumed. Matrix-type relationships within most core departments long ago superseded the rigid, command-like, hierarchies of which the Home Office under Sir Charles Cunningham (Permanent Under-Secretary, 1957-66) was perhaps the last example. Moreover the creation during the 1970s of such organizations as the Property Services Agency and the Defence Procurement Executive - each headed by a (second) permanent secretary but within the embrace of the DoE and the MoD respectively - marked a further challenge to former hierarchical arrangements. Nevertheless these earlier agencies did not involve the extensive devolution of responsibility to line managers envisaged under Next Steps.

What, then, is the relationship now envisaged between agencies and their core departments; and what are the evident and likely consequences for departmental hierarchies? The official position is that agencies should have the maximum freedom compatible with expenditure limits and within the parameters of 'robust' performance targets and departmental policies - all of which agency chief executives will have a hand in formulating. The onus will be upon departments to justify interference rather than upon agency chief executives to claim their independence (Office of the Minister for the Civil Service, 1990, p. 5). The structures envisaged have been variously described. The Government has referred to a 'federal structure of more autonomous units' (Office of the Minister for the Civil Service, 1989, p. 5). In evidence to the TCSC Norman Lamont, then Chief Secretary to the Treasury, talked about disconnecting agencies from their linkages with parent departments (Treasury and Civil Service Committee, 1990, Q. 209). Sir Peter Kemp described agencies as being 'semi-detached ... still quite close to the core ... (not) totally detached' (Treasury and Civil Service Committee, 1991, Q. 417). Meanwhile, one of the chief executives, Mike Fogden, has described the framework document for his Employment Service Agency as a 'bill of rights' (Treasury and Civil Service Committee, 1990, Q. 87).

All of this seems to reflect the unsettled, transitory, nature of things at present. Much will obviously depend upon the extent to which agencies become unplugged from their sponsoring departments. Perhaps the worst-state scenario for core departments would be to recede into some kind of managerial no-man's land, overshadowed by agencies on the one hand and by ministers together with their topmost advisers on the other. Even this assumes the paradigm of a unilateral relationship between each individual agency and its core department. In this respect the notion, already mooted, of internal markets could herald a yet greater challenge. An agency would then be able to sell its services to different departments, just as each department would be free to buy-in from agencies sponsored by other departments, or indeed from outside the civil service. Core departments would lose their sense of ownership. Indeed they may cease, so to speak, even to be majority shareholders in the agencies they nominally sponsor. The consequences for the core would be profound. It is difficult to see how, in these circumstances, core departments could exercise any meaningful supervision, either in matters of management or of policy.

In practice there is no sign so far of any such cataclysm, though there are no firm historical data against which comparisons may be made (Hogwood, 1993, p. 13). At the same time, the Fraser Report found evidence of frustration over the number of detailed and comparatively trivial management decisions which still have to be referred back by agencies to their core departments and to the Treasury (Efficiency Unit, 1991, para. 3.19). Clearly, departments are not letting go to the extent initially envisaged. Relationships between agencies and departments have therefore not yet been tested to anywhere near their limit. The new managerialism has not, so far, seriously challenged traditional forms and structures. Yet there is already some evidence of limited change. According to the former Next Steps Project Manager there is a perceptible trend from an hierarchical system to one in which the minister and the agency chief executive are in a quasi-contractual position (Treasury and Civil Service Committee, 1990, Q. 170). This the TCSC interpreted as meaning that chief executives are more directly responsible to their ministers than to their departmental hierarchies (Treasury and Civil Service Committee, 1990, para. 26). Such would be consistent with Kemp's earlier statement that there was no intention to put any 'fudge' between chief executives and ministers (Treasury and Civil Service Committee, 1989, Q. 34).

In the short-run core departments are unlikely to be left out in the cold, if only on account of the need for sustained financial stringency. Thus the Fraser Report described how approval to exceed delegated expenditure had been granted to an agency chief executive by a core department official three grades his junior (Efficiency Unit, 1991, para. 3.7). It is not uncommon for Treasury officials to deal with their more highly graded counterparts in the spending departments and this could become the pattern for routine relationships between core departments and their agencies. This assumes, first, that such relationships are not deliberately overturned as constituting a threat to the whole philosophy of Next Steps; second, that core departments remain sufficiently staffed to maintain such supervision. We must therefore look at the size, shape and structure of the core.

The Size, Shape and Structure of the Core Departments

The Ibbs Report envisaged 'a relatively small core' to service ministers and to manage business through the sponsorship of agencies (Efficiency Unit, 1988, para. 44). Three years later the Fraser Report called specifically for a 25 per cent reduction in the aggregate numbers employed by core departments in their 'personnel and finance divisions and in any support services not provided on an untied and full cost basis' (Efficiency Unit, 1991, para. 2.14). In subsequent evidence to the TCSC Sir Angus Fraser explained the three reasons underpinning this recommendation (Treasury and Civil Service Committee, 1991, Q. 375). First, that there should be staffing reductions in the core departments commensurate with the need for agencies themselves to establish personnel and finance services support for their operations. Second, small cores were a feature of successful organizations outside the civil service. Third, that a small core would encourage the desired 'hands-off' approach. The Government was quick to endorse the notion of staff reductions in the core departments. In a written reply to the House of Commons on 16 May 1991 the Prime Minister explained that, in consequence of the shift from day-to-day involvement and towards 'strategic advice and direction', the number of people 'at the centres of departments' can be reduced (Official Report, 1990-1, col. 248). Inasmuch as they are typically involved in day-to-day matters this could imply corresponding reductions in the numbers of junior ministers and perhaps a change in their role, too.

The extent to which long term shrinkage in the core is both possible and likely will, again, depend upon the pattern of agency-departmental connections that evolve. Observers are far from unanimous as to which model is the most likely. Some see an end-game resembling the Swedish system of very small core departments with a multiplicity of hived-off agencies doing most of the work (Fry, 1988, p. 433). Others have denied any such possibility in the absence of a reformed system of public law incorporating judicial review procedures comparable to those in Sweden (Metcalfe and Richards, 1990, p. 230). Others again have seen closer resemblances with the US federal government inasmuch as traditionally unified departments may adopt more segmented, intra-departmental, structures (Dunleavy and Francis, 1990).

Other things being equal, the greater the amount of work devolved and the more remote the supervision exercised, the greater the scope for staffing reductions in the core. But other things rarely are equal. Pam Alexander, Vice-President of the First Division Association (FDA), has warned of the danger of an additional layer of bureaucracy arising from the need for core departments to monitor the activities of agencies (Treasury and Civil Service Committee, 1988, Q. 192). Indeed the Fraser Report acknowledged that, in the short term, the creation of agencies often imposed additional burdens upon core departments, involved as they are in the formulation of agency agreements, target-setting and evaluation. But it remains unclear as to what exactly is meant by the short term. Nor is it clear as to whether reductions in the core departments are supposed exactly to compensate for the support services required by agencies in addition to their operational components, so maintaining existing overall manpower levels; or whether a non-compensatory (i.e. smaller) reduction in the core could be tolerated, bringing a modest increase in total manpower levels; or whether reductions in the core should more than compensate to facilitate and to reflect the new streamlined management, thus making possible reductions in the total size of the civil service.

Whichever is the case, we should expect at some stage to see certain reductions in core staffing levels over and above the operational components extracted to form the new agencies. Of this there is no sign at present as can be seen from the figures in Table 1. These figures indicate the numbers of ministers and senior civil servants within selected core departments. All sections or divisions within these departments which were subsequently removed to form agencies are excluded from the 1987/88 figures as, of course, are agencies themselves from those for 1993. This allows proper comparability between the two sets of figures. The four departments chosen are those more than half of whose staff are engaged in agencies. We must bear in mind that the core departments in question have all to some extent been re-organized during the period of agency creation. Such re-organizations may have taken place in any case but they cannot have been entirely unaffected by the creation of agencies. Of course many of the agencies sponsored by these departments - even the big, politically sensitive ones such as the Social Security Benefits Agency - enjoyed a discrete identity prior to full agency status. Their creation as agencies may therefore have had less impact upon the size and structure of the core than have the effects upon, say, the DTI of its assumption in 1992 of many of the functions of the former Department of Energy. It is interesting to note that the DTI is the only one of the four departments in which there has been a reduction (of nearly 7 per cent) in the number of officials.

Such are the complexities and subtleties of organizational change - and of the work undertaken within sections of departments that remain structurally stable - that precise comparisons are difficult, even over a five year period. Yet, organizational complexities and subtleties notwithstanding, it is clear that Fraser expected some manifest reduction, the only uncertainty being about the time-scale. And it is equally clear that, overall, there is little evidence of such contraction, either in the number of officials or in the number of ministers. It may be that only if agencies are carved out from areas of work closer to the heart of departments and if the degree of autonomy achieved by, say, HMSO is to become the norm will there be contraction in the core on the scale called for by Fraser. This would then have consequences for the roles of senior officials within the core, a critical topic to which we must now turn.

Table 1 **Numbers of ministers and civil servants (by grade) in comparable sections of certain core departments before (1987 and 1988) and after (1993) the creation of agencies**

A. Ministers

Grade	1987/1988					1993				
	EDG	DSS	DTI	DTr	Total	EDG	DSS	DTI	DTr	Total
Sec of State	1	1	1	1	4	1	1	1	1	4
Ministers/ Under Secs	3	3	5	4	15	3	4	5	4	16
Parly. Priv. Secs.	1	2	1	2	6	1	2	3	1	7
Other	-	-	-	1	1	-	-	-	1	1
					26					28

B. Civil Servants

Grade	EDG	DSS	DTI	DTr	Total	EDG	DSS	DTI	DTr	Total
1	1	1	1	1	4	1	1	1	1	4
1A	1	-	-	-	1	-	-	-	-	0
2	2	2	9	5	18	3	2	6	4	15
3	9	8	37	16	70	13	9	30	17	69
4	5	-	4	6	15	2	-	8	9	19
5	53	29	118	70	270	52	33	112	70	267
Priv. Secs	5	4	9	5	23	6	6	9	6	27
					401					401

EDG = Employment Department Group [1,3]
DSS = Department of Social Security [2]
DTI = Department of Trade and Industry [1,2,4]
DTr = Department of Transport [1]

1. Excludes regional offices
2. Excludes Solicitor's Office
3. Figures for 1988 exclude the Small Firms Division
4. Figures for 1993 exclude the Small Firms Division and sections/ divisions drawn from the former Department of Energy

Source: Civil Service Yearbooks, 1987-1993

The Changing Roles of Senior Officials Within Core Departments

It was one of the Fulton Committee's main complaints that senior civil servants paid too much attention to their role as ministerial advisers while devoting too little time to the management of their departments (Fulton Report, 1968, para. 18). Ibbs broadly confirmed the accuracy of this picture twenty years later, reflected in the now famous words of a deputy secretary that 'the golden route to the top is through policy not through management' (Efficiency Unit, 1988, para. 4). Sir Peter Carey claims that the first genuinely managerial job he had was upon becoming Permanent Secretary at the DTI/Department of Industry during the 1970s. He bemoaned the fact that his progress through the hierarchy had given him little preparation for this role (Carey, 1984, p. 82). Certainly management has had a low status in Whitehall, though things are now changing. This low status is in part the product of an 'impoverished concept' of management, associating it with lower level work (Metcalfe and Richards, 1990, p. 216). In part, too, it springs from the constitutional imperatives of the ministerial department. Everything is done, nominally at least, in the name of the minister. Ministers, in turn, look to their senior officials for advice and support - almost to the point of a dependency relationship in some cases. Certainly relationships between ministers and senior officials are usually close ones, sometimes closer and with franker discussion than pertains between ministers and their Cabinet colleagues (Headey, 1974, p. 153; Wass, 1984, p. 58; Theakston, 1987, p. 105).

Ministers, then, are and are likely to remain the focal point for most senior core department officials. Neither the Ibbs Report nor any of the subsequent official pronouncements have denied this. Indeed Ibbs wanted to increase rather than to diminish the 'crucial skill' of the senior civil servant in helping ministers 'to handle politics and political sensitivities effectively' (Efficiency Unit, 1988, para. 6). In fact Ibbs and other upholders of Next Steps have unleashed a three-pronged assault: first, to enhance the management role of officials within the core; second, to encourage a strategic rather than a day-to-day supervisory management style; third, to separate this role from that of policy support for ministers. Questions arise as to the extent to which such objectives are compatible in principle, obtainable in practice and, if so, at what (if any) cost.

The management role of officials within core departments was neatly expressed by Ibbs in that: '... their task will no longer be the detailed prescription of operational functions: it will be the definition of a rigorous policy and resources framework within which the agency management is set free to manage operations ...' (Efficiency Unit, 1988, para. 25). Hayden Phillips, then a Treasury Deputy Secretary, told the TCSC that this would require of senior officials skills and knowledge quite different from that required in the past (Treasury and Civil Service Committee, 1990, Q. 56). Committee members found some evidence that core departments were beginning to concentrate on strategy and planning rather than on routine issues (Treasury and Civil Service Committee, 1990, para. 59). This suggests either that core officials are more adaptable than is usually acknowledged; or that changes prior to Ibbs were already quite well advanced in this direction; or that it has been possible until now to accommodate a modest shift of emphasis without fundamentally recasting the roles of senior officials. The latter is to imply that the real test is yet to come. Certainly the separation of the policy role from that of strategic management could impose acute conflict for senior officials in the core departments.

The difficulty of separating policy from administration is widely acknowledged in the literature. Yet the whole Next Steps philosophy is, according to one account, built over this particular 'fault-line' (Hood and Jones, 1990, p. 80). Sir Peter Kemp acknowledged the inherent tensions for those in the core departments (Treasury and Civil Service Committee, 1989, Q. 32). These tensions - implicit in any core-agency relationship - are heightened by two features of the new arrangements: the role of agencies in policy making; and the high public profile of agency chief executives, including their accountability to Parliament.

Agency chief executives are already making their contribution to departmental policy. In itself there is nothing remarkable about this. It merely formalizes what has long been the reality - the input to policy from many different quarters and levels within Whitehall. Policy making senior civil servants within core departments are quite accustomed to this. But now there is a change, however subtle it may be: one which is potentially far-reaching. For while they may remain at the centre of broad policy formulation, core officials now know that agency chief executives can appeal directly to the minister. Ministers will no doubt be guided by their permanent and deputy secretaries, to whom chief executives in any case technically report. But the policy roles of those below deputy secretary, or grade 2, level seem uncertain.

Similarly, core officials are involved in establishing framework documents; in setting, monitoring and evaluating agency targets and performance levels. Thus core officials will be enmeshed in management (of a general nature) while chief executives become part of the policy process - a kind of crossover as counterweight to the growing specialization, differentiation and possible polarity between agencies and their core departments. Such is the essence of official reassurances given to those who are concerned that Next Steps will drive a wedge between policy and administration (Treasury and Civil Service Committee, 1989, Q. 275; Butler, 1990, p. 6). These anxieties may prove ill-founded. But there may be a price to be paid for building the bridge between policy and administration. As Chapman (1991, p. 2) says, officials will sometimes have to hold the ring when 'the interests of ministers, their staff and their customers are not precisely the same'. The likelihood of such incongruence of interests will be increased not only because chief executives have a hot line to their ministers but because they are directly accountable to Parliament.

The broader issues of public and Parliamentary accountability lie beyond the scope of this chapter. There may indeed be implications for ministers, hence for constitutional propriety, if high profile chief executives contradict the official line, either in action or in words; or if, in explaining failure to meet targets, they point to lack of funds or of other vital support from the department. Again, core officials would stand exposed to the crossfire within Whitehall, unable (as of course at present) to do other than tuck in behind the minister when faced by Parliamentary Select Committees. In this respect particular questions arise about the role of the permanent secretary as accounting officer.

For some time now the sovereign role of the permanent secretary (together with certain others) as accounting officer has been under challenge (Chapman, 1979, pp. 125-128). Sir Peter Middleton's defence of the permanent secretary as the sole accounting officer was the last bugle-call for a principle which, established over a hundred years ago but consolidated and codified by Sir Warren Fisher in 1920, had nearly run its course. Agency chief executives now share this role with permanent secretaries as agency and departmental accounting officers respectively. In one sense this no more constitutes a qualitative change than does the now commonplace appearance before select committees of other senior and middle-ranking officials. So far, in practice, the new arrangements betray little evidence of tensions incapable of accommodation by experienced and sensible permanent secretaries and chief executives. But from time-to-time they are bound to get at cross purposes, rather in the way that departmental accounting officers have occasionally discharged their role as custodians of probity and regularity to the frustration and embarrassment of ministers. The higher profile of agency chief executives and their greater numbers will increase the likelihood of such incongruence between themselves and the permanent secretaries. The revised *Accounting Officer Memorandum* issued by the Treasury in 1990 and already under review simply fails to recognize either the movement that has taken place or the full implications for permanent departmental heads (Committee of Public Accounts, 1990). It assumes a degree of control and *de facto* authority among permanent secretaries that they probably no longer possess and which in future they will almost certainly not be able to exercise *vis-a-vis* agencies. This will be so especially where agencies have their own votes, or become trading funds, or where added independence is the result of internal market arrangements.

Next Steps therefore has consequences for the roles of permanent secretaries as well as for those below this level. Some have even called for the abolition of the office of permanent secretary and its replacement by 'a layer of top departmental executives through which all subordinates report' (Williams, 1989, p. 260). This seems unlikely to happen in the foreseeable future. Yet the clarification of roles, declared to be one of the possibilities opened up by Next Steps, may prove unattainable without either fragmentation within the core or the artificial separation of policy and administration. These dangers have been recognized to the extent that the mobility of staff between agencies and core departments has been heralded as a necessary corrective.

Career Patterns - Mobility between Core Departments and Agencies

The desirability of staff movement between agencies and core departments has become a near universal mark of faith. The Ibbs Report called for a policy of secondments so to secure '... a balanced expertise in policy, the political environment and service delivery which too few civil servants possess at present' (Efficiency Unit, 1988, para. 28). Sir Peter Kemp thought it desirable that very senior staff should move to and fro (Treasury and Civil Service Committee, 1988, Q. 63); and that the permanent and deputy secretaries of the future in the mainstream civil service should have had 'worthwhile and effective stints in an agency' (Treasury and Civil Service Committee, 1989, Q. 19). Such interchange has been endorsed by the TCSC and accepted by the Government (Treasury and Civil Service Committee, 1988, para. 28; Office of the Minister for the Civil Service, 1988, p. 5). Support has also come from the FDA as part of its campaign to uphold the concept of a unified career service within a national pay framework (Treasury and Civil Service Committee, 1988, Q. 183).

Only tentatively and obliquely have reservations been expressed about the idea of transferability. The TCSC, in upholding the notion, were nevertheless glad to have from the Head of the Civil Service an assurance that good managers would not be subjected to enforced periods back in the core departments where their skills would not be put to such good use (Treasury and Civil Service Committee, 1989, para. 35). The Fraser Report, again while encouraging transfers as a means of fostering closer relationships between agencies and their core departments, warned that there should be no cutting across the responsibilities of chief executives for the good management of their agencies (Efficiency Unit, 1991, Annex A, p. 23). Conversely it could be held that excessive mobility may dilute the core, having implications for its sense of identity, an issue considered more fully below.

If the desirability of mobility is for the moment broadly accepted, then three main questions remain for discussion. First, do present indications, such as they are, suggest the fulfilment of the type of career patterns sought? Second, what are the possible and likely obstacles to their fulfilment? Third, to what extent can such obstacles be overcome without destroying the essence of Next Steps?

Present indications offer few clues as to the future extent of staff mobility between agencies and core departments. We must remember that few of the agencies created so far were ever the springboards for promotion to top posts in the core departments. It is not surprising, then, that among the sixteen agency chief executives so far to have vacated their posts only two, one an under secretary, the other now a deputy secretary, have returned to the Whitehall core. Of the other fourteen, eight have retired, two have transferred to higher graded agency headships, one is on secondment to a private company and three have left the civil service altogether of whom one has become Chief Executive of the London Chamber of Commerce and Industry. At lower levels there is localized evidence of diminished transferability between the DVLA and the Department of Transport (Treasury and Civil Service Committee, 1991, para. 47). Otherwise there is little firm evidence.

We must then ask - what are the likely obstacles to mobility? Sir Frank Cooper claims that the qualities required to work closely with ministers are different from those required of managers (Treasury and Civil Service Committee, 1988, p. 97). This implies not only a practical obstacle but a principled objection to the type of career mobility now sought. As such it has received little attention compared with the implications of the breakdown of national uniform pay scales. For if agencies are able to make their own appointments, to set their own establishments, even to strike their own pay deals, will not transfers be more difficult to achieve? Will not mobility be further frustrated if, as has been predicted (Greer, 1992, p. 223), agencies exploit these freedoms and begin to recruit in their own image while developing a polarization of roles between themselves and their core departments? And if transfers are frustrated will not this lead to the 'fossilized', policy-centred, core that Sir Peter Kemp was so keen to prevent?

The official answer is that '... enabling staff to transfer freely does not require common grading structures throughout the civil service' (Office of the Minister for the Civil Service, 1991, p. 7). The TCSC seem satisfied that a civil service based 'to a lesser extent than at present on standardized, service-wide grades' may still be compatible with transferability (Treasury and Civil Service Committee, 1989, para. 57). History, experience and logic give some credence to such a view. The mobility of senior officials between core departments for which Whitehall is fabled evolved prior to the establishment of uniform grading. Such movement, though, was less common, more concentrated in the senior grades and tended to be associated with random, personalized, factors (Barberis, 1989, pp. 415-428). Logically there is no compelling reason why civil servants could not transfer between agencies and core departments which operated different grading schemes in the same way as individuals move from one private company to another. What really counts is not that grading schemes should be common but that they should be compatible. Here perhaps the greatest challenge may arise from the need to offer salaries well above Whitehall levels in order to attract people to agencies from outside the civil service. It is difficult to see how such people could subsequently be assimilated to regular posts within core departments. For the moment this does not present itself as a major problem in that most of the agency heads were civil servants immediately prior to their appointment as chief executives.

If in the long run flexibility of grading is not to impede transferability between agencies and core departments one (or both) of two requirements may emerge: the extension of open competition to include the filling of individual senior positions in core departments; and/or centrally supervised, if not centrally directed, manpower planning and career development. Open competition has been used to fill many of the agency headships. The Government has promised that this will in future be the norm for such appointments. It is an anomaly that senior posts within core departments should not be filled in the same way. The existence of an anomaly is in itself rarely sufficient to effect a change of policy. But practical imperatives may be a more powerful stimulant. The adoption of direct open competition within core departments may prove necessary in order to overcome the obstacle of heterogeneous grading systems and in the absence of planned career development. Otherwise an ever more insular mandarin elite will be the result of mobility confined to a slimmer and narrower core. Open competition for posts in core departments could therefore become one of the most visible consequences of Next Steps. It seems more likely than the other possibility - centrally-directed career planning, which is now out of favour (Efficiency Unit, 1991, para. 3.8; Office of the Minister for the Civil Service, 1989, p. 7). This begs questions about the consequences of recent changes in recruitment to the civil service.

As from 1991 the Recruitment and Assessment Services Agency (RAS) has assumed, on behalf of the Civil Service Commissioners, responsibility for much of the day-to-day recruitment, including that of fast-stream entrants. It is clear that (core) departments are more heavily involved than formerly, at least in recruitment beyond the confines of the fast-stream. It is a specific policy objective that selection should continue to be on the basis of fair and open competition (RAS, 1992, p. 8). But critics remain unconvinced that the new arrangements will sustain '... the high standards previously expected and achieved by the Civil Service Commission, and so much admired in other countries' (Chapman, 1992, p. 3). For if the highly centralized recruitment for direct entry across the board was heavy-handed and becoming an anachronism, then the near abandonment of a common system will at the very least place in jeopardy the former virtues of predictability and comparability between departments. It may even bring an absolute decline in quality. It will be more difficult in future to know what calibre to expect, say, in an executive officer or a grade 7 civil servant. This could have implications for promotions within the core and, especially, for transfers within and between core departments and between core departments and agencies. At the same time the fast-stream could strengthen its grip upon promotions to senior positions if it alone bears the imprint of common recruitment. This, again, could make for a more insular elite corps.

Meanwhile the TCSC has criticized the absence of an overall strategy in the implementation of Next Steps. This begs questions about the role of the central departments - the Treasury and the Office for Public Service and Science (OPSS) (formerly the OMCS) in particular - about which a few observations are now appropriate.

The Central Departments

As observed by one Cabinet minister, then temporarily on the back-benches: 'The Civil Service has outgrown the power of official control from the centre' (Heseltine, 1990, p. 50). If this be so, then there are two realistic responses: to decentralize and delegate in line with this reality; or to re-equip the centre to exercise the necessary control. The Next Steps philosophy favours decentralization and delegation. The Ibbs Report argued that core departments should at once both delegate to agencies and be freed from detailed control from the centre, especially from the Treasury (Efficiency Unit, 1988, para. 30). The Fraser Report confirmed these sentiments, arguing for a reduction in the size of central as well as of core departments (Efficiency Unit, 1991, para. 2.15). The Government has stated that central functions include 'responsibilities for public expenditure and value for money and for ensuring that basic standards and rules of propriety are maintained'. This may, it says, involve some monitoring together with overall control and co-ordination (Office of the Minister for the Civil Service, 1991, p. 3). Such statements reflect the caution with which central supervision is to be relaxed. Norman Lamont told the TCSC that the Treasury would only acquiesce in delegation where framework agreements were tight and where value for money was the likely result (Treasury and Civil Service Committee, 1990, Q. 214).

With such ambiguity it is not surprising that the Treasury has been involved not only in laying down the principles for framework agreements but also in supervising all the specific agency targets set so far (Treasury and Civil Service Committee, 1991, Qs. 395 and 401). In criticizing this practice the TCSC has shrunk from advocating the model of unbridled freedom from Treasury control, either for agencies or for core departments. Rather it has called for a new style of central control - more general, strategic, supportive of core departments but essentially regulatory. This would require that the roles of the Treasury and the OPSS be more clearly defined. Equally, the TCSC has expressed reservations about the capacity of the centre itself either to define or to carry through any such change of role, especially for the co-ordination of personnel policy (Treasury and Civil Service Committee, 1988, para. 30). The Next Steps Project Team were told by a number of permanent secretaries that the centre is fragmented. A management board to co-ordinate overall strategy was recommended in an internal report written in 1987 by Sir Kenneth Stowe (Flynn, Gray and Jenkins, 1990, p. 165). This assumes that there is an overall strategy to be co-ordinated.

Stowe's recommendation was rejected. Some would argue that, in consequence, the centre of government and the core departments of Whitehall stand in danger of fragmentation. At present the evidence suggests a retention, in practice, of detailed supervision within the skein of nominal delegation. But the policy is to let go eventually. If this is not to result in administrative anarchy there will need to be some corresponding co-ordination and integrative impetus from the centre, not to negate but to harness the energies supposedly released by Next Steps. Perhaps more important in this respect than formal machinery is Whitehall's traditional mechanism for integration - homogeneity, a sense of common identity and a certain public service ethos. It is this integrity, arguably underpinned by the notion of a unified career service, which now begs our attention.

The Integrity of the Core - Challenges to the Whitehall Ethos

While the Fulton Committee launched its now famous onslaught on Whitehall's alleged insular elitism it sought nevertheless to retain the notion of a unified career service (Fulton, 1968, para. 134). By contrast the Ibbs Report saw the concept of a career in a unified civil service as an obstacle to proposals for accountable management which otherwise resembled those of Fulton. Technically a unified service is possible in the sense of common grades and conditions across all the departments without having the majority of officials serve their entire careers in Whitehall - and *vice-versa*. But in Britain these two notions have been closely linked even if, historically, their application has not always been coterminous. And alongside the notion of a unified career service - if, again, only imperfectly - rest the essential values and characteristics which have given the British administrative elite its identity. These values and characteristics have been widely discussed. They include, among the values, political neutrality, impartiality, fairness, propriety and a sense of public duty activated by a homogeneity, common identity and *esprit de corps* which are said to be the central characteristics. If these values and characteristics are indeed to be found anywhere in the civil service they will be found in the core and central departments. Any attack upon such values and characteristics, or upon notions of a unified career service with which they have been associated, may therefore seem to be an attack upon the integrity of the core and central departments.

It is important, therefore, to be clear about the nature of the attack launched by Next Steps and about the precise targets, intended or otherwise. Supporters of Next Steps have tried to train their attack upon the notion of a unified career service; to inject a dose of managerialism without necessarily destroying or weakening the accompanying values or characteristics. In a much-quoted phrase Sir Robin Butler described the civil service as 'unified but not uniform', implying some commonality in an otherwise variegated pattern of pay and reward systems (Treasury and Civil Service Committee, 1989, Q. 320). Sir Angus Fraser was less circumspect in telling the TCSC that '... a "unified Civil Service" really is not compatible with the way we are going' (Treasury and Civil Service Committee, 1991, Q. 344). Significantly, though, he denied that this implied the abandonment of common standards, by which he meant 'codes and principles, of things like loyalty, impartiality, fair and open competition in recruitment, promotion on the basis of performance and merit' (Q. 343). Elsewhere he has written that, even with the adoption of Next Steps, the civil service would continue to be held together by 'certain common codes and principles of doing business and by the unity of its purpose in serving collective Cabinet government' (Efficiency Unit, 1991, Foreword). His claim is simply that such codes and standards do not require for their fulfilment uniform pay and conditions. At the same time he and others have argued that the abandonment of such uniformity merely franks what is already the reality - that departments are heterogeneous and that the notion of 'a service-wide system appropriate to everyone is becoming increasingly a fiction' (Treasury and Civil Service Committee, 1991, Q. 342).

Those sceptical of Next Steps may see, at one level, a lack of understanding if not disingenuity in any such attempt to isolate the notions of a unified career service from the values and characteristics with which it has been associated. At another level they perceive in the managerial emphasis of Next Steps a more direct attack upon those values and characteristics. This managerial emphasis, together with the accompanying structural changes, will, it is claimed, have an effect on administrative ethics, including the disaggregation of the public interest so that it becomes 'no more than the sum of interests of the public' (O'Toole, 1990, p. 339). This utilitarianism could have as one of its consequences the inculcation among officials of a narrower, self-focusing rationality to replace the detached brokers of yesteryear, especially if the competition implicit in internal markets advances close to the core. This could present a threat to traditional notions about public bureaucracy. Despite its stodginess, its formality, its general clumsiness such bureaucracy remains as 'one of the great social inventions' and 'an integral support of liberal democracy' (Rhodes, 1991, p. 554). Such a pivotal role rests heavily upon core departments and upon officials who work in core departments - the apex of the state bureaucracy. And while for some the prognostications are equivocal, for others the signals are already quite clear. According to one such critic 'the British civil service, as a distinct institution of the public service, identifiable primarily through certain characteristics and qualities ... no longer exists' (Chapman, 1992, p. 4).

Many, though, remain content for the moment with less dramatic but nevertheless important claims about the consequences of the new managerialism exemplified by Next Steps. Hood distinguishes between Sigma-type and Theta-type values, broadly corresponding to the new managerial and to the traditional public administration values respectively (Hood, 1991). As Hood says, though, it is yet far from clear as to whether the new managerialism is to be achieved, or can only be achieved, at the expense of Theta-type values. There is so far no conclusive empirical evidence that Next Steps has destroyed the integrity of the core departments in terms of the central values and characteristics with which they are associated. Of course some changes are perceptible. There is a stronger inclination towards managerialism among lower level officials, though by no means the product solely of Next Steps (Gray et al., 1991, pp. 41-42). At the same time it has been suggested that the structures associated with Next Steps may enhance the personal welfare of senior officials by removing them from many of the routine management responsibilities. Thus core departments of the future may 'accord much better with senior officials' preferences for working in small, elite, high status and collegial staff organizations close to political power centres ...' (Dunleavy, 1989, p. 270).

There are nevertheless some measurable if modest signs of decomposition within the Whitehall elite. Twenty four people have risen to permanent secretaryships since the publication of the Ibbs Report. While fourteen were public school products, only twelve - proportionately fewer than was typical during the previous twenty years - had an 'Oxbridge' education. More significantly only half had spent their entire careers in Whitehall, while eleven had served as private secretaries to Cabinet ministers. Needless to say such information, while interesting, hardly constitutes incontrovertible evidence of cultural change in the Whitehall core.

It is therefore too early to say to what extent the integrity of the core - its central values and characteristics - lies exposed to any serious threat from Next Steps. Cultural changes are likely to lag behind most of the other consequences sketched in this paper which may be concluded by drawing together some of the main themes.

Conclusions

At the outset two analytical distinctions were noted: one between consequences already evident and those likely or possible as the result of Next Steps; the other between that which is inherent to Next Steps and that which may be circumstantial but not logically inevitable in its adoption.

So far, few firm and far-reaching consequences have been manifest. There is some limited evidence that core departments are adopting a more strategic role, though many - the Treasury included - remain heavily involved in day-to-day supervision of agencies. There has been some re-organization within those core departments in which agencies have been more widely created, though there are no signs so far of the staffing reductions called for by the Fraser Report. Nor have there been any reductions at the political/ministerial level. There has been little mobility between core departments and agencies of the kind considered necessary for Next Steps to succeed, though this undoubtedly has something to do with the nature of the agencies created so far. Nor is there much evidence of a new breed of core department official, though there is some suggestion that the alleged insularity of the past has already been tempered. In particular, those who head core departments are now less likely to have spent their entire careers in the civil service.

Most of the consequences for the core remain in the categories of 'likely' or 'possible'. Much depends upon the degree of independence finally attained by the agencies. This will probably vary. In particular, the advent of internal markets would have far-reaching implications, making likely a number of consequences which otherwise remain mere possibilities. It is difficult to see how, in these circumstances, core departments could retain any sense of ownership or sponsorship of agencies. Officials below, say, grade 2 could in any case become caught in a kind of managerial no-man's land between ministers and agencies. The permanent secretary's role as accounting officer, already in effect redefined, could become more limited, perhaps untenable beyond the confines of the core. Yet the policy roles of officials within the core will remain central, albeit shared with the agency chief executives.

Time only will tell whether it will be possible at once to separate out and to harmonize the functions of policy and those of administration and management. It is possible, if not likely, that the two broad functions may become further divorced, leaving the core with a more narrowly focused policy role. At any rate it is not only possible but very likely that officials within the core will experience intense role conflict. Much store has been set by the transferability of staff from agencies to the core, and *vice-versa*. The abandonment of uniform grading (inherent to Next Steps) need not be an obstacle to such mobility, though it could prove to be an obstacle in certain circumstances. It will become an obstacle unless open competition is adopted for the filling of all core as well as agency posts - at least in the absence of any planned career development. Extensive, centrally controlled, career development seems unlikely because it is explicitly contrary to present policy and because central departments are not equipped to perform such a function. One of the more serious possible consequences for the core and central departments is that they may be unable to play the co-ordinating, integrative, role made ever more critical by the centrifugal tendencies associated with Next Steps.

It may of course be possible to have some of the benefits claimed for Next Steps without sacrificing the traditional civil service public administration values and characteristics of which core departments are the chief custodians. Next Steps *may* place in jeopardy these traditional values and characteristics. But another possibility suggests itself. This recognizes that core departments have already undergone some change - modest change for sure, not necessarily at the sole behest of Next Steps. The history of the last hundred and more years is the history of continuous, at times almost imperceptible but nevertheless steady, change at the heart of Whitehall - more so than critics are apt to admit. Yet rarely does Whitehall yield all. As it changes so also it preserves, drawing seductively into its citadel those who once seemed to threaten its total destruction.

Without doubt Next Steps constitutes Whitehall's leap in the dark. Only time will tell whether the comparatively rapid and visible activity of the last few years will be sustained: whether the new agencies continue to develop their roles having established their identity and when the process of agency creation comes to an end. There have been a complex of factors shaping the whole process and it has been difficult sometimes to know from where exactly the critical impetus has come. What if anything, for example, will be the significance of Kemp's replacement as Permanent Secretary (OPSS) by the seemingly more emollient Richard Mottram? It is therefore as yet too early to say whether Whitehall can contain the potentially centrifugal tendencies as the core struggles to retain its traditional poise, its integrity, its role as the central pillar of the state apparatus; or whether the energies unleashed by Next Steps will mark a decisive loss of initiative for the centre, a bureaucratic democratization as agencies seek their own identities, develop their unique cultures and establish an independence of spirit which proves irreversible.

Parliamentary Accountability

BARRY J. O'TOOLE AND RICHARD A. CHAPMAN

Sir Ivor Jennings, acknowledged by many to be the most authoritative writer on British constitutional law and practice, believed that the doctrine of individual ministerial responsibility to Parliament 'is the most essential characteristic of the civil service' (Jennings, 1959, p. 499). By encouraging senior managers in the civil service to 'show real qualities of leadership, [to have] the ability to back their judgement and to take and defend unpopular decisions' (Efficiency Unit, 1988, para. 35) the Next Steps programme may have fundamentally undermined that doctrine. The essential characteristic of the civil service may no longer be the accountability of ministers to Parliament; it may rather be that the essential characteristic is now the zealous application of the 'doctrine' of value-for-money and accountability to customers. While ministers pay constant lip-service to adherence to cherished constitutional values, there seems to have been a considerable weakening of commitment to, and devaluation of the structure and operation of, Parliamentary accountability. This chapter is an attempt to clear the smokescreen and discover the actuality of Parliamentary accountability of British government now. Mr William Waldegrave MP has recently argued that accountability has been strengthened by making services more responsive to consumers and that a 'democratic gain' has been achieved (Waldegrave, 1993, pp. 9-10). Is that really the case or might it be argued that there is in fact a 'democratic deficit'?

The Traditional Perspective on Parliamentary Accountability

In effect, the doctrine of individual ministerial responsibility to Parliament has always been the working convention which governs the relationship between ministers and their civil servants. The doctrine, which simply stated means that the minister and the minister alone is responsible to Parliament for everything that his officials either do or refrain from doing, facilitates both the party political impartiality and the anonymity of officials. Together, these facets of the doctrine 'give protection to the advice civil servants give to ministers, thus allowing it to be free, frank and comprehensive; and ... give the minister the confidence that he has the loyalty of his officials' (O'Toole, 1989, p. 151).

Of course, it is unrealistic to believe that ministers can know about everything that happens in their departments. Only the most politically salient issues or other issues of major importance reach the minister's desk. This has always been the case, and has always been recognized to be the case by constitutional and political commentators (see Jennings, 1959, p. 499). All other decisions, indeed most decisions, are taken by civil servants, who have no constitutional personality of their own and who always act in the minister's name. It is up to the officials to know what the minister's policy is and it is up to the minister to make known that policy to them. They can then act according to that policy. If the policy leads to political problems then clearly that is anyway a matter for the minister. If the civil servants make a mistake they are subject to internal disciplinary procedures. In all circumstances, however, external accountability is to Parliament.

This system of accountability means that in a very real sense the minister is the personification of his department. Parliamentarians have a real person, a public person, to whom they can address the grievances of their constituents. They have someone they can embarrass politically and thus someone over whom they can exercise some form of political control. Moreover, by being able to exercise some form of control over the person who represents, and very publicly represents, the department, they have some form of control over the department. The consequence is that it would be a very foolish minister who did not make sure that, while he cannot know everything, his civil servants know what they are meant to be doing. It also means that if anything does go wrong the minister will take firm action to make sure that whatever went wrong does not go wrong again.

Perhaps the most controversial aspect of the doctrine of ministerial responsibility is that of the question of ministerial resignations, or at least the refusal of ministers to resign. It is argued that because ministers have refused to resign when things have gone wrong, then this is indicative that the doctrine has broken down. This line of argument is somewhat blinkered. It would be unreasonable in any case for ministers to resign over most of the problems which arise in their departments.

Moreover, it would be foolish for commentators to expect ambitious people such as politicians to throw away lightly the opportunities offered by ministerial office. The point of the doctrine is not the ability of Parliament to force ministers to go; the point is the ability of Parliament to ensure that departments act in accordance with the known policy of the government as approved by Parliament. In other words, the doctrine is to the advantage of both ministers and Parliament, and allows for the democratic control of public officials.

All this is not to say that there have been no problems with the doctrine of ministerial responsibility. Recent events have displayed only too well the weaknesses. The Westland debacle, the Ponting affair, the Tisdall case, the 'arms for Iraq' scandal and others have all indicated that, when it suits them, ministers can use constitutional conventions for ambiguous ends and are only too happy to hide behind their officials. The doctrine has been under stress for most of the post-Second World War period; and the watershed came in 1971 with the controversy surrounding the Vehicle and General Affair, when the Vehicle and General Insurance Company collapsed, leaving many motor car owners uninsured, despite the company having been monitored by the Department of Trade and Industry. There is no need to go into the details of the affair here, except to note that a named civil servant working in the DTI, who was unable at the time of the Tribunal of Inquiry to defend himself (because he did not know he was going to be accused) was accused in the Tribunal's report of 'negligence' (Vehicle and General Tribunal, 1972, paras. 319-322; for discussions see Chapman, 1973; O'Toole, 1989, pp. 144-52). What was startling was that the Secretary of State for Trade and Industry, Mr John Davies, did not accept any responsibility for what had happened. This may well have been in line with the Report of the Tribunal, which had exonerated ministers, but this is hardly the point. As Mr Edmund Dell commented at the time, the Tribunal had taken 'a narrow and legalistic view of what constitutes the responsibility of ministers'. He argued that ministers had responsibility for the fact that 'over many years ... the Insurance Companies Division of DTI was left lacking the resources of experience and expertise to do its job properly' (Dell, 1972). This very point might have some relevance today, when the policy and resources frameworks within which agencies operate are clearly the responsibility of ministers, who can nevertheless claim that operational matters are the responsibility of chief executives. Indeed, from this perspective it is fascinating to note that the Secretary of State even went so far as to say that the officials named in the Tribunal's Report would 'in no way be forbidden' from speaking publicly in defence of their position (Official Reports, 1971-72, col. 55). That was then a clear denial of ministerial responsibility; and if we accept the most recent comments of ministers about their belief in ministerial responsibility then they presumably believe that the then Secretary of State had misinterpreted the constitutional position. However, the practice *is* that agency officials do appear in public, do make public pronouncements and do defend their positions in public. This is a matter to be addressed later in this chapter.

A fascinating aspect of the Vehicle and General affair was the reaction of the First Division Association (FDA), the union of the under secretary accused of negligence. They established a sub-committee on Tribunals of Enquiry, which produced two reports, the second of which was entitled *Ministers and the Civil Service* (FDA, 1973). It highlighted the speech of the then Home Secretary in the debate on the Vehicle and General affair. In that speech, the Home Secretary had affirmed that a minister:

> is responsible for all the actions of his department: taking blame for anything bad as he takes praise for anything good that it does ... He was also responsible for seeing that there was a system by which he was informed of important matters which arose; for minimising the danger of errors ...; and for the general efficiency of the department. He added that although a Minister could not supervise action on all the letters which reached his department, he was still responsible to Parliament if he failed to ensure that mistakes were not made.

However, 'he did not explain why the Tribunal had not examined Ministers...' and had accepted that in a Tribunal of Inquiry it was inevitable that there would be an ascription of responsibility to individual civil servants (FDA, 1973, para. 3; O'Toole, 1989, p. 148). The FDA believed that, while ministers had stated that no precedent had been set, the situation was nevertheless very confused. The major recommendation of the subcommittee was that there should be an urgent review of the respective responsibilities of ministers and civil servants. The questions to which this review should address itself were: the extent of the accountability to Parliament of civil servants; the effects of the creation of very large departments; the need for an adequate definition of responsibilities; the extent of the convention of anonymity; and the circumstances in which civil servants could take responsibility for their actions (FDA, 1973, para. 9; O'Toole, 1989, p. 151). These questions are remarkably similar to questions that might be asked today about the Next Steps programme. In the 1970s and 1980s, however, despite the worries of the FDA, there was little doubt about the answers.

The Next Steps and Parliamentary Accountability

Despite questions about the ways in which ministers have discharged their responsibilities to Parliament, it is true to say that, by-and-large, the doctrine of ministerial responsibility remained, until the Next Steps programme, intact. Even the introduction of the relatively influential departmental Select Committees of the House of Commons did not undermine the doctrine that it was still ministers who answered to Parliament and it was still ministers who were the public manifestations of their departments. Civil servants remained largely anonymous, ministers took both the credit and the blame for the actions of those civil servants, and citizens knew where the 'buck' stopped. The creation of agencies, the proliferation of so-called citizen's charters and the possibility of 'contracting out' civil service activities have all served to make the situation much less clear.

The Next Steps report itself was, in this matter as in most others, really rather ambiguous and superficial. It laid great emphasis upon the importance of ministers and their relationship to Parliament, yet clearly had little understanding of constitutional practice, political reality or administrative imperative. Consider paragraph 6 of the report:

> ... senior civil servants inevitably and rightly respond to the priorities set by Ministers which tend to be dominated by the demands of Parliament and communicating government policies. In this situation it is easy for the task of improving performance to get overlooked, especially where there is, as we observed, confusion between Permanent Secretaries and Ministers over their respective responsibilities for the management of service delivery ... Nevertheless the ability of Ministers supported by their senior officials to handle political sensitivities effectively is a crucial part of any government's credibility. Changes in the management process should therefore aim to increase rather than diminish this crucial skill (Efficiency Unit, 1988, para. 6).

It is to be wondered how many ministers and permanent secretaries the project team 'observed' on such an intimate basis as to be able to detect such 'confusion'; indeed, it is to be wondered, given the necessity these days to measure everything, what measurements were used by the team to gauge this confusion. Moreover, if it is 'inevitable' and 'right' that the work of senior officials should be driven by the need to respond to ministers who in turn respond to Parliament, what is the use of, let alone the need for, management change?

The report, of course, suggests that there is a dichotomy between policy work and the management of policies produced in consequence of that work. The corollary is that ministers and their senior advisers should confine themselves to policy, while administration can be left as an entirely separate function. This is surely an outdated and superficial view. Surely, the policy/administration dichotomy died with Woodrow Wilson? Policy and the implementation of policy are intimately linked and it is anachronistic to suggest otherwise. However, the fundamental premise of the Next Steps report reasserts the anachronism. This is clear from several parts of the report. For example:

> The main strategic control must lie with the Minister and the Permanent Secretary. But once the policy objectives and budgets within the framework are set, the management of the agency should then have as much independence as possible in deciding how those objectives are met. *A crucial element in the relationship would be a formal understanding about the handling of sensitive issues and the lines of accountability in a crisis.* The presumption must be that ... [management] must be left as free as possible to manage within that framework. To strengthen operational effectiveness there must be freedom to recruit, pay, grade and structure in the most effective way as the framework becomes sufficiently robust and there is confidence in the capacity of management to handle the task (emphasis added; Efficiency Unit, 1988, para. 21).

This very excerpt from the report underlines the irrelevance of attempting to re-invent the policy/administration dichotomy. Which minister is going to stand back and allow civil servants to deal with any 'crisis' that may arise in his or her department or its agencies? Dealing with crises is precisely what ministers are for. Indeed, some of them welcome the opportunities offered by crises to display their own competence as politicians.

This superficial and dated approach is then followed by the most important statement in the report about accountability:

> Placing responsibility for performance squarely on the shoulders of a manager of an agency also has implications for the ways in which Ministers answer to Parliament. Clearly Ministers have to be wholly responsible for policy, but it is unrealistic to suppose that they can actually have familiarity in depth about every operational question. The convention that they do is in part the cause of the overload we observed. We believe it is possible for Parliament, through Ministers, to regard managers as *directly* responsible for operational matters and that there are precedents for this and precisely defined ways in which it can be handled (emphasis added; Efficiency Unit, 1988, para. 23).

These 'precisely defined ways' are outlined (though not specified) in an annex to the report entitled: 'Accountability of Ministers and Parliament on Operational Matters'. The relevant paragraph reads:

> The precise form of accountability for each agency would need to be established as part of drawing up the framework for agencies. Any change

from present practice in accountability would, of course, have to be acceptable to Ministers and to Parliament. It is axiomatic that Ministers should remain fully and clearly accountable for policy. For agencies which are government departments or parts of departments ultimate accountability must also rest with Ministers. What is needed is the establishment of a convention that heads of executive agencies would have delegated authority from their ministers for operations of the agencies within the framework of policy directives and resource allocations presented by Ministers. Heads of agencies would be accountable to Ministers for the operation of their agencies, but could be called - as indeed they can now - to give evidence to Select Committees as to the manner in which their delegated authority has been used and their functions discharged within that authority. In the case of agencies established outside of departments, appropriate forms of accountability to Ministers and to Parliament need to be established according to particular circumstances (Efficiency Unit, 1988, Annex A, para. 3).

This seems somewhat confused. On the one hand it is 'axiomatic' that ministers remain 'fully and clearly accountable to Parliament' for policy and resources matters; on the other, 'precise forms' of accountability for each agency need to be established in the framework for the agency, and a 'new convention' needs to be created. That new convention would allow something which already happens! Has anything changed? Or has everything changed? The report itself assumes that everything is clear, and the relevant paragraph is somewhat surprising:

> The recommendations we have made should *ensure that authority and responsibility for operations will be clear and Ministers will know who is accountable to them. The confusion we observed about the role of Ministers should be substantially resolved. Inevitably and rightly it is open to a minister to get involved in any part of his or her department's business,* but in a well managed department this should normally be necessary by exception (emphasis added; Efficiency Unit, 1988, para. 49).

The actual work of agencies since the report indicates that the matters it says will be clear have not become clear at all.

Agencies in Action: Accountability to Parliament

In the various *Next Steps Briefing Note* publications of the Efficiency Unit, the following paragraph usually appears:

Agencies are fully accountable to Parliament through their respective Ministers. Next Steps *has enhanced* accountability to Parliament, as well as providing much more information for customers, staff and the public, through the requirement for Agencies to publish their framework documents, annual targets, annual reports and accounts, and where appropriate, their corporate and business plans (emphasis added; Efficiency Unit, 1993b, para. 15).

Leaving aside the obvious questions about how the publication of these various documents can possibly enhance accountability to Parliament, this simplistic and assertive approach begs more questions than it answers. What is the relationship of ministers to Parliament with reference to agencies? What is the relationship of ministers to chief executives? What is the relationship of permanent secretaries to chief executives and to ministers with reference to agencies? What is the relationship of permanent secretaries to Parliament? What is the relationship of chief executives to Parliament? What is the general relationship of departments to agencies? What is the relationship of ministers, permanent secretaries, departments, chief executives and agencies to the Treasury? And what is the relationship of the Treasury to Parliament with reference to agencies? All these questions are fundamental to an understanding of Parliamentary accountability in the Next Steps era.

There are a number of places to look for answers to these questions, but the obvious starting point is with ministers and their senior officials. It is, after all, the convention of ministerial responsibility, the working convention which governs the relationship between ministers and civil servants, which has always been at the heart of Parliamentary accountability.

On 18 February 1988 Mrs Margaret Thatcher, then Prime Minister, made a statement about the Next Steps programme in the House of Commons, which heralded the creation of agencies. She had this to say about accountability: 'Each agency will be accountable to a Minister, who will in turn be accountable to Parliament for the agency's performance' (Official Reports, 1987-88, col. 1157). This statement was reiterated by the most senior of senior officials, the Head of the Home Civil Service, Sir Robin Butler, when he appeared before the Treasury and Civil Service Committee during its first consideration of the Next Steps programme. He gave evidence to the Committee on 29 June 1988 and said:

The structure of accountability will remain the same, in the sense that there will be reporting through Ministers to Parliament and there will be ... no change in that.

This seems straightforward enough, except that he went on to elaborate, and in the process introduced an element of confusion. He thought that:

> Where ... there will be a change ... is that there will be a clearer definition of responsibility of chief executives which will make it easier for Parliament ... to know what their responsibilities are and to question them about them.

To rectify this element of confusion he then proceeded with the following corrective:

> ... that should not be confused with saying that a chief executive becomes directly responsible to Parliament - he does not. If Parliament wanted to criticise the activities of a chief executive it would not be for Parliament to dismiss that chief executive, it would be a matter for the Minister. If Parliament was dissatisfied with the action that was being taken it would then take it up with the Minister. I think the structure of accountability remains; its operation will be changed and, I hope, improved (Treasury and Civil Service Committee, 1988, Q. 277).

This surely can have done little to have cleared the confusion associated with Parliamentary accountability and the Next Steps. Would it, for example, be acceptable for Parliament to publicly criticize named civil servants for their official actions, and, in effect deny ministerial responsibility? Would it be proper to call for the resignation of chief executives? Would ministers still be accountable through Parliamentary questions for the activities of chief executives? None of these, or other, questions really received an adequate answer from the Head of the Civil Service. Moreover, apart from this one answer being inherently ambiguous, this was only one of many answers which talked about giving agency chief executives more freedom and promising less interference from ministers and senior officials in the 'core' departments. For example, Mr Richard Luce, who was then Minister for the Civil Service, said at the same session that 'For [the Next Steps] exercise to succeed ... then there must be maximum freedom on day-today operational matters for the Chief Executive' (Treasury and Civil Service Committee, 1988, Q. 302). Or again, Mr Michael Heseltine's suggestion, given at his appearance before the Committee on 22 June 1988, that: 'If you really want accountable units, you want them as far removed from the disciplines of the classical public sector arrangements as possible' (Treasury and Civil Service Committee, 1988, Q. 201). All of this only served to make the issue even more confusing, as indeed the Treasury and Civil Service Committee pointed out. However, the Report of the Committee itself added to rather than cleared the confusion.

The Treasury and Civil Service Committee's Eighth Report of the 1987-88

Parliamentary Session, which was the first report of the Committee on the Next Steps programme, was generally supportive, not to say enthusiastic, about the aims of the programme. The Committee thought that the objectives of the programme would be 'more likely to be achieved the more decentralized an agency is' (Treasury and Civil Service Committee, 1988, para. 32). It believed, however, that:

> The more freedom to make decisions is delegated the more important become the financial and budgetary systems which enable the efficiency and effectiveness of the agency to be monitored ... We ... urge... the Government to ensure that the difficulties in producing ... measures of efficiency can be overcome, so that the pace of reform is not unnecessarily slowed ... If the level of resources given to an agency is properly related to the objectives and targets set and the internal financial and management systems are adequate, there should be no need for further monitoring by the departments (Treasury and Civil Service Committee, 1988, para. 34).

The Committee went much further than this in its endorsement of the 'hands-off' approach to core departments' involvement in the activities of their agencies. It suggested, for example, that:

> instead of handing out freedoms to managers as they prove themselves capable of using them responsibly the Government should formally adopt the policy that managers will be free to take all decisions for their organizations, within the policy they are assigned to carry out, except where the wider needs of the Government must override that assumption (Treasury and Civil Service Committee, 1988, para. 36).

Notwithstanding the phrase 'the wider needs of the Government', which is certainly a sufficiently vague expression to cover most purposes, and would give ministers sufficient discretion to enable them to interfere with the operations of their agencies, these passages from the Treasury and Civil Service Committee's report unquestionably indicate the enthusiasm which the Committee had for the Next Steps programme. However, the question of accountability did feature in the report, and the enthusiasm which it displayed for the traditional role of Parliament and its committees was equally striking! The report is thus as confusing and contradictory as the utterances of the ministers and senior officials who gave evidence, for example:

> We do not regard Parliamentary accountability as a cost which must be weighed in the balance against the benefit of effective management. It is not only important in its own right, it is also an extremely effective pressure for

improvement (Treasury and Civil Service Committee, 1988, para. 39).

or again:

> We regard Parliamentary scrutiny of agencies to be the best guarantee, in
> addition to effective monitoring by the Government itself, of improved
> performance ... Ministers will, and must, remain clearly accountable on the
> floor of the House just as they will remain answerable to Select Committees
> (Treasury and Civil Service Committee, 1988, para. 43).

While it is clear that the Committee was primarily concerned in these passages
with ministers' responsibility for policy, strategic objectives, the formal directions
given to agencies, the monitoring of performance and the level of resources, it
nevertheless recognized the difficulties of separating such matters from day-to-day
activities and the cases of individual citizens. The most important passage on these
matters reads thus:

> We believe... that there is a dilemma in the case of matters for which the
> Chief Executive is responsible. The House needs to assess the risk that Chief
> Executives' freedom of manoeuvre ... will be constrained if Ministers
> continue to answer questions in great detail about the activities which are to
> become the responsibilities of the agencies themselves. Where decisions are
> made which affect individuals ... there will always be cases which need to be
> raised with the Minister, whether because of an anomaly in the rules or for
> some other reason. This does not represent a constraint on managerial
> freedom, but an essential check on possible abuses (Treasury and Civil
> Service Committee, 1988, para. 44).

This passage, along with the passage which refers to chief executives being
allowed to manage except where 'the wider interests of the Government' are
concerned, implicitly recognizes that the policy/administration dichotomy is
unworkable.

Nevertheless, despite this implicit acknowledgement of the difficulty of having
both managerial and ministerial freedom, the Committee still manages to reinforce
the nonsense. It refers, for example, to the so-called 'Osmotherley Rules', the
Memorandum of Guidance for officials appearing before Select Committees, which
indicates that civil servants are accountable 'through' ministers and are subject to
the instruction of ministers. The Committee believed that these rules applied to
chief executives, but suggested that:

> ... the Government should reconsider the position ... The traditional system

of accountability does not seem to us to be entirely consistent with the increased delegation of responsibility to individual civil servants ... We conclude that there must be a modification of the present formal arrangements for accountability. The Chief Executive should give evidence on his own behalf about what he has done as head of an agency. But if, during the course of questioning, a Select Committee is not satisfied with the answer a Chief Executive gives, or finds that a Chief Executive has acted outside his or her responsibility, the proper course of action will be to take the matter up with the Minister, who will then be able to go into the matter in depth, remain accountable, and subsequently give an explanation to the Committee, which can if appropriate, report to the House (Treasury and Civil Service Committee, 1988, para. 46).

Like Janus, the Treasury and Civil Service Committee looked both ways. On the one hand managerial freedom was a good thing, and to be encouraged; on the other, ministers were still to be fully accountable to Parliament. 'We certainly do not advocate abandoning the principle of ministerial accountability', reads paragraph 47 of the Report, 'but modifying it, so that':

the Chief Executive who has actually taken the decisions can explain them, in the first instance. In the last resort the Minister will bear the responsibility if things go badly wrong and Parliament will expect him or her to put things right, but the process of Parliamentary accountability should allow issues to be settled at lower levels wherever possible (Treasury and Civil Service Committee, 1988, para. 47).

The question must be, was this not the case when there were no such things as agencies or chief executives? The government's reply to the report was somewhat platitudinous:

The Government agrees with the Committee about the importance of Parliamentary Accountability. The Government does not envisage that setting up Executive Agencies within Departments will result in changes in existing constitutional arrangements. The further delegation to managers inherent in the Next Steps concept concerns internal accountability within departments and does not conflict with external accountability of Ministers to Parliament.

Nevertheless, even this bland statement came with some qualification:

Establishing Executive agencies ... will however involve some developments in the way in which external accountability is discharged. These involve the publication of framework documents ... and the expectation that Members of Parliament may often wish to deal directly with Chief Executives on operational matters for which they have delegated authority. Ministers will continue to deal directly with inquiries about matters of policy or levels of resources, and with any cases when a Member of Parliament specifically seeks a reply from a Minister.

The Government's reply to the Select Committee's Report also commented on the relationship between chief executives and Select Committees:

Chief Executives' authority is delegated to them by Ministers who are and will remain accountable to Parliament as a whole (and its Select Committees). The Government ... believes that the general rule must continue to be that civil servants who give evidence to Select Committees do so on behalf of their Ministers. In practice, where a Committee's interest is confined to day-to-day operation of an Agency, Ministers will normally regard the Chief Executive as being the person best placed to answer on their behalf (Office of the Minister for the Civil Service, 1988, p. 9).

There appears to be some element of ministers both having their cake and eating it. On the one hand, they remained fully accountable to Parliament for everything; on the other, operational matters should be referred to chief executives. This pattern was repeated each time the Treasury and Civil Service Committee examined progress in the Next Steps programme. This can be illustrated with reference to the controversy surrounding Parliamentary Questions.

This problem was first raised by the Treasury and Civil Service Committee in its 1990 Report *Progress in the Next Steps Initiative*. The Committee specifically referred to the Employment Service Agency, the framework document for which contained the following paragraph:

The Secretary of State will continue to answer questions from Members of Parliament on matters concerning the Agency, but will encourage them to contact the Chief Executive or other appropriate Agency managers direct on individual cases or operational issues (Employment Service, 1990a, para. 4.3).

The Treasury and Civil Service Committee referred to an adjournment debate of the House of Commons in May 1990 when the Minister of State had explained how the system worked in practice in relation to Parliamentary Questions: the minister decided whether the question concerned a strategic, resource or operational matter;

the question would then be answered by the minister if it referred to a strategic or a resource allocation matter; if it concerned an operational matter then it would be passed to the chief executive, who would then reply to the Member; at the Member's request a copy of the reply would be placed in the Library of the House of Commons (Treasury and Civil Service Committee, 1990, para. 67). This, the Committee felt, left something to be desired:

> Although we agree that this system recognizes the delegated responsibility of the Chief Executives, and should on many issues, provide full and prompt answers, it has some disadvantages ... Replies from the Chief Executive ... are not freely available to those outside the House, nor is it clear that they would attract Parliamentary privilege in the same way as written answers published in the Official Report. Many answers on operational matters might have wider implications than the individual cases concerned (Treasury and Civil Service Committee, 1990, para. 68).

The Committee recommended that if such problems persisted the Government should consider introducing an 'appropriate system' whereby the replies of chief executives arising from Parliamentary Questions could be published (Treasury and Civil Service Committee, 1990, para. 70).

The Government's response was to decide that all replies of this kind should be placed in the House of Commons Library and its Public Information Office. They would thus, said the Government, 'be in the public domain and available to the public on request' (Office of the Minister for the Civil Service, 1990, p. 13). It also accepted the Committee's concern that some day-to-day operational matters might have wider implications than just for individual cases, and indicated that:

> Where a case is of wider interest or it is desirable that a reply should be covered by Parliamentary privilege, the Minister may decide to reply to a written Parliamentary Question so that the full response is published in Hansard (Office of the Minister for the Civil Service, 1990, p. 14).

This response was not, however, satisfactory, either to the Treasury and Civil Service Committee or to the Committee on Procedure. That Committee recommended that 'in future, replies from agency chief executives in response to parliamentary questions referred to them by Ministers should appear in the Official Report' (Select Committee on Procedure, 1991, para. 125).

The Treasury and Civil Service Committee agreed, primarily because the 'Excessive use of Ministers' powers to refer questions had needlessly increased suspicion of the Next Steps initiative ...' (Treasury and Civil Service Committee, 1991, para. 81). The Committee argued that operational matters referred to chief executives were unexpectedly wide in their scope and the practical difficulties with the current arrangements had not been resolved. The solution offered by the Select Committee on Procedure was therefore the preferred solution. However, it was not until October 1992 that these recommendations were implemented for the House of Commons and November/December 1992 for the House of Lords. The answers usually contain more information than a conventional ministerial answer would contain, and come in different formats from different agencies. The procedure, though not the policy, is constantly under review, and the 1993 review resulted in a more uniform style of presentation across agencies and a reduction in the amount of statistical and supporting material made available.

Another area of controversy relates to the financial accountability of Next Steps agencies, in particular the role of accounting officers. Traditionally, the accounting officer of a department was the permanent secretary, who received from the Treasury a letter of appointment requiring him to be accountable for the department's allocation of funds, if necessary before the Public Accounts Committee. The practice of appointing the permanent secretary as accounting officer dates from at least as far back as 1920, when the Cabinet approved the so-called Baldwin Council's *Interim Report on the Position of Accounting Officers* (PRO, 1920). The position of accounting officer allows the permanent secretary to remind the minister that the department should not be asked to spend money for any purpose which does not have specific Parliamentary approval. The appointment of the permanent secretary in this context meant that there was complete clarity about financial accountability. The Next Steps programme introduced an element of confusion.

In May 1989, Sir Peter Kemp, then Next Steps Project Manager, explained the position as far as the financial accountability of agencies was concerned:

> Whether there is a single or a split vote [allocation of funds by Parliament], the man in charge of the Agency would either be 'the Accounting Officer', which is a technical title for the person who has a Letter of Appointment from the Treasury who looks after the whole vote or, if it is part of a vote, he would be 'the Agency Accounting Officer' and he would have a letter of appointment from the Permanent Secretary, in effect delegating to him accountability for that part of the vote (Treasury and Civil Service Committee, 1989, Q. 24).

This arrangement, which had, in fact, been announced on 10 November 1988 in the House of Commons, was reiterated in a special Treasury document entitled *The Financing and Accountability of Next Steps Agencies* (HM Treasury, 1989). It simply stated that chief executives will:

... be appointed Accounting Officers or Agency Accounting Officers... Where the Agency has its own Vote, the Treasury will appoint the Chief Executive as Accounting Officer under existing procedures. However ... the government has also accepted that where an Agency does not have its own Vote and is financed from one or more Vote subheads the departmental Accounting Officer will designate the Chief Executive as Agency Accounting Officer (HM Treasury, 1989, para. 4.5).

This seems a relatively straightforward statement of the position. When an agency is a department in its own right, or exists outside the normal departmental structure, and thus has a separate Parliamentary vote of supply, then the chief executive is the accounting officer. Where an agency exists within the normal departmental structure but has a separate vote within the overall vote for the parent department, then the permanent secretary is the departmental accounting officer and the chief executive is appointed by the permanent secretary to be the agency accounting officer with delegated responsibility to be accountable for spending the agency's vote. However, even in 1991 the Treasury and Civil Service Committee felt that 'There appears to be some uncertainty about the respective responsibilities of the Permanent Secretary as Accounting Officer of the Department and the Chief Executive as Agency Accounting Officer' (Treasury and Civil Service Committee, 1991, para. 86). Sir Geoffrey Holland, then permanent secretary at the Department of Employment, explained how he believed the system worked in practice:

> I would regard in the new structure the Chief Executive of the Employment Service as accountable for the vote expenditure as being the person who would answer [questions on day-today activities, structures, numbers of staff in post, training etc.] ... with myself giving some view about what steps I had taken to assure myself their systems were up to scratch across the piece. I would talk therefore about the assurance or otherwise which my head of internal audit gave and whether I had myself instructed further things to be done (Treasury and Civil Service Committee, 1991, Q. 153).

What seems now to be the case is that in agencies which are parts of departments, whose budgets are part of votes allocated to those departments, there is something of a dual responsibility. The permanent secretary remains accounting officer, appointed by the Treasury, and has overall accounting responsibility. The permanent secretary delegates accounting responsibility for agencies within the department to the chief executives as agency accounting officers. The agency accounting officers are accountable to the permanent secretary as accounting officer, who remains accountable to Parliament for the whole vote, but who delegates responsibility for answering questions about agencies' votes to the agency accounting officers. They answer those questions *on behalf* of the accounting officer. It is up to the accounting officer to ensure that the agency accounting officers have systems for ensuring that the agencies spend within the limits and specifications imposed by Parliament.

A third area of controversy concentrates on the position and role of chief executives in relation to ministers and departments. Although they are usually civil servants, their position is quite different from others in the civil service. Most importantly, they are usually appointed on fixed term contracts, which may or may not be renewed. Secondly, unlike permanent secretaries, but in common with most grades in the civil service, they are subject to performance related pay. Thirdly, they are appointed to specific jobs not grades and are not usually part of the official hierarchy. In particular they are more directly responsible to ministers than to the departmental hierarchy. As Kemp explained on 10 July 1990 when giving evidence before the Treasury and Civil Service Committee:

> We are moving from a hierarchical system to a system in which the Minister and the Chief Executive are in a quasi-contractual position ... The Minister has specifically designated some of his powers to the individual to carry them out on his behalf (Treasury and Civil Service Committee, 1990, Q. 170).

The committee decided that it agreed with the then Project Manager that this should be the position (para. 71), and the Government in its reply to the Report of the Committee made a full statement about it:

> A clearly defined relationship between a Minister and an Agency Chief Executive is indeed at the very heart of the Next Steps. That relationship is a key aspect of every Agency Framework Document. As the Government said in Cm 524, the Framework Document (and surrounding arrangements) by its nature normally cannot be a legal document. But the principles are well established. The Minister determines the overall strategy of the Agency and how it fits into and contributes to his departmental policy; and agrees the resources allocated to the Agency and its annual targets; approves the appointment of the Chief Executive and his or her remuneration package; and specifically delegates to the Chief Executive responsibility for managing the Agency on a day-to-day basis within that context, making arrangements to monitor performance as appropriate. The bargain is that in return for the resources - assets, people and finance - that can be made available and the maximum possible freedoms and flexibilities appropriate to the needs of the business, the Chief Executive delivers what the Minister asks. The transparency of the system enables the Chief Executive's success or

otherwise in this to be seen publicly, and for appropriate consequences to follow (Office of the Minister for the Civil Service, 1990, p. 7).

The problems arise, of course, when the resources made available are not sufficient to carry out the tasks assigned. This was one of the problems highlighted by the Vehicle and General Affair, when the minister theoretically responsible absolved himself of that responsibility. Much the same seems to have happened more recently in the case of the Child Support Agency, which is responsible for ensuring that absent fathers meet the financial responsibilities associated with maintaining their children. Resource constraints seem to have led to policy problems. The problems arose from the fact that the primary, but largely unpublicized aim of the agency seems to have been to save money on the social security budget. To this end it seems to have pursued those fathers who were already known, and already paid maintenance, to get them to pay more, rather than those who had not yet been traced and who were not paying anything. Apart from the strategic decision to concentrate on a particular group, it was also the case that the resources provided to the agency to pursue its ostensible and public aims and objectives seem to have been inadequate for that task. Clearly, these are matters for ministers, yet it was appearances of the chief executive of the agency before the Social Services Select Committee which received most media attention; little attention was focused on the Social Services Secretary or on other ministers in the DSS. This surely seems odd in a system which still proclaims itself to be based upon the accountability of *ministers* to Parliament? The question must be, are ministers now more or less likely to absolve themselves of their responsibilities, and follow what seems to be a precedent from the Child Support Agency? (For a discussion of this case see *The Independent*, 7 December 1993).

Parliamentary Accountability and the Next Steps

The concept which is at the very heart of the Next Steps programme, and indeed of subsequent citizens charter and market testing initiatives, is that of the dichotomy between policy and administration. While that concept has been recognized by most commentators to be bankrupt, nevertheless it is the foundation stone upon which management reform in the civil service is being built. Ministers and senior officials make policy; they then farm out that policy to their semi-autonomous agencies or they 'buy' the administration of that policy from bodies outside the public service. The claim is that ministers and their senior officials can concentrate on making 'sound' policy while the agencies and other bodies can be given the managerial freedoms necessary to put those policies into effect 'efficiently'. The quasi contractual or indeed fully contractual relationships between ministers and the agencies which their departments sponsor allow the ministers to monitor those agencies to ensure that they are operating within the limits set. Ministers are accountable to Parliament for the policies and the frameworks within which the policies are carried out; 'operational' matters are for the agencies. Such relationships, it is claimed, add 'transparency' to the accountability process. The question remains, however, where does policy end and administration begin? It is a question which gives considerable scope for ministers to pick and choose what they are going to be accountable for, yet at the same time retain the control they so desire.

It may be argued that the closest parallel in recent history to the relationships between departments and agencies was the position of the nationalized industries. The Acts of Parliament which established the nationalized industries more or less followed the same principles which seem to be being applied to the Next Steps agencies, the basic principle being an arms length relationship between the sponsoring department on the one hand and the agency or the industry on the other. In the case of the nationalized industries the minister appointed the chairman and senior executives, issued general policy guidelines and allowed the management freedom to carry out day-to-day operational tasks. At least that was the theory. In practice, ministers consistently intervened in the running of the nationalized industries for the purposes of pursuing policy aims, be they directly linked to the work of the industry concerned or wider social and economic aims.

This is made quite clear in William A. Robson's seminal study of the nationalized industries (Robson, 1962, especially chapters VI, VII, VIII and IX). He notes, for example, that the general injunction of the legislation setting up the various corporations was that 'the appropriate minister may ... give public corporations "directions of a general character as to the exercise and performance by the corporations of their functions in relation to matters which appear to him to affect the national interest"' (p. 139). In addition, ministers were given specific powers over all nationalized industries in general in regard to matters considered to be of special importance (p. 140). Moreover, they had other powers in relation to particular corporations (p. 140). All this, and other factors, made it evident to Robson that the government possessed:

> very extensive legal powers of control over the public corporations. Their full extent [was] not altogether clear, for the question of exactly what is meant by the expression 'directions of a general character' is open to doubt; and so too is the question of what the national interests demand (p. 141).

Robson showed clearly that ministers played a major role in both the strategic and the operational management of the nationalized industries, yet they had more or less *carte blanche* to refuse to answer Parliamentary Questions about the public corporations. These general observations, and his investigations into the operations of certain specific industries led Robson to the following conclusion:

> Ministers have carefully hidden their activities, doubtless from a desire to avoid having to answer in Parliament for the great variety of matters about which they intervene or are consulted by the public corporations, but for which they do not wish to be responsible either to Parliament or the public (p. 142).

Perhaps it was similar thoughts about the relationships between ministers and Next Steps agencies which led to questions from members of the Treasury and Civil Service Committee based upon the experience of the nationalized industries. The following exchange between Mr John Watts MP and Peter Kemp highlights the concern some MPs had about the precise point Robson made so astringently in 1962:

> Watts: But the principle of Ministers having the ultimate responsibility is maintained, so we will not find with Agencies as we do for example with British Rail, that the Transport Minister can say 'That is not a matter for the Department; that is a matter for British Rail' ... Kemp: If I can just put a slight gloss on that, not with Agencies set up within the Civil Service ... If you quangofied it or something, then something different might happen, but if you went down that path you would need legislation and Parliament could say whether it liked the new apparatus or not (Treasury and Civil Service Committee, 1989, Q. 23).

This was a disingenuous reply. It is clear that ministers, while not quite saying in some circumstances 'this is not a matter for the department', have nevertheless said that it is not a matter for them but for the relevant agency chief executive. If he were writing today Robson might have said about ministers and Next Steps Agencies what he said in 1962 about ministers and nationalized industries: 'Their main preoccupation has been to exercise power while avoiding responsibility in public' (Robson, 1962, p. 160). Moreover, of course, the market testing programme, with the implications it has for the possible privatization of certain parts of the civil service is not necessarily dependent upon specific legislation.

The question of the relationship of market testing and accountability to Parliament is an extremely important one. The possibility of certain tasks being carried out by non-public service organizations has always been implied by the Next Steps programme. It was raised in the original Next Steps document and has been flagged ever since in the evidence of ministers and officials to the Treasury and Civil Service Committee. Paragraph 19 of the Efficiency Unit's 1988 report specifically states that 'An "agency" of this kind may be part of the government and public service, or it may be more effective outside of government'. More obliquely, it was in the annex of the Next Steps report, on accountability, that the possibility was again raised. It referred, for example, to 'agencies which are government departments or parts of departments' (implying that agencies could exist outside of the normal government machinery), and later in the same paragraph it referred to 'agencies established outside departments', where 'appropriate forms of accountability would need to be established according to particular circumstances' (Efficiency Unit, 1988, Annex A, para. 3). Presumably in the case of fully privatized parts of the public sector these appropriate forms of accountability would be in the form of contracts negotiated between departments or agencies and the private firms concerned. Such forms of accountability can hardly be said to fit in with current constitutional practice. So long as any firm was carrying out the requirements of a freely negotiated contract no minister would be able to interfere with the work of that firm either in individual cases, or operating methods, or in terms of policy. The only sanction available would be the non-renewal of the contract. It may be argued that terms could be negotiated which would allow the minister to intervene: but which private sector firm would sign such a contract? If a contract was not renewed because of such difficulties, which other private sector firm would enter into a relationship with such a perfidious partner?

These are mundane questions. More importantly, if ministers do accept the restrictions on their powers which such contractual arrangements imply, what channels might be available for the redress of grievances by individual citizens, and can there be any real guarantees about confidentiality, equity of treatment, personal safety, the national interest and a whole host of other issues? Whatever its defects, which are clear and manifold, the traditional system of Parliamentary accountability based upon hierarchical systems of unified authority at least provide some of the benefits which more pluralistic modes of accountability, such as those now being introduced without much debate into the civil service, manifestly do not provide. The only criterion which private sector organizations hold dear is that of profit. It is clear that they will not enter into contractual relations with government unless they are fairly satisfied of reasonable returns. It would be madness for them to act in any other way (as indeed many of the ideologues on the Government's benches will vehemently argue). It could be argued, of course, that unless these companies provide a decent service for their 'customers' they will not do well, in other words that there is an 'accountability' to 'customers'. It could be counter-argued that (a) there can be no precise definition of who are the customers of public services, and (b) again following the arguments of the free-market ideologues, the benefits of private sector provision come with competition, of which there will be none once contracts have been awarded.

In addition, the question of quality calls into question the effectiveness of the government's screening process for would-be service contractors. *The Government's Guide to Market Testing* lays down three main criteria which must be established, after the so-called 'prior options' have been examined, for a private firm to be awarded a contract: (a) the firm's capacity for carrying out the work; (b) its experience in similar work; and (c) its financial stability (Efficiency Unit, 1993a). These seem reasonable enough, but are they adequate? It may be argued that on several occasions they have proved inadequate. For example in April 1993 the BBC broadcast a particularly disturbing *Public Eye* documentary, entitled 'Profits from Punishment', which made startling allegations about the various reforms taking place in the prison service. In particular it described the controversial career of Mr Don Hutto, the American behind the overseas operations of a private prison company in the United States called the Corrections Corporation of America (CCA). The CCA is the main organization involved in the successful bid for the contract to run Blakenhurst Prison, which will be the first privately run prison for convicted criminals in the United Kingdom. The programme alleged that various prison organizations in the United States, both state run and private, with which Hutto had been involved at a senior level, had, on numerous occasions, run foul of the law. In particular, prisons in Texas, Arkansas and Virginia had been found guilty of civil and human rights violations, and, in at least one instance, of imposing 'cruel and unusual punishments' in contravention of the requirements of the Constitution of the United States. Injunctions were not served personally against Hutto, but he was usually the most senior person involved. In addition, at least one of the American prisons in Hutto's charge has been criticized for its lax methods of personnel recruitment. In the case of Silverdale Penitentiary such laxity had tragic consequences. A female inmate in that prison died in 1987 because none of the medical staff knew that she was pregnant. While no wilful neglect was found nevertheless the County Commissioner did remark that there was human error by inexperienced staff. Hutto's involvement in these cases was not known by the civil servants negotiating the contract for Blakenhurst prison. It may be wondered whether, had they known, the contract to run Blakenhurst prison would have been awarded to the organization of which he is the head.

The same programme also investigated the recent performance of Group Four Security, both in its prisoner escort service and its management of the Wolds Remand Centre. Here it alleged that there were various drug related problems within the prison. The medical staff and management interviewed in the programme seemed either to be unaware of them or to be inadequately trained to deal with them. More worryingly, the programme discovered that a civil servant who had at one time been heavily involved in negotiating the prisoner escort service contract with Group Four was now working for them. While no evidence of wrongdoing was uncovered, there may nevertheless be, with this and other cases cited by the programme, some cause for concern (BBC, 1993). They all seem to indicate the possible future dangers associated with private organizations operating services which were previously well entrenched in the public service. These are apart from the dangers of corruption, waste and inefficiency referred to in the 1994 *Report* from the Public Accounts Committee, which the Committee associates with the loosening of the hierarchical controls found in 'traditional' government departments. While there may be requirements for private firms to provide certain basic levels of service, and incentives exist in terms of contract renewal, there is already empirical evidence (not just from the limited central government experience but in local government too) that there are greater incentives to do the job as quickly and as cheaply as possible, often cutting corners and perhaps leading to health, security and other problems. In such circumstances the traditional methods of Parliamentary accountability will be useless since they will have been jettisoned. Ministers will not be answerable in Parliament because they will have contracted the responsibility out. In addition, of course, they will have little control.

It is perhaps this loss of control more than anything else which might limit the scope of contracting out. From this perspective the Next Steps agencies are the ideal organizational innovation for ministers: they apparently retain control while being legitimately able to deny, or at least defer, responsibility for a whole host of so-called 'operational matters'. As William Plowden and Gavin Drewry pointed out in their evidence to the Treasury and Civil Service Committee in 1988:

> ... the division of responsibility between departments and agencies, and thus between policy and its execution ... is bound to make harder the tasks of scrutiny ... ministers will be able to side-step criticism on the floor of the House by washing their hands of responsibility for operational activities of the agencies (Treasury and Civil Service Committee, 1988, Volume II, Memorandum submitted by the Director General and the Research Officer of the RIPA).

or, as the First Division Association put it, with more feeling and with a more direct interest:

> It is our view that ministers will be unable to resist interfering in the management of agencies for political reasons ... [If] ministers adopt a genuinely hands-off approach they will be unable to answer to Parliament and civil servants will need to have a more direct relationship to select committees scrutinising the use of public funds by those agencies. We fear that senior civil servants ... will find themselves cast in the role of scapegoats when things go wrong. Senior civil servants are unable to speak in public ... without jeopardising political neutrality (Treasury and Civil Service Committee, 1988, Volume II, Memorandum submitted by the Association of

First Division Civil Servants).

While the evidence for civil servants compromising their political neutrality is somewhat limited, there is already scope for suggesting that the FDA's prediction about scapegoating is already manifesting itself. The Child Support Agency and its problems provide a case in point.

The proceedings of the Treasury and Civil Service Committee have been very helpful in clarifying some of the problems associated with accountability and the Next Steps. In particular, the relationship of agency chief executives with their ministers and departments, and their role as accounting officers or agency accounting officers, is now clearer as a result of the Committee's persistence. There is also greater clarity in the relationships of chief executives and ministers in relation to Select Committees and the nature of Parliamentary Questions, again because of the work of the Committee in this area. What remains unclear is how the policy/administration dichotomy is to be resolved. We are told that ministers remain accountable to Parliament for policy and resources questions, and delegate responsibility for the administration of this policy to chief executives and agencies. That seems clear enough. But who decides where policy ends and administration begins? It is ministers. That too is clear enough. What it means, however, is that ministers are responsible for what they want to be responsible for *and* retain control of everything. They can both have their cake and eat it. Parliament is left only with the stale crumbs that ministers feel in their generous moments they can throw away. It is beside the point for Waldegrave to point out that only 28% of the people of Cleveland, Durham and Yorkshire mentioned 'accountability' as one of their criteria for assessing public services, compared to 54% mentioning 'cost and quality of service' (Waldegrave, 1993, p. 3).The fact is that government is not simply about delivering services to 'customers'. Surprisingly enough, it is about governing. Governing in a democracy requires *above all else* accountability. So long as ambiguity remains about the extent and nature of accountability, then there will remain the question of the 'democratic deficit'. In government, accountability is not to customers, it is to citizens. Furthermore, it is not just to citizens individually, it is to the society of which each individual citizen is an integral part.

Next Steps: The End of Whitleyism?

BARRY J. O'TOOLE

The creation of the Civil Service National Whitley Council must stand as one of the great achievements of British industrial relations. While Whitley himself did not originally envisage that the recommendations of his Committee could be applied to non-industrial organizations, it is, in fact, in non-industrial organizations that the principles of Whitleyism have witnessed their most important triumphs. In the civil service in particular, the introduction of Whitleyism heralded more than half a century of good industrial relations. Events in the late 1970s and early 1980s rather damaged the reputation of government as a good employer; but then industrial relations generally had suffered the consequences of the long period of economic decline. In addition, the advent of Thatcherism did little to foster a sense of good-will between employers and the representatives of those they employed. Nevertheless, in the civil service Whitleyism remained, and, on the basis of a shaky truce, reasonable relations between government and trade unions re-established themselves. However, the emergence of some of the implications of the Next Steps programme has made that truce even shakier. Some now see the possibility of the break-up of the national, unified, career civil service, the creation of which the introduction of Whitleyism both accompanied and assisted; and with that break-up, the end of Whitleyism.

The Principles of Whitleyism and their Application in the Civil Service

Whitleyism emerged from the alarm of the War Cabinet at the outbreak of serious labour unrest and strike action in heavy industry during 1916. This unrest seemed to augur badly for the War effort, and in an attempt to ameliorate the situation a sub-committee of the Reconstruction Committee was established with the Liberal MP J.H. Whitley as Chairman. The terms of reference for this sub-committee were to investigate the relations between employers and employed and to make recommendations for their improvement. The underlying principle of what became known as Whitleyism is simply stated: that there should be joint consultation between employers and their employees and 'the regular consideration of matters affecting the progress and well-being of the trade from the point of view of all those engaged in it, so far as this is consistent with the general interest of the Community' (Whitley, 1917). This joint consultation would take place in standing industrial councils, created for the purpose by the government on an industry by industry basis. They would consist of representatives from both sides of the industries concerned. Consultation would take place at three levels, the national, the district and the works levels.

The Whitley Report was enthusiastically supported by the Ministry of Labour, and received the full endorsement of the Cabinet in September 1917 (Ministry of Labour, 1917). However, it was less well received by the industries and trade unions it was aimed at improving the relations between. The trade unions in particular 'remained obstinately suspicious' (Chapman and Greenaway, 1980, p. 90). The trade unions, that is, which did not represent civil servants remained obstinately suspicious. Amongst the trade unions which represented civil servants the reaction was quite different. As Chapman and Greenaway point out in their discussion of the introduction of Whitleyism, and as others have also pointed out, the civil service unions 'showed an unwelcome interest' and were 'determined not to let the opportunity for change slip by' (Chapman and Greenaway, 1980, pp. 85-100; see also Humphreys, 1958; Parris, 1973; and White, 1933). Thus, despite initial resistance by the Treasury and the Government, Whitleyism was established in the civil service, in 1919.

The order which Whitleyism brought to civil service industrial relations contrasts sharply with the chaos by which they were characterized previously. Of course, this was partly due to the rather disparate and diffuse nature of the service before the reforms of the post-World War I period. The civil service prior to the reforms stimulated by the various committees and commissions of the years between 1850 and 1920 was essentially a series of more or less autonomous departments, each having its own 'method' of dealing with industrial relations matters. As one commentator has remarked management was authoritarian 'tempered with a degree of paternal benevolence' (Gladden, 1956, p. 112). For the people who worked in these departments there was no established or bureaucratic means of airing grievances, except that of 'petitioning', that is of presenting grievances to immediate superiors. As the departments became more bureaucratic so grew the bureaucratization of petitioning. In other words the growth of government led to greater scope for protective association on the part of clerks led to the creation of trade unions. As the nineteenth century wore on the number of trade unions increased, but were generally confined to departments. Despite the resistance of senior officials and of governments civil service unionism continued to expand in the nineteenth century; and in the first years of the twentieth century this expansion seemed to move more and more towards the creation of service wide unions. Indeed, in 1906 the first civil service union was recognized, the Assistant Clerks Association. It largely remained the case, however, that when the Treasury was approached by staff associations about pay and related matters by the various staff associations, they were always referred back to the heads of their various departments (Kelly, 1980, pp. 91-97; O'Toole, 1989a, pp. 9-17). It was both the establishment of Whitleyism and the appointment in 1917 of the Civil Service Conciliation and Arbitration Board for Government Employees which forced the Treasury to come to terms with service-wide bargaining. In particular the terms of reference of the Arbitration Board were to deal with classes of employees, and there was specific mention made to representations by associations and to attempts to settle differences by conciliation before resource to arbitration (Humphreys, 1958, pp. 78-98). Following this it was almost inevitable that the Treasury, as finance department, should enter into negotiations with recognized unions (O'Toole, 1989a, p. 10).

At the same time as these industrial relations developments it also became clear that there was a more concerted move towards the creation of a unified, career civil service. There had been a number of committees, commissions and Royal Commissions examining the nature of the civil service, starting with the famous coupling of Sir Stafford Northcote and Sir Charles Trevelyan and culminating in the MacDonnell Royal Commission on the Civil Service which reported in 1912. All these commissions and committees had stressed the need for a more unifying central control of the civil service, giving central importance to the role of the Treasury. The War meant that the recommendations of these bodies could not be acted upon; at the same time it became clear that the unification of the service was inevitable. Various internal reports endorsed the moves towards greater central control by the Treasury, and after the War the scene was set for the unification of the civil service. Indeed, in 1919 Sir Warren Fisher was appointed as the Head of the Home Civil Service, and vigorously promoted unification over the ensuing twenty years (Chapman and Greenaway, 1980, pp. 100-115; O'Halpin, 1989; O'Toole, 1989b). This unification both assisted and was assisted by the introduction of Whitleyism into the Civil Service.

Industrial Relations in the Civil Service

The first few years of the new civil service industrial relations system were not easy. There were wrangles about the construction of the Whitley Councils and about their role and the scope of their powers. Of particular importance were questions about the role of ministers and that concerning who was to be considered employer and who employee. These questions being resolved (Heath, 1919; Ramsay, 1919) the Whitley system could be established. The Civil Service National Whitley Council had 54 members, with six officials - the Chairman, the Vice Chairman and two secretaries each for the National Staff Side (NSS, the employees representatives) and the Official Side. Local and departmental Whitley Joint Councils were also established and 'they seem very quickly to have provided a valuable mechanism for mutual understanding between departmental heads and their staff' (Chapman and Greenaway, 1980, p. 96). The original terms of reference of the National Council, never amended, were:

> to secure the greatest measure of co-operation between the state in its capacity as employer, and the general body of civil servants in matters affecting the Civil Service with a view to increased efficiency in the public service combined with the well-being of those employed: to provide machinery for dealing with grievances, and generally to bring together the experience and different points of view of representatives of the administrative, clerical and manipulative Civil Service (quoted in Mackenzie and Grove, 1957, p. 143).

As Mackenzie and Grove point out 'There is very little that this excludes, and the scope of the Council has depended largely on the general state of feeling in the Service' (p. 143).

The first few years of the new system were characterized by the Official Side being 'lukewarm' and the Staff Side 'aggressive' (Mackenzie and Grove, 1957, p. 143), and this was more than emphasized because of the General Strike of 1926. Civil Servants did not take part in the strike but the General Purposes Committee of the NSS passed the following resolution on 3 May 1926:

> That advice be given to all civil servants not to volunteer to perform during the crisis [of the General strike] any work other than their own normal duties, and to report to the headquarters of their [staff association] ... any attempt to cause them to perform any work outside the normal duties of their

class or grade. Pending a further communication, however, all civil servants should obey the orders of competent authorities, making protest in proper form, if such orders conflict with the principles stated above.

This resolution was sufficiently militant to be the excuse of the Association of First Division Civil Servants (FDA) to leave the NSS on the grounds that 'it is the duty of every civil servant ... to inform his department superiors that he is ready to perform whatever work the Government consider it to be to the national advantage that he should perform' (FDA, 1926; O'Toole, 1989a, pp. 30-35). The FDA did not rejoin the Whitley system until 1946. However, of much more import to the Whitley system was the other major repercussion of the General Strike for all trade unions, the passing in 1927 of the Trade Disputes and Trade Unions Act. Clause V of that Act required the Treasury to issue regulations with regard to civil service staff associations which in essence meant their status as independent trade unions was ended. The regulations which were issued, the Civil Service (Approved Associations) Regulations 1927 (SRO 1927, Number 800), required (i) that after 31 December 1927, no established civil servant should be a member, delegate or representative of any organization of which the primary object was to influence or affect the remuneration and conditions of employment of its members unless a 'certificate of approval' was in force certifying that the organization was an approved association; and (ii) that membership of the association must be confined to persons employed by or under the Crown. The Act also made it illegal for civil service staff associations to affiliate 'directly or indirectly with any political party or organization'. The Act was repealed in 1946, along with the Treasury regulations. In practice 'there are now no restrictions except those imposed by the good sense of civil servants' (Mackenzie and Grove, 1957, p. 135). All national civil service trade unions are now affiliated to the TUC, the last to join being the FDA in 1977 (O'Toole, 1989a).

In 1957 Mackenzie and Grove were able to observe that 'it is difficult to imagine circumstances in which it would be good tactics to attempt to further a claim [by official strike action]' (p. 141). In the 1970s and the 1980s the staff associations clearly disagreed with them.

The 1960s and 1970s saw a growing tendency for public sector trade unions representing professional people of equivalent status and salary to low to middle ranking civil servants both to affiliate to the TUC (see Table 1) and to take industrial action, including strike action. Of the latter tendency a few examples will illustrate the point. As early as 1961 the National Association of Schoolmasters (NAS) struck in protest at its exclusion from the Burnham Committee which negotiated teachers' salaries. The National Association of Teachers (NUT) also took strike action in selected areas in 1961 over the pay of its members (although at that time it also denied the usefulness of the strike sanction). The NUT took strike action again in 1967 and in 1969-70, again over pay. NALGO, the organization representing local government officers, the local government equivalents of civil servants, took its first strike action in 1970.

Table 1 Public Sector Affiliations to the TUC [1]

Organization	Year of affiliation
Association of HM Inspectors of Taxes (AIT)	1977
Association of University Teachers (AUT)	1976
Civil and Public Services Association (CPSA)	1946
Civil Service Union (CSU)[2]	1946
Confederation of Health Service Employees (COHSE)	1946/1974
First Division Association (FDA)	1977
Institute of Professional Civil Servants (IPCS)(now IPMS)	1976
Inland Revenue Staffs Federation (IRSF)	1946
National and Local Government Officers Association (NALGO)	1964
National Association of Schoolmasters (NAS)	1968
National Union of Public employees (NUPE)	1943
National Union of Teachers (NUT)	1970
Society of Civil and Public Servants (SCPS)[2]	1975

[1] Not all public sector unions are listed here, only those representing civil servants and occupations of similar status to civil servants. Some organizations have changed their names.

[2] The CSU and SCPS merged in 1988 and are now the National Union of Civil and Public Servants (NUCPS)

Although most civil service unions have been affiliated to the TUC since 1946 when such affiliations were made possible again by the repeal of the 1927 Trade Unions and Trade Disputes Act, and although civil servants have never been statutorily forbidden from taking industrial action, it was not until 1973 that the tendency amongst other public sector unions to take industrial action manifested itself in the civil service (although post office workers represented by the Civil and Public Services Association and the Society of Civil Servants resorted to strike action in 1970). This is not to say that certain civil service unions had not considered industrial action prior to 1973. Indeed, as early as 1961- 2 the Civil Service Clerical Association (CSCA, the forerunner to the CPSA) had actually planned a work to rule to take place on 17 January 1962 (which did not in the end take place). Following this threat of industrial action there were calls at the 1962 and 1963 annual conferences of the Association to adopt a strike policy, (CSCA, 1962, p. 354; CSCA, 1963, p. 306) although no such policy was adopted until 1968 when a motion for the adoption of a strike policy was carried overwhelmingly (CSCA, 1968, p. 229). Similar moves were adopted by the Society of Civil Servants which in 1970, at the annual conference, passed by a narrow majority a resolution to use militant action, including strike action and the setting up of a fighting fund (SCS, 1970, paras. 34 and 39). The reasons for these moves were essentially concerned with the pay policies of the Wilson Labour Government in the late 1960s (Kelly, 1980, pp. 106-109).

The civil service industrial action in 1973 was also concerned with pay, and again unrest was caused primarily by pay policies, this time those of the Heath Conservative Government. Under the Pay Research system most non-industrial civil servants were due to a pay rise in January 1973. Pay in the civil service had not been revised under pay research since 1 January 1971 for the majority and there was thus the possibility of large 'catching up' increases. The Government, however, refused to pay any increases until after the end of their pay freeze. The Civil and Public Services Association arranged protest meetings, as did the Society of Civil Servants, who, in addition, launched a campaign to educate the public about civil service problems. On 8 January 1973 the Prime Minister received a deputation from the civil service unions but nothing emerged from this. On 10 January members of the CPSA and SCS staged walkouts, and rallies and protest meetings were organized throughout the country. The Government still refused to act and the CPSA, the SCS and the Customs and Excise group staged a one day national strike on 17 February 1973. The unions estimated that 75 per cent of their members took part, but government departments put the figure much lower (about 50 per cent). Following the one day national strike there were selective strikes all over the country and this sporadic campaign of protests lasted until April. Settlement was reached by November.

This was the first time in the history of the civil service that there had been official strike action.

However, of much greater import were the strikes and other forms of industrial unrest in the civil service in 1978-9, in 1981 and in 1984 and onwards following the GCHQ 'Affair'. In 1978-9 the civil service unions, in common with other public sector unions, became increasingly impatient with the incomes policies of the Labour Government. They were particularly annoyed by the non-payment of awards due in consequence of agreements reached after pay research, and the Society of Civil and Public Servants (SCPS) and the Civil and Public Services Association called selective strikes and short all-out one day stoppages during 1978-9 as part of their campaign. All the civil service unions decided to join the protest with a one day strike on 2 April 1979, when it became clear that the

Government's offers were in the words of the First Division Association 'totally unacceptable'. The consequence of this action was that the unions believed that the Government made a 'satisfactory offer' (FDA, 1980, para. 52).

The industrial action in 1981 was much more significant. It was precipitated, as far as the unions were concerned, by the Conservative Government's unilateral suspension, and later abolition, of the Civil Service National Pay Agreements and of the Pay Research Unit (PRU). In February 1981, following the Government's decision, the Council of Civil Service Unions (CCSU - the successors to the NSS) presented a common pay claim. The amount claimed was 15 per cent with a minimum cash increase of £10 per week. The Government's response was to offer 6 per cent and to express a willingness to talk about the future - but with no guarantee about arbitration or a return to an agreed pay system. The CCSU inaugurated a campaign of industrial action, including a one day stoppage on 9 March and selective strikes thereafter, which turned out to be the longest national industrial dispute since 1926, lasting some twenty one weeks. The action sought to stop the flow of revenue to the Government, and the strikes affected the nation's defences, the administration of justice and, towards the end, the payment of benefits to the elderly, the sick and the unemployed. The settlement eventually reached involved an extra half of one per cent on the Government's original offer to be distributed as £30 per head; a commitment on the part of the Government to negotiations in 1982 without predetermined cash limits; a concession that if there was failure to reach an agreement in 1982 there would be reference to the Civil Service Arbitration Tribunal; and the setting up of an inquiry into non-industrial Civil Service pay under the chairmanship of Sir John Magaw, a retired Lord Justice of Appeal (O'Toole, 1989a, pp. 177-180).

The bitterness of the 1981 industrial action, and the distrust engendered on both sides, may have been partly responsible for the next major industrial relations problem in the Civil Service, the notorious GCHQ Affair. On 25 January 1984, the then Foreign Secretary, Sir Geoffrey Howe announced in the House of Commons that all civil servants working at the Government's Communications Headquarters (GCHQ) were to cease to have the right of access to industrial tribunals or to belong to independent trade unions. The announcement affected about 7,000 staff, and according to *FDA News* of February 1984 'General Secretaries were only given ten minute's notice of the announcement in the Commons'. Each member of staff at GCHQ was issued with a form setting out two options. They could either agree to give up their right to belong to a trade union along with their right of access to Industrial Tribunals and receive a cash payment of £1,000 (less tax); or they could apply for transfer to another civil service job, thereby retaining these rights and not receiving the £1,000. Anyone who refused to complete this option form or who, after electing to leave GCHQ, refused to accept an alternative posting, would be dismissed. The staff at GCHQ were also told that from 1 March 1984 they would only be allowed to join a departmental staff association, confined to GCHQ staff and approved by the Director of GCHQ. The ensuing legal battle and industrial campaign continues even now, with victories on both sides. However what has happened is that, while working relationships remain, industrial relations in the civil service have been badly soured by this event. Coming after the unilateral abolition of the National Pay Agreements and of PRU that sourness was all the more bitter.

It is against this background that the trade unions response to the Next Steps needs to be considered; and it is with these points in mind that the question of this paper, whither Whitleyism, should be assessed. Industrial relations in the civil service may well be returning to the pre-1919 situation. And this may well reflect the possibility of the civil service itself returning to that situation which so many committees, Commissions and Royal Commissions thought to be so detrimental to the efficiency of the public service.

The Trade Unions and the 'Next Steps'

It could be argued that the most important passage in the Ibbs Report is that 'To strengthen operational effectiveness, there must be freedom to recruit, pay, grade and structure in the most effective way' (Efficiency Unit, 1988, para. 21). As the report recognizes the implication is that 'the central responsibility for pay and conditions of service, and the associated negotiations with national trade unions, will be progressively and substantially reduced' (Efficiency Unit, 1988, para. 45). These two passages, and others, raise important questions about personnel management in the British civil service, with its long tradition of open competition, fair treatment of candidates, and good, or at least satisfactory conditions for those employed in government service. They raise enormous questions about the unified nature of the service and about the state of industrial relations therein.

In an article published in 1982, long before the Next Steps, Peter Jones, then Secretary of the Council of Civil Service Unions, made the following comments:

> One way of introducing more realistic forms of accountability could be in using the operational agency system developed in Sweden. We already have in theory at least, three such agencies in our own Civil Service: the long established Board of Inland Revenue, and Customs and Excise, and the more recent Property Services Agency. Operational Agencies, with management boards responsible for carrying out services as laid down by ministers and Parliament, could concentrate on carrying out those services with some degree of freedom from the more transient considerations [of Parliamentary accountability]. The relatively low cost of administration against the overall cost of the services provided, particularly noticeable in revenue areas, could

be the measure of effectiveness - with freedom to move into new areas without artificial manpower constraints, if this could be shown to be cost effective. Would Ministers and Parliament be prepared to see this degree of freedom given to public service managers? I doubt it. But perennial cries for greater efficiency, concern about staff numbers and arbitrary manpower cuts would perhaps be better received if some attention were given to the other side of the equation (Jones, 1982, quoted in Jones, 1991, p. 22).

Peter Jones' 1990 (published in 1991) description of the official attitude of the civil service unions was that it was one of 'cautious neutrality' (Jones, 1991, p. 22); and he pointed out that Sir Robin Butler, the current Head of the Home Civil Service, has said of the trade union leaders that 'they have shown a very constructive attitude to change'. According to Jones the reason why the unions have taken this attitude is:

The same reason that we have welcomed other measures - for example the Fulton Report - which were designed to improve standards of management in the Civil Service. Given proper safeguards on essential matters such as maintaining *joint consultation and industrial relations procedures, and current pay, pensions and personnel management arrangements* we see scope in the agency concept for better management, better use of financial resources, better services to public and better treatment of staff (emphasis added) (Jones, 1991, p. 22).

Since Jones made these observations it has become more and more clear that the safeguards he called for have not been forthcoming - and the reason largely emanates from the attitude of the Government, and of senior management within the service, towards the unions. As Jones also argued, carrying through the sort of changes involved in the creation of agencies requires the co-operation of the workforce, particularly when the aim is to improve the quality of service (Jones, 1991, pp. 22-23). However, the Next Steps programme is being implemented by a Government which, certainly in the years of Mrs Thatcher, failed to recognize the contribution which staff in general and civil servants in particular can make. Even Lord Rayner is conscious of the lack of trust which the Government which he advised had towards its civil servants, particularly in relation to the reforms he had been so heavily involved in. He has spoken of:

the failure to understand the scale of what was involved together with a persistent refusal to use the Civil Service properly. You have to help, congratulate and lead those who are involved in bringing about change.

He went on to express regret that so many civil servants who were fully committed to better management and with whom he had worked closely in Government had left the Service:

> There is enormous quality in the Civil Service. It is a pity [Mrs Thatcher] took too much advice from theoretical people and too little from the talent that existed in the Service (Rayner, 1991).

According to an Institute of Public Policy Research (IPPR) report commissioned by the trade unions the drain of officials from the civil service referred to by Rayner was 'a direct result of the low morale and disillusionment caused by Government policy in the first two Thatcher administrations' (IPPR, 1991, p. 49). The unilateral abolition of the established and agreed system of pay determination in 1981, the consequent strike, and the arbitrary withdrawal of trade union rights for civil servants at GCHQ, all served to create an atmosphere of enormous hostility. This hostility extended beyond matters solely related to industrial relations. Many civil servants saw the retrenchment of the 1980s as an attack on the services they provided, and also, naturally, as a threat to their job security. Privatization, contracting out, budget limitations, all affected the morale of civil servants; as did the hostility of the Government to civil servants and to civil service unions. Thatcher's hostility to the civil service and the Government's prior commitment to a continuing reduction in public spending had fundamental implications for the implementation of the Next Steps programme (IPPR, 1991, p. 50*)*.

This chapter, however, is concerned with those matters which are primarily the concern of industrial relations: the future of collective bargaining and joint consultation; civil service pay; and the future of the career civil service. As Mr John Garrett MP succinctly put it in his evidence to the Treasury and Civil Service Committee:

> The proposal to give agencies full responsibility for recruitment, pay, grading and organization is a particularly radical change. Presumably, this is the beginning of the end of a unified Civil Service with common conditions of service and establishment procedures. Agencies will be expected to establish their own pay rates, which will no doubt vary with location, and staff will be expected to make their careers in an agency. Trade union negotiations will be moved to an agency basis - and no doubt the unions will have noticed the observation ... that 'benefits' should result from the proposals and that five per cent of Civil Service running costs amounts to £630 million. Since the greater part of running costs is in staff salaries the implication must be that the government expects substantial reductions in staff numbers or wage costs or both (Treasury and Civil Service Committee,

1988, Memorandum from John Garrett MP, para. 12).

These are the very issues which have exercised the civil service trade unions. They have also, however, been very concerned at the implications of Next Steps for bargaining structures and procedures.

As the IPPR points out existing structures of collective bargaining are clearly challenged by the development of agencies. This is so at the national and at the departmental/agency level. If agencies have the right to recruit, pay and grade according to the needs of their customers and the type of work that they are involved in this has implications throughout the civil service. In addition, of course, an agency may wish to have individual contracts with its staff, particularly the senior staff, and these contracts can be individual specific in relation to responsibilities, performance targets, assessment and remuneration. It is true, as the IPPR report notes, that even where such contracts are negotiated, there remains an interest conflict between employer and employee (IPPR, 1991, pp. 53-54). Indeed, there may in these circumstances be a *greater* need for collective representation. However, the nature of the role of a union would be inherently different, more concerned with appeals procedures than with collective bargaining.

Unfortunately for the trade unions, some of the agencies take quite a different view. For example in the Royal Mint not only have there been moves to introduce personal contracts for senior staff but also hints that the unions representing them - in this case the Institute of Professional and Managerial Staff (IPMS) and the National Union of Civil and Public Servants (NUCPS) - are to be 'de-recognized' (CCSU, 1992). These fears have been exacerbated by more recent moves towards privatization and contracting-out. The unions are also alarmed by what is happening elsewhere in the service. It seems that as far as agencies generally are concerned, chief executives:

> have been noticeably harassed by the Next Steps Unit to produce their own distinctive pay and grading structures - regardless it would seem of whether or not the Agency needed new structures or the Chief Executive desired them. 'Something new' is the Unit's cry - nothing which looks like the existing structure and pay system will do (CCSU, 1992).

This generalized concern is particularly highlighted in the case of Her Majesty's Stationary Office (HMSO). This agency was the first to completely disassociate itself from the mainstream civil service collective bargaining and joint consultation procedures. From the unions' perspective it created a precedent, and for them a worrying precedent. The 1991 pay settlement there was, according to B. Brett, an 'unacceptably low across the board settlement' and 'would undoubtedly increase unions' suspicions of the Treasury's proposals for wider change in Civil Service pay arrangements' (CCSU, 1991c).

Even at the level of the unions' representation of individual officials there seems to have been a change of attitude, or at least of procedure, on the part of the Official Side of the civil service. In particular the unions have expressed unhappiness at the prospect of appeals procedures changing so that the permanent secretary of a department could delegate the hearing of appeals to the chief executives of the agencies for which that department is responsible. The CCSU is reported as having told Sir Peter Kemp, then Next Steps Project Manager, during a joint meeting that permanent secretaries 'had a responsibility for the department as a whole which permitted them to take a broader view than Chief Executives'. It believed that, in terms of natural justice, the appellants would feel the need to go outside the agency 'to ensure their consideration was not unduly influenced by the Agency's operational commitments'. Kemp said that the proposal would be 'an enabling measure':

> However, the proposal was in keeping with the Government's general policy of giving managers in departments and agencies the discretion they needed to carry out their work effectively. His view was that when a Chief Executive was responsible for the day to day management of particular staff he or she should also be responsible for considering appeals by them (CCSU, 1991c).

In line with this philosophy, the philosophy that managers in departments and agencies should be allowed the discretion necessary to carry out their work effectively, the framework documents for the agencies allow for 'flexibility' in all aspects of the industrial relations procedures in those agencies. This has so worried the unions that articles appear on the subject in the CCSU's monthly *Next Steps Newsletter*. For example in March 1991 the following appeared:

> Given the attack on collective bargaining being insidiously sustained throughout the service, we would do well to take seriously what is happening to local Whitley Constitutions in agencies ... The variations proposed in some agencies can seriously undermine local negotiations and sever links with departmental TUS's. Sometimes a Whitley Committee needs to be established : don't wait too long ...

The article goes on to suggest what the most contentious issues are, and to make sure that certain prescriptions should be followed. In particular the chief executive should be in the chair, there should be lay trade unionists from other parts of the *department*, there should be clear details of the functions of the council, and care should be taken to ensure that the agency council's aims and objectives are compatible with those of the departmental council (CCSU, 1991a).

A specific example of discontent in relation to the industrial relations procedures arose in the Central Statistical Office (CSO) Agency. Article 7.9 of the framework document says that:

> The Director is responsible for ensuring effective staff relations within the Department. As *part* of these arrangements there will continue to be a Whitley Committee system through which recognized trade unions will be consulted as appropriate. The arrangements for staff relations will be periodically reviewed in the light of the developing needs of the Agency (emphasis added).

One trade union official in the CPSA thought this 'woolly' and that it 'could be open to a greater degree of interpretation' than some other framework documents. John Ellis, then General Secretary of the CPSA sent the internal memorandum on which these thoughts appeared to Peter Jones in the hope that the issues might be raised with the Next Steps Project Manager. Ellis was particularly unhappy about the Whitley machinery being only 'part' of the staff relations procedures and that the system would be open to review (CCSU, 1991b).

If there has been concern about the constitution of Whitley Councils in the agencies there has been even greater concern with wider constitutional matters, albeit that this concern has been expressed from a trade union perspective. The wider constitutional matters in question relate to the future of the unified career civil service. On this question worry and anger is widespread amongst the civil service unions.

The reforms of the inter-War years created a unified civil service. Under the guidance of Sir Warren Fisher and Sir Edward Bridges the foundations laid by the famous Northcote Trevelyan Report and by the numerous reports which followed theirs, could be built upon. The common recruitment procedures, developed by the independent Civil Service Commission provided the services of people who were well qualified for positions of general responsibility in all departments. The introduction of Whitleyism and the modernization of industrial relations procedure facilitated the change. The role of the Treasury was transformed from penny-pinching to being at the heart of the drive for efficiency in government. This unified civil service meant that those becoming part of it had a career for life. The service offered job security, appropriate career development and a remuneration package which included a pension on retirement. For the government as employer it offered stability and flexibility in staffing.

In a real sense the Next Steps programme can be seen as a return to the civil service as it was before 1914. Just as agencies are semi-autonomous so too were departments. Just as agencies may have a degree of control over pay and conditions so too did departments. Just as the agencies have agency specific industrial relations procedures so too did the departments. Some even see the contemporary changes as a return to the civil service as it was pre-1870, before the establishment of the Civil Service Commission - and in the sense that the Civil Service Commission no longer exists and departments and agencies now do their own recruiting, they may be correct (see Chapman, 1991a). It is these aspects of the Next Steps initiative which have increasingly come to alarm the trade unions.

This alarm has been demonstrated both publicly and in private. For example the National Union of Civil and Public Servants (NUCPS) debated the following two motions at their 1991 Annual Delegate Conference:

> 1. That this Conference reaffirms its opposition in principle to the Next Steps. Conference believes that the main goal of Next Steps is not improvement in quality of service to the public but rather cost cutting and the break up of the national Civil Service ...
>
> Conference reaffirms its view that the interests of both civil servants and the public are best served by a national, unified, career Civil Service, which is adequately funded, fully accountable to Parliament and responsive to the needs of the public ...
>
> Conference instructs the NEC to: assist Groups and Branches in agency negotiations to defend Civil Service wide pay and conditions, Civil Service status, interchangeability, the Whitley Structure and recognition of existing trade unions and accountability of agencies to Parliament.
>
> 2. That this Conference notes with concern the Prime Minister's endorsement on 16 May [1991] of the Fraser Report *Making the most of the Next Steps* ...
>
> Conference further instructs the NEC to take all measures necessary to defend members whose jobs are threatened and to build a wide-ranging campaign of opposition to the break up of the service (NUCPS, 1991).

The reasons behind this public expression of alarm are more eloquently and reasonably expressed in a letter from Peter Jones to the Next Steps Project Manager, sent after the matters it raises were discussed at the CCSU Major Policy Committee on 6 August. The letter read in part:

> You will be aware of our continuing concern to ensure that there are no barriers to flexible movement throughout the Service ... We are most anxious

to ensure that agencies do not become enclosed employment ghettoes, and that both management and staff can continue to benefit from the interchange of career opportunities that has served the Civil Service so well up to now. With this in mind, we are most apprehensive about both the short term and the longer term effects of the recent announcement by the Chancellor about 'pay flexibilities' ... the trend of current Official Side thinking seems to spell real danger to the notion of a coherent pay and grading system - with obvious consequential dangers so far as freedom of movement is concerned (CCSU, 1991d).

The announcement by the Chancellor which Jones refers to is, in fact, of momentous importance for the future of the unified civil service, even though it was made only as a written response to a Parliamentary Question. It makes Jones' reference to real danger look an understatement.

The statement begins quite innocuously, with reference to the Civil Service Pay Agreements which have 'provided useful stability in Civil Service pay'. It becomes more ominous as the statement proceeds, with the following observations : 'that any organization must be able to adapt to changing needs' and 'The Government now wants to introduce more flexible pay regimes for the civil service, both nationally and locally'. The Chancellor argued that:

The new pay systems must meet the needs and objectives of departments and agencies; they must be demonstrably beneficial to the citizen, fair to the employee and linked to the delivery of high quality public services; and they must be affordable.

He continues that while:

Progress has already been made in providing for pay flexibility ... the Government have concluded that the agreements as they stand do not provide a framework that is fully capable of meeting the needs of the 1990s. It has informed the unions that it wishes to negotiate changes to them.

There were three new elements which the Chancellor wished to see emerge from the negotiations. First:

a range of forms of performance related pay ... over time performance will come to determine a larger proportion of the pay bill ...

Secondly, measures:

further to enable responsibility for pay bargaining to be delegated to civil
service departments or agencies, to allow them wider discretion in relation to
their pay and grading regimes. Alternative pay and grading structures will be
approved when they are expected to produce value for money benefits
greater than through centrally controlled negotiation.

And thirdly, provisions:

to give an option to those departments and agencies for which such extensive
discretion is not appropriate to negotiate for themselves flexibilities of their
own within the total of the overall central pay settlement agreed by the
Treasury (Chancellor of the Exchequer, 1991).

The situation was formalized by the Civil Service (Management Functions) Act
1993, and *The Next Steps Briefing Note* of April 1993 announced that the
arrangements called for by the Chancellor of the Exchequer have indeed been
negotiated:

Following the Chancellors' announcement on 24 July 1991 the Government
has re-negotiated the pay agreements with the NUCPS, CPSA, IPMS,
NUCPS/PMS/FDA/AIT (for grades 5-7) and industrial JCC, to facilitate
greater delegation, and put into place new performance pay arrangements.
All agencies have been encouraged to review their pay and grading
arrangements in the light of these changes and to consider delegation where
it will lead to value for money through more cost effective use of the pay
bill. The 17 largest agencies (including the two new Prison Service
Agencies) and the two Revenue Departments are all expected to have taken
responsibility for their own pay bargaining by 1st April 1994 (Efficiency
Unit, 1993b, para. 25).

It is now the case that most agencies are indeed semi-autonomous. Some will
soon be totally autonomous, in the sense of being completely privatized. Taken
together with other statements from official sources, and other changes which have
received scant attention (like the complete re-organization of civil service
recruitment - see Chapman, 1991a, 1993) these new pay agreements seem to spell
the end of the unified career civil service.

Trade Unions and the Next Steps : The End of Whitleyism?

The system of collective bargaining in the civil service, known as Whitleyism, dates back to 1919. The theory, as envisaged by Whitley, is of a system which encourages joint consultation at all levels of the organization. In the civil service there are local and departmental Whitley Councils and the National Whitley Council. The system allows for the representation of employees through the intermediary role of trade unions, unions which staff have traditionally been encouraged to join by all governments. The consequence of this encouragement is a very high degree of union density, and thus an ability on the part of the unions to claim that they are representative of the workforce. As the IPPR Report states Whitleyism 'offers a channel for discussion between management and staff to ensure that changes are introduced in ways which maximize the chance of success' (p. 53).

For most of the history of the civil service the principle of joint consultation on important matters has worked well. The consequence has usually been that the benefits argued by the IPPR have indeed accrued. Whenever major changes have been introduced the staff side of the Whitley machine has usually been consulted at every stage of the process of change. Indeed, the changes may well have been facilitated by the Whitley machinery. This was true of changes in the organization of the civil service after both World Wars (Chapman and Greenway, 1980, pp. 71-122); it was true of changes introduced by the Tomlin and Priestley Royal Commissions, both of which concentrated on industrial relations matters (O'Toole, 1989a, pp. 37-53 and pp. 95-113); and it was true of the changes which came about as a result of the Fulton Committee (Chapman and Greenaway, 1980, pp. 123-182; O'Toole, 1989a, pp. 120-143).

The 1970s and 1980s, however, witnessed a sea-change. Partly this was due to economic circumstances; and partly, more latterly, to an ideological distrust of trade unions. Economic circumstances led to the relative decline of civil service pay and to the suspension of agreed principles of pay determination (O'Toole, 1989a, chapter 7 and appendix 2). Ideological distrust led to the arbitrary abolition of those principles and a failure, in the view of the unions, to replace them with an adequate system. Distrust between the two sides of the Whitley system grew, and while Whitleyism largely remained intact, the relationship was certainly less intimate.

This has been especially true in relation to the Next Steps. While Peter Jones could say in 1990 that the attitude of the unions was one of 'cautious neutrality', it is clear in 1994 that the situation is very different. This is so because the safeguards which Jones called for in 1990 and 1991 have simply not been forthcoming. Indeed, there seems to have been an accelerated move towards the undermining of traditional systems of collective bargaining. Worse still, from the union perspective, they seem to be being cold shouldered. This is admirably portrayed in a CCSU document about the 'management flexibilities' which the Treasury is consistently trying to encourage: (CCSU, 1991e).

This is at the very heart of the question in hand. Whitleyism is about consultation - it is about being involved in the management of change. That involvement does not seem to be occurring - at least not as much as in the past. Even where consultation has taken place, the Next Steps Project Team seem keen to underplay the role of the unions. In fact the word 'unions' hardly now appears in many of the documents related to the Next Steps programme the rather old fashioned phrase 'staff-side' has replaced it.

Does the Next Steps programme herald the death of Whitleyism? The answer must be, in some senses yes; in some senses no. The machinery and the vocabulary of Whitleyism remain: there are departmental, local and agency Whitley Councils; and national procedures of joint consultation and collective bargaining continue. However, the nature of the agency system (if system be the word) is such that the end of the unified career civil service is not just in sight, but almost upon us.

The reforms in the recruitment methods coupled with the wholesale transfer of discretion with regard to pay, grading and structure to agencies and even departments does mean that there will soon no longer be a career civil service in the sense understood by Sir Warren Fisher or Sir Edward Bridges or even Sir Ian Bancroft or Sir Robert Armstrong. With the end of the unified civil service we shall also see the end of national Whitleyism. Of course, in the agencies and the departments there will be industrial relations procedures of some sort. It remains to be seen whether, even if the word 'Whitleyism' is applied to those procedures, the spirit of Whitleyism can survive.

The spirit of Whitleyism lies in the phrase 'joint consultation'. More or less since its inception the Whitley machinery of the civil service has ensured at least some measure of co-operation between staff and their employers. That is, until recent times. As this chapter notes the Next Steps programme was conceived and is being implemented against a background of distrust between the unions and the Government. To some extent joint consultation had already begun to disintegrate. The Next Steps programme seems, at least to the unions, to have accelerated that disintegration. What they see - and what empirical evidence suggests is the case - is a return to the pre-World War I situation. In other words, civil service unions will once again be 'petitioning' the quasi-autonomous heads of quasi-autonomous agencies. The unions may well be forgiven if they believe that the sort of 'managerialism' this implies does not sit easily with the spirit of Whitleyism.

Lessons from the Antipodes

JONATHAN BOSTON

Introduction

Next Steps is but one of many programmes of public sector reform which have been pursued within the OECD since the early 1980s (OECD, 1990). Clearly, the structural and managerial changes already brought about by Next Steps have been significant, and indeed rank as one of the most important reforms to the civil service during the twentieth century. Moreover, the Conservative Government's reforming zeal is far from exhausted, and further policy changes, including the decentralization of wage bargaining and the contracting-out of a large number of departmental functions, are currently in the process of formulation and implementation (Prime Minister, 1991). Nevertheless, when compared with developments in some other parts of the world, the Next Steps reforms appear to be relatively modest and restrained. Certainly, they have been less radical and comprehensive than the recent public sector reforms in New Zealand.

The purpose of this chapter is to examine Next Steps from the perspective of policy changes in New Zealand, arguably the most advanced case of what has been termed 'the new public management' (Aucoin, 1990; Hood, 1991; Hood and Jackson, 1991). The chapter is divided into three sections. First, it briefly sketches the main changes to the management of the public sector in New Zealand since the mid 1980s. Second, it compares these changes with the Next Steps programme and highlights some of the key policy differences. Third, it outlines a few of the lessons which emerge from New Zealand's recent experience that may be of relevance to the management of the British civil service, particularly in the light of the Conservative Government's most recent reform proposals (Efficiency Unit, 1991; Prime Minister, 1991b).

New Zealand's Public Sector Reforms: A Brief Outline

Initiated by the fourth Labour Government (1984-90) and subsequently pursued by the fourth National Government (1990-), New Zealand has undertaken a remarkably comprehensive programme of economic, social and political reforms. The public sector reforms, which have formed a key part of the broader reform agenda, have been very much in keeping with the doctrines of the new public management (Boston et al., 1991; Chapman, 1989; Hood, 1990; Scott, Bushnell and Sallee, 1990; Wistrich, 1992). Hence, there has been a marked shift from the use of input controls and bureaucratic rules to a reliance on detailed output measures and performance targets, various responsibilities have been devolved from central agencies to departmental managers, new reporting, monitoring and accountability mechanisms have been introduced, and a strong preference has been given to private ownership, contracting-out, and contestability in the provision of public services. Further, the use of short term labour contracts, performance agreements, and performance-linked remuneration has been greatly extended, and there have been determined efforts to curb public expenditure and improve efficiency via cost-cutting, load-shedding and cuts in staffing levels. To quote from a recent report reviewing New Zealand's state sector reforms, the intention has been to put in place a policy framework based on 'Clear, prior specification of intended performance, appropriate delegation of decision-making authority, subsequent monitoring of achievement and the careful application of incentives and sanctions' (Steering Group, 1991, p. 60). The overriding objectives of this reform programme, as in many other OECD countries, have been to reduce public expenditure, enhance the efficiency and effectiveness of the public sector, improve the quality of the goods and services provided by public agencies, and ensure that providers are responsive to the needs and interests of their consumers.

Given the widespread and far-reaching nature of the public sector changes in New Zealand, it is not possible to outline them in detail here. Briefly, however, the major changes can be summarized as follows:

a) There has been a systematic and extensive programme of commercialization (i.e. the placing of publicly-provided goods and services on a full cost-recovery or user-pays basis). This policy has been applied to a wide range of services including: agricultural advisers, data from the Statistics Department, weather information from the Meteorological Office, the use of facilities in National Parks, and various health and educational services.

b) Wherever possible commercial functions have been separated from non-commercial functions and the commercial functions have been placed in independent profit making organizations known as state-owned enterprises (SOEs). Originally, nine such SOEs were established under the State-Owned Enterprises Act (1986), but since then many more have been added including the country's three international airports, major ports, TV and Radio networks, etc. In recent years the research and development activities undertaken by various government departments have been re-organized into Crown Research Institutes and the country's major hospitals are being turned into Crown Health Enterprises. In each case the new enterprises are expected to compete for the available state and private sector funds and operate as successful businesses.

c) A major asset sales programme was commenced in 1988. Since then over 20 SOEs and other substantial state assets have been sold, representing nearly two-thirds of the state's commercial assets. Further asset sales are under consideration including parts of the electricity industry, Coalcorp, Landcorp, Works and Development Corporation, and various local authority trading organizations.

d) A wide range of government services have been contracted out to private sector suppliers. Recently, the government investigated the possibility of contracting-out the policy advice functions of departments (which would, of course, end the concept of a public service as traditionally conceived), but has so far decided not to proceed with the idea (State Services Commission, 1991).

e) Wherever feasible, the provision of policy advice has been separated from executive functions (including the delivery of publicly-provided goods and services, together with regulatory, policing and assessment functions). On the one hand, this has led to the establishment of large number of relatively small policy ministries (e.g. the Ministries of Cultural Affairs, Defence, Education, Environment, Forestry, Health, Housing, Maori Development, Pacific Island Affairs, Research, Science and Technology, Youth Affairs and Women's Affairs). On the other hand, it has resulted in the establishment of a number of departments with mainly operational responsibilities (e.g. the Department of Conservation, the Education Review Office, the National Library, the Serious Fraud Office, and the Department of Survey and Land Information), together with a range of non-departmental agencies (boards, commissions, etc.). This decoupling process, combined with the separation of commercial and non-commercial functions, has so far resulted in the abolition (or privatization) of 16 departments and the creation of 22 new departments.

f) As a result of the State Sector Act (1988) and the Employment Contracts Act (1991) there have been major changes in the conduct of industrial relations in the public sector. In particular, the practice of having a central employing authority in the form of the State Services Commission (SSC) has been abandoned and instead departmental chief executives are now their own employing authorities, and thus responsible for pay fixing and conditions of employment. Effectively, this has ended the concept of a unified public service. To date, however, wage bargaining has not been completely decentralized, and the SSC continues to play a role in co-ordinating state sector industrial relations. Further, there has been a substantial move away from permanent employment to fixed-term contracts, not merely for senior departmental managers (i.e. departmental chief executives and members of the Senior Executive Service (SES)), but also for many other departmental employees. There has also been a marked shift away from fixed salary scales to flexible scales and performance-linked remuneration.

g) Major financial management reforms were introduced in the late 1980s and early 1990s via the Public Finance Act (1989). Among the more important changes have been a shift from a programme-based to an output-based appropriation system, the removal of numerous input controls, the introduction of accrual accounting throughout the public sector, the imposition of a comprehensive capital charging regime, the production of a Crown balance sheet of assets and debts, and the introduction of a new reporting and monitoring regime.

h) A central feature of the reform programme has been the emphasis placed on the relationship between ministers and departmental chief executives. To this end, chief executives are now required to sign annual performance agreements with their portfolio minister(s), and their performance is reviewed annually by the SSC. Also, in the interests of assisting ministers to hold their departments to account, the National Government has experimented with the use of management boards comprising senior private sector executives.

i) These changes in the public sector have not, of course, been undertaken in isolation. Rather, they have been part of a much broader and systematic economic and social reform agenda. This has included the introduction of an essentially monetarist-type macroeconomic policy stance, a comprehensive microeconomic liberalization programme covering virtually all major sectors of the economy, substantial changes to the structure and operations of local government, and significant changes in education, health, housing and social welfare policies (characterized by a greater emphasis on targeting, large cuts in the real value of most welfare benefits, the separation of purchaser and provider roles, and a move away from in-kind assistance in favour of cash subsidies).

Judging from the evidence currently available, there can be no doubt that the impact of the changes in public sector management have been significant (see Boston et al., 1991; Steering Group, 1991). For example, the total number of staff employed in the core state sector (i.e. central government departments and ministries) has fallen from more than 80,000 in the mid 1980s to around 45,000 in 1991, and is expected to fall to less than 40,000 by the mid 1990s (Hunn, 1991, p. 12). Moreover, this reduction in staffing levels has not been solely due to contracting-out, privatization and natural attrition. There have also been thousands of redundancies. In some cases, more than a third of departmental staff have lost their jobs. Such outcomes, together with the huge re-organization of the machinery of government, have necessarily had a marked impact on careers paths, departmental morale, and organizational cultures, as well as significant social and regional impacts in some instances.

More positively, there is also evidence of major improvements in labour productivity and profitability in the SOE sector (Duncan and Bollard, 1992; Scott, Bushnell, and Sallee, 1990, pp. 148-50). The Coal Corporation, for example, reduced its staff numbers by around 50 per cent while at the same time increasing its output of coal. Similarly, the Electricity Corporation, the largest SOE, reduced its unit costs of production by 23 per cent between 1987 and 1989, and has significantly increased its output of electricity per employee. Most SOEs have also provided evidence of improvements in consumer service (e.g. faster delivery of mail, speedier phone connections, etc.). To date, there has been no comprehensive research undertaken on the impact of the various policy changes on the quality of departmental outputs. Until robust evidence is available, assessments of the benefits or otherwise of the reforms must be treated with caution. Nevertheless, such studies as have been undertaken indicate that those most closely involved with the reform process, namely senior department officials and government ministers, believe that in most cases departmental performance has improved since the mid 1980s (Steering Group, 1991).

Next Steps: Comparisons and Contrasts

The Next Steps programme closely parallels many of the recent New Zealand reforms. In both countries there has been a strong emphasis on separating policy advice and executive functions, though the methods adopted for achieving this purpose have been somewhat different. Whereas in New Zealand executive functions have been hived off into separate departments and agencies, in Britain the new executive agencies have, so far, been retained within the organizational boundaries of their parent departments. Another feature common to both reform programmes has been the decentralization and delegation of power within the civil service. As a result, the role and importance of input controls has been reduced and instead much greater reliance has been placed on output targets and performance indicators. Other important similarities include the emphasis on contracting-out and user-pays, the greater attention given to consumer satisfaction and responsiveness, an increased reliance on explicit contracts rather than implicit understandings, loyalty and trust, and changes to the structure of incentives facing civil servants, in particular the growing reliance on fixed-term employment, open competition, and performance-linked remuneration. Not surprisingly, too, the reform programmes have generated very similar problems (e.g. the difficulty of specifying and measuring outputs and outcomes, the difficulty of developing meaningful performance indicators, the political and practical constraints in applying the new regime of rewards and sanctions, etc.). There are also some important similarities in the way the reforms in the two countries have been pursued, in particular the relatively limited opportunities for public debate and the extent to which they have been driven from the centre - by the Prime Minister and the Efficiency Unit/Project Team in the case of Britain, and the Minister of Finance and the Treasury in the case of New Zealand.

But despite such close parallels, there are also striking differences in the origins, nature and scope of the reforms in the two countries. It is not possible here to provide a detailed account of such differences, but some of the main contrasts are worth highlighting. The focus here will be on machinery of government issues, changes in personnel policies and the decentralization of management responsibilities, with little attention being given to financial management reforms.

1. The Theoretical Underpinnings of the Reform Programmes

From a New Zealand perspective, one of the most notable features of the recent reforms to the British civil service is the absence of any serious attempt on the part of the Government or its advisers to justify their policy proposals on the basis of a coherent and comprehensive theoretical framework. To be sure, some use has been made of the recent managerialist literature (e.g. Peters and Waterman, 1982). But the contemporary social science literature dealing with such issues as human motivation, organizational design, governance arrangements, incentive structures, accountability regimes, policy making, and the management of change appears to have been almost entirely ignored, or at least has been deemed to be largely irrelevant to the business of providing a public justification for the policies adopted. For example, the key documents outlining the rationale for Next Steps, such as the Ibbs Report (Efficiency Unit, 1988) and the Fraser Report (Efficiency Unit, 1991), are virtually devoid of any reference to theoretical issues, and draw neither on the older traditions of organizational theory and public administration (see Chapman, 1988; Jordan, 1992), nor on the more recent theoretical insights arising from the 'new institutional economics' or the 'new economics of organizations', as it is variously called. This latter literature embraces a number of strands including agency theory and transaction cost analysis (Moe, 1984; Perrow, 1986; Williamson, 1985). Even more surprising is the fact that the some of the reformers appear to regard the absence of any attention to theory as a virtue. For example, Diana Goldsworthy, a member of the Next Steps Project Team, has commented in her account of the origins and implementation of Next Steps that the residential courses held by the Project Team for departmental and agency representatives have concentrated on 'developing practical solutions rather than indulging in theorising' (1991, p. 35). Later in the same document she makes a similarly dismissive remark about theory: 'Above all, reforms that will work in practice and produce results must be based on detailed knowledge of what actually happens in an organization, not on theories about what should be happening' (p. 39).

By contrast, the reformers in New Zealand, particularly those in the Treasury (1984, 1987), have drawn heavily on a range of theoretical literature in developing their policy proposals. In particular, extensive use has been made of the new institutional economics and public choice theory (Scott and Gorringe, 1989). Moreover, the reformers have been keen to ensure that their theoretical framework is coherent and robust, and that the reforms proposed and introduced are not merely well founded in theoretical terms, but also well integrated, internally consistent and mutually reinforcing. As a product of this approach, considerable effort has been expended in attempting to think through policy questions from first principles (e.g. Is this function or activity really necessary or justified? Is it currently being undertaken in the most efficient and effective way? Is there a continuing role for the state, and, if so, of what does this comprise? etc.). The importance attached to theory is readily apparent from even a cursory reading of the major documents outlining the reform agenda (Treasury, 1987; Steering Group, 1991). Further, the influence of public choice and the new institutional economics is very plain from the justifications that have been given for the various reforms that have been introduced. Thus, the separation of policy advice and executive functions has been justified primarily on the grounds that this will assist in preventing producer (or bureaucratic) capture. Likewise, the new accountability regime is firmly grounded in agency theory - as is evident from its overriding preoccupation with the clarification of principal-agent relationships, the avoidance of situations in which agents are required to serve multiple, and potentially conflicting, principals, and the design of incentive structures that maximize the chances of agents acting in accordance with the interests of their principals. Similarly, the questions of organizational design and the possibilities of contracting-out have been addressed from the perspective of transaction cost analysis, with its emphasis on minimizing the transaction costs involved in the design, monitoring and enforcement of contracts.

It should not be implied from these remarks that the Next Steps reformers have been unwise to rely primarily on pragmatic rather than theoretical considerations in developing their proposals. After all, not all theories are useful or relevant for the management of the public sector, and even the best of theories can be poorly understood or wrongly applied. Further, theoretical arguments can sometimes be advanced dishonestly to provide a cloak of intellectual respectability or legitimacy for a course of action which has been chosen for essentially self-interested reasons. Nevertheless, the lack of attention by the British reformers to contemporary theoretical developments in economics, political science and other social science disciplines certainly stands in marked contrast to developments in New Zealand and warrants further analysis and explanation. The current British indifference to theory and abstract ideas is, of course, consistent with long-standing civil service traditions (Chapman and Greenaway, 1980, pp. 189-95). Also, the apparent failure of the various theoretically-orientated reforms of the 1960s and 1970s (e.g. planning, programming, budgeting systems, programme analysis review, management by objectives, zero-based budgeting, etc.) may simply have reinforced this negative attitude. Like their British counterparts, senior New Zealand public servants have not been known in the past for their interest in theory. The current emphasis on using theory to guide policy is, therefore, a relatively recent phenomenon, and seems to be due, at least in part, to the growing influence of economists and the particular kind of higher education which many of these economists, especially those in the Treasury, have received.

2. The Role of Detailed Blueprints

Just as the British reformers have eschewed theory, so too have they avoided the development of detailed blueprints or comprehensive plans to guide the Next Steps programme. Certainly the former Project Manager, Sir Peter Kemp, believes that the general goals of the reforms were clearly spelled out - in terms of improving the efficiency, effectiveness, responsiveness and accountability of departments and changing the culture of the civil service. But the method for achieving these goals was left relatively open-ended. Hence, as many commentators have observed (Flynn et al., 1988; Jordan, 1992), the process of designing and implementing the new executive agencies and determining their structure, mandate, financial management regime and so forth has been conducted in an ad hoc and incremental fashion, with an emphasis on flexibility, improvization and organizational pluralism - essentially 'a make it up as you go' approach.

Again the contrast with New Zealand is striking. To start with, there has been a conscious and serious effort to develop an overall policy framework for the management of the state sector. The most detailed and sophisticated such attempt was set out in the Treasury's briefing papers to the incoming government, prepared in the months leading up to the 1987 general election and subsequently published under the title *Government Management* (1987). In addition to this broad and wide ranging blueprint, ministers and officials have given considerable attention during each stage in the reform programme to the development of a consistent, robust and comprehensive policy framework before embarking on the process of implementation. This occurred, for example, prior to the establishment of SOEs, the changes to public sector industrial relations, the introduction of the financial management reforms, and introduction of the reforms to particular sectors - environmental administration, education administration, and health administration. The aim, in each case, has been first, to get the policy framework 'right', and second, to ensure that vested interests are unable to undermine or hijack the reform agenda during the implementation phase. This is not to suggest, of course, that changes of an essentially ad hoc or incremental nature have been absent or that there has been no interest in learning and adjusting to, the impact of the reforms. Nor have the reformers pursued a rigid set of policy proposals irrespective of their political consequences (although the political tolerance levels have been much higher than has been customary in New Zealand). On the contrary, as one might expect, things have frequently worked out differently to the reformers' intentions, and significant policy adjustments (and reversals) have been required for one reason or another during the implementation phase. Nevertheless, when taken as a whole it is remarkable how closely the broad sweep of the public sector reforms in New Zealand have conformed to the grand designs of their instigators.

3. The Process of Change

Not only has Next Steps lacked a detailed blueprint, the Conservative Government has to date implemented the programme by means of executive decisions rather than seeking a specific legislative mandate. There is, therefore, no legislation defining the nature of an executive agency, specifying the nature and scope of framework documents, and setting out the accountability framework under which agencies must operate (i.e. their reporting obligations, the nature of the monitoring regime, the responsibilities of ministers, permanent secretaries and chief executives, etc.) (Greer, 1992a). This is very different to the situation in New Zealand where all the major reforms were based on specifically-designed empowering legislation. Chief among these legislative initiatives were the State-Owned Enterprises Act (1986), the State Sector Act (1988), and the Public Finance Act (1989). But there were also a host of more narrowly focused Acts dealing with the reforms in particular sectors. There was, of course, no need in the case of Next Steps to introduce new legislation since machinery of government changes of this kind are usually initiated by Orders in Council. Moreover, the absence of specific legislation has enhanced the flexibility of the programme. Against this, however, it reduced the opportunity for Parliament to debate the reforms at an early stage and their exposure to detailed public scrutiny.

As far as the process of policy implementation is concerned, another striking feature of Next Steps is the fact that it has had such a limited impact on employment levels in the civil service, at least to date (Greer, 1992b, p. 225). So far as is known, the establishment of executive agencies has not resulted in any compulsory redundancies, although in some cases staff have been re-deployed or taken early retirement (e.g. the Recruitment and Assessment Services Agency and the Defence Research Agency). To be sure, there was a considerable reduction in the overall size of the civil service during the first half of the 1980s prior to Next Steps. But again large scale redundancies were avoided during this period, with staff reductions being achieved by natural attrition or privatization. By contrast, as noted earlier, many of the machinery of government changes in New Zealand have had severe staffing implications.

4. The Willingness to Fudge

Judging by the particular kind of agency approach adopted under the Next Steps reforms, British policy makers are more willing than their New Zealand counterparts to fudge difficult issues and, more specifically, to live with ambiguous accountability relationships. This is evident from the decision to establish executive agencies *within* their parent departments rather than hiving them off into separate departmental or non-departmental organizations. Under the approach adopted, agency chief executives face multiple, and potentially competing principals. That is to say, they report directly to their departmental minister and yet at the same time serve under their sponsoring department's permanent secretary, who, in turn, reports to the same minister. Such dual accountability is bound to generate problems from time to time. Similar tensions also arise from the fact that executive agencies are meant to be relatively autonomous and free standing - supposedly in the interests of greater efficiency and effectiveness - and yet are still subject to a substantial range of controls, imposed either by the Treasury or their sponsoring department. Thus, for example, the negotiation of agencies' framework documents and performance indicators has involved not merely the individual agencies and their portfolio minister but also the relevant sponsoring department and the Treasury. Not surprisingly in these circumstances, the Fraser Report (Efficiency Unit, 1991) noted that there was continuing frustration over the number of detailed and comparatively trivial management decisions which agencies are required to refer back to their core departments and to the Treasury. Equally important, because executive agencies are located firmly within departments and their chief executives report to a minister, rather than a board of directors or a group of Commissioners, they are still bound (at least in theory) by the doctrine of ministerial responsibility. This necessarily carries with it certain implications for management autonomy and makes behind-the-scenes political interference in management decision making highly likely.

In New Zealand there has been no denying the fact that conflicting values and imperatives are part and parcel of the management of the public sector. Hence, it is accepted, for example, that there will always be tensions between the quest for decentralization, in the interests of managerial autonomy, and the desire for centralization, in the interests of co-ordination, integration, the minimization of risks, and so forth. Yet from a New Zealand perspective, the Next Steps programme - with its inbuilt dual accountability, the attempt to reconcile agency autonomy and traditional notions of ministerial responsibility, the idea of having distinct and separate organizations operating within another organization, and the emphasis on maintaining supposedly free-standing units within a unified civil service - seems a little untidy, to say the least. This is not to suggest that the approach is unworkable: virtually any organizational arrangement can be made to work given the necessary good will and capacity to compromise. But it is difficult not to agree with Hood and Jones that the Next Steps approach is a somewhat unsatisfactory 'half-way house arrangement' and that it is unlikely 'to constitute a formula for a new stable system of public management' (Treasury and Civil Service Committee, 1990, p. 78; 81).

There is not the space here to outline in detail how the New Zealand approach to public sector reform has attempted to overcome the kind of fudging exhibited by Next Steps. But a number of points are worth highlighting. First, the New Zealand reformers, in keeping with the dictates of agency theory, have made a concerted effort to avoid organizational arrangements which entail some form of dual or multiple accountability. This means, for example, that departmental chief executives are directly, and solely, accountable to their portfolio minister for the conduct of such executive functions as remain within their departments. Second, there has been an attempt to clarify the relationship between ministers and those organizations for which they have some form of responsibility, and to make transparent (generally in legislation) the nature of the accountabilities involved. In some situations this has led to a revision and re-defining of the traditional notion of ministerial responsibility. Third, in the interests of minimizing intra-organizational conflicts, departments have been restructured so as to reduce the number of situations in which they are faced with conflicting interests or the pursuit of conflicting values.

5. Alternative Forms of Organizational Pluralism

As should be evident from the preceding discussion, both the Next Steps reformers and their New Zealand counterparts have accepted the need for organizational pluralism within the public sector. In other words, it is agreed that the public sector must undertake a wide variety of tasks and that it is desirable, in terms of efficiency and accountability, to design organizations to suit the particular functions required of them. To this end, it is accepted that some public organizations, in the interests of democratic accountability, need significant ministerial oversight and involvement, whereas others, in the interests of independence from the executive, need to be protected from undue ministerial interference. Such a situation necessarily leads to the conclusion that there can be no single or uniform accountability regime throughout the public sector. Where the British and New Zealand reformers have differed, therefore, is not in their attitude to the need for organizational pluralism, but rather in the form of organizational pluralism which they have embraced.

In the case of Britain, there has been a willingness to experiment with a wide range of organizational forms within a departmental framework, and hence within the bounds of direct ministerial responsibility. Moreover, the new organizations that have been formed within departments have all been called 'agencies', regardless of their function, degree of autonomy, or degree of commercialization. Indeed, as Kemp has stressed, evidently with enthusiasm:

> there is no blueprint for agencies. Each must be set up specifically to deal with a particular task or tasks. Each of the framework documents for the agencies so far launched is different ... some chief executives have powers to manage certain grades of staff; for others, the financial regimes differ according to the degree to which the agency generates revenue, while some have powers to carry revenue over between financial years (1990, p. 189).

Such is the variety of agencies under Next Steps that some are fully commercial and have the status of a self-funding trading organization (under the Government Trading Funds Act 1973), while others have no commercial functions at all.

In New Zealand, by contrast, there has been an attempt, still in the process of implementation, to design a number of different kinds of public sector organizations and to ensure that the organizational form takes a proper regard for the kind of functions which are being performed and the environment in which the organization operates. In particular, attention has been given to such variables as the degree of commercialization and market contestability which is possible, the nature and extent of the organization's social responsibilities, and whether the organization is primarily in the business of providing policy advice, undertaking regulatory or policing functions, or providing services to the public. This has resulted in the establishment of a number of distinct types of organizations (e.g. ministerial departments, SOEs, Crown Research Institutes, and Crown Health Enterprises), all with a mandate, financial structure and accountability regime appropriate to the nature of their task. Under this approach, there is certainly scope within particular organizational categories for the adoption of different management styles and for some variation in the degree of autonomy from Treasury control, but there has been nothing like the variety that is apparent with respect to the new executive agencies in Britain.

6. The Application of Agency Principles to the Core Civil Service

A final contrast lies in the extent to which the core (or headquarters) part of government departments have been affected by the process of reform. In Britain, many of the policy changes that have been applied to executive agencies have not been applied, or else have been applied less fully, to the core. This is most apparent with respect to the management of senior staff. Unlike agency chief executives, permanent secretaries have not been placed on fixed-term contracts. Nor are they subject to performance-based remuneration. And nor are their jobs or those of their senior colleagues subject to open competition. In New Zealand, by contrast, the positions of departmental chief executives and other senior staff are advertised widely (often internationally) and the successful applicants are employed on renewable fixed-term contracts (for up to five years). Moreover, chief executives are required to negotiate an annual performance agreement with their portfolio minister(s), their performance is assessed annually, and their remuneration package contains a performance-related component (Boston, 1992).

From an international perspective, the use of annual performance agreements is relatively novel and involves a shift away from a reliance primarily on mutual trust to a quasi-contractual relationship between chief executives and ministers. Under the new procedures, chief executives prepare a draft agreement (at about the time of the annual budget) which is then discussed with their minister(s) before being signed by both parties. In most cases the agreement is based on the relevant department's corporate plan for the coming financial year, but usually other matters of particular importance to ministers will also be included. Ministers are expected to meet with their chief executives on a regular basis to assess their progress in achieving the objectives contained in the agreement. At the end of the financial year the SSC uses the agreement as a key benchmark for assessing the performance of chief executives. As part of this exercise, the views of ministers and external referees are sought together with written self-evaluations prepared by each chief executive. Remuneration levels are then adjusted, within certain parameters, to reflect the level of performance achieved.

Lessons from New Zealand

Given such differences, what lessons, if any, do New Zealand's reforms have to offer? This is, of course, a large and complex issue and can only be touched on fleetingly here. It must be stressed at the outset that the evidence concerning the effectiveness and implications of New Zealand's reforms is neither abundant nor uncontroversial (Boston et al., 1991; Steering Group, 1991). For one thing, most of the reforms are very recent and some are still in the process of implementation. For another, there are serious methodological difficulties in assessing many of the reforms. Moreover, even if the evidence were more plentiful and less contentious, there are well known dangers in drawing conclusions from the experiences of a single country and then using them as a basis for policy in another, perhaps very different, context. But while bearing these reservations and qualifications in mind, the public sector changes in New Zealand since the mid 1980s do suggest a number of tentative conclusions.

First, there is no need to establish separate executive agencies or hive off the delivery functions of departments in order to improve an organization's performance. This is not to suggest that hiving off is necessarily wrong. Rather the point is that there are a range of instruments available for enhancing departmental performance of which machinery of government changes are but one. Thus, as explained earlier, New Zealand policy makers have made use of various instruments including the decentralization of responsibility for choosing most inputs to departmental chief executives, better performance specification, the clarification of accountability relationships, improved financial management systems and information systems, changes to the incentives facing departmental managers and so forth. In all likelihood, it has been changes of this nature rather than the shifting of organizational boundaries that has contributed most to improving departmental outputs.

Second, the appropriate relationship between the provision of policy advice and the task of implementation - whether it be regulation, the delivery of services, or the allocation of government grants - requires careful analysis. Recent experience in New Zealand suggests that a sharp, cut-and-dried separation is not always desirable (Ewart and Boston, 1993). Indeed, attempts to enforce an artificial separation between policy advice and administration (or execution) can have harmful consequences, especially where policy advisers require detailed operational knowledge in order to tender competent advice (as is the case, for example, in such areas as foreign policy, defence policy, and law enforcement). In any case, agencies and departments responsible for executive functions are likely to retain an important policy advice role in many instances.

Third, the form organizational pluralism adopted in New Zealand has resulted in certain cases in the establishment of a plethora of new agencies. As an example, the break up of the Department of Education in 1989 led - in line with the organizational principles underpinning the machinery of government reforms - to the creation of no less than 10 separate agencies. Not only can institutional fragmentation of this nature have negative consequences for policy development and co-ordination, it also imposes substantial transitional costs (e.g. consultants reports, redundancy pay, the need for new management information systems etc.) not to mention the potentially negative implications for staff morale and institutional memory. Overall, it can be argued that the New Zealand reformers have placed too much emphasis on organizational realignments and bureau shuffling, some of which have secured little, if any, evident gain.

Fourth, there is little evidence to date from New Zealand on how the placing of senior civil servants, including departmental heads, on fixed-term, performance-linked contracts and the opening up of such positions to competition from the private sector has affected such things as inter-departmental mobility, the public service ethos, or the behaviour of those directly concerned. Nevertheless, the damaging consequences for the public service feared by some traditionalists do not appear to have materialized. Moreover, such evidence as is available suggests that senior departmental staff have adjusted to the new policy regime with few difficulties, and that the concepts of fixed-term employment, performance-related pay and performance agreements now have the support of the vast majority of ministers and their senior advisers (Boston, 1991; Steering Committee, 1991). One factor possibly contributing to this state of affairs is that the new policy framework has not led to a flood of job applications from the private sector, nor a significant number of private sector appointments (e.g. only 6 per cent of the members of the SES have been appointed from outside the public service). This, however, is hardly surprising. The nature of the work of senior policy advisers and departmental managers in the core public sector is quite different from the management of a private firm and, as a consequence, the respective labour markets are relatively distinct (though, of course, there is some overlap in areas like corporate affairs, including financial management and human resource management). Further, there are always likely to be political and fiscal constraints on making the salary packages of senior departmental staff attractive to high fliers in the private sector. It is interesting to note, in fact, that since the introduction of more flexible employment conditions in New Zealand in 1988, the gap between the average remuneration levels of public sector managers and their private sector counterparts has actually widened.

The new policy regime for senior departmental staff has not, however, been without its problems. Implementing the new chief executive performance agreements, performance assessment system and performance-linked remuneration have all generated certain difficulties. Also, the move to fixed-term contract employment can have potentially destabilizing consequences for the public service. For example, as a result of the new policy it is expected that in 1993 some 30 per cent of SES positions will come up for renewal (in some departments the percentage is much higher than this). As the authors of the recent review of the state sector reforms have observed, 'No matter how confident senior managers are of contract renewal, they will almost certainly start casting around towards the end of their term - if only to increase their bargaining strength. This can pose a risk to the employing organization' (Steering Group, 1991, p. 85). Related to this, fixed-term employment also has potentially negative implications for succession planning and human resource development (pp. 75-8).

Finally, the State Sector Act effectively ended the concept of a unified public service by giving departmental chief executives responsibility for the recruitment and management of their own employees. This has led since 1988 to a much greater use of fixed-term employment and the termination of unified salary scales and conditions. How this has affected inter-departmental mobility and the values and ethos of departmental employees remains uncertain, though the retention so far of a service-wide superannuation scheme has reduced the potential barriers to movement between departments. Despite the emphasis on delegating management responsibilities to the departmental level, a significant degree of central oversight has been maintained by the SSC in the area of collective bargaining. The main rationale for this has been to avoid a ratcheting up of pay rates as a result of departmental managers settling industrial agreements at too high a level (with flow-on implications for other departments). How serious such a problem would be under a fully decentralized bargaining model, however, remains uncertain. Nevertheless, there are reasons to doubt, given the nature of industrial relations in New Zealand - with high union density in the public sector and a tradition of rigid occupational relativities - whether a reliance on cash limits alone would be sufficient to prevent excessively high settlements occurring in particular departments with subsequent spillover effects throughout the public sector. This issue will clearly be exercising the minds of British policy makers as the quest for a more decentralized system of pay determination within the civil service gathers momentum.

Conclusion

Although the Ibbs Report claimed that its recommendations would bring 'fundamental and radical' changes to the operations of the British civil service (Efficiency Unit, 1988, p. 13), from a New Zealand perspective the changes so far introduced appear to be neither fundamental nor radical. Admittedly, Next Steps has brought about real and important changes in the machinery of government, the delegation of responsibility to agency managers, and the system of contract specification and performance appraisal. But by comparison with New Zealand, the implications for civil servants have so far been much less substantial, with few staff reductions and few being placed on fixed-term contracts. Similarly, the degree of central control over civil service appointments and conditions of employment remains much greater than is now the case in New Zealand. Of course, defenders of the British reforms can justifiably respond that Next Steps is but part of a continuing programme of public sector renewal. It is not the end of the journey but a prelude to more radical changes, including further privatization and much more extensive contracting-out. Yet while this is not denied, the conclusion still remains that in organizational and management terms Next Steps has been much less revolutionary than some of its defenders would like to claim.

The Next Steps to Market Testing?

BARRY J. O'TOOLE AND GRANT JORDAN

There has been what many view as a management revolution in Whitehall. While it is unclear whether the insurgents have won there have certainly been casualties. It may well be that the unified career civil service, both in concept and in actuality, is one. Yet another may well be both the concept and the actuality of public service. The question must surely be whether the changes which have threatened these previously cherished aspects of public life have improved the management of government.

The Next Steps programme is only part of the revolution, albeit the most radical, extensive and vital part. That programme must be seen both as building upon the Rayner Efficiency Strategy of the early 1980s, including the Financial Management Initiative, and as laying the foundations for the current changes, or at least providing part of the framework within which those current changes are able more easily to take place, even if they may be seen by some as being contrary to the Next Steps programme. The two most significant of those initiatives since the onset of the Next Steps programme have been the Citizen's Charter and the Market Testing programme associated with *Competing for Quality,* the title of the White Paper which has set in train a process of 'defining what are the tasks of Government and how they can best be delivered' (Mottram, 1993, p. 3).

Next Steps to Citizen's Charter

The Citizen's Charter is essentially about setting standards for public service organizations and putting in place mechanisms by which the 'customers' of those organizations are able to obtain some sort of redress when those standards are not met. There are, according to Diana Goldsworthy, the Deputy Director of the Citizen's Charter Unit, in a speech to the Annual Conference of the Public Administration Committee at York in 1993, six principles attaching to the Charter: first, explicit **standards** for the levels of service; secondly, **consultation** with the 'customers' in setting those standards; thirdly, the ready availability of clear **information** about the services, the targets set and the results; fourthly, **openness** about whether targets are being met and about the people providing the service; fifthly, a **complaints** procedure which is swift, 'user friendly' and effective in providing remedies when things go wrong; and finally, **value-for-money**. Goldsworthy notes the 'simplicity, indeed the childlike nature of these principles', but points out that this simplicity 'should not disguise their radical nature and their fundamental importance to the delivery programme'. Indeed, they can and do apply to every public service, interpreted and tailored to fit each of the vast variety of individual services and their customers .

This is where the organizational changes of the Next Steps programme have proved so useful, for, as Richard Mottram, the Permanent Secretary of the Office of Public Service and Science, has pointed out, 'Agencies provide an important vehicle for the delivery of Charter principles'. He has given three examples: the Jobseeker's Charter of the Employment Service, 'which includes an easy to use complaints procedure with a target of five working days for response to written complaints'; the Ordnance Survey Superplan, 'whereby detailed maps are plotted out in an agent's shop to the customer's specification from digital data which is continuously updated'; and the Charter Mark awarded to Companies House, which had 'reduced the time taken for its premium search service to 20 minutes instead of an hour'. (Mottram, 1993, p. 5). Cynics might argue that these are minor examples, but of course such cynicism might be part of the 'sneering by the chattering classes' to which Goldsworthy disparagingly refers. Perhaps the Next Steps programme and the Citizen's Charter have indeed facilitated a welcome sea-change in the administrative culture, and the cases Mottram refers to, and no doubt many others, could not have happened without them.

Next Steps to Market Testing

The more important reform is the *Competing for Quality* initiative and the associated Market-Testing programme. These processes have implications which go right to the heart of a fundamental question both for political theorists and for citizens: what is the scope of government? In the words of Mottram, 'Clearly, it is possible to define some tasks as close to the heart of Government and functions for which it must be responsible ... and to separate out provider functions where ownership and delivery by public servants is less compelling' (Mottram, 1993, p. 3). Market testing is designed to help in the consideration of where the line should be drawn.

Market testing is a matter of costing the support services for government, previously provided 'free' by government departments or agencies, so that the users of those services can decide whether to seek them internally or externally (i.e. from outside the civil service). In other words departments and agencies 'charge' for their services, managers have budgets to 'purchase' them and can choose which supplier (in-house or external) provides the best 'value for money'. Thus, in market testing, 'an activity currently performed in-house is subject to competition' (Efficiency Unit, 1993a, para. 1.10).

Before an activity is considered as a possible candidate for market testing a number of 'prior options' are considered. It is at this point that the questions about what government should be doing become explicit. *The Government's Guide to Market Testing* sets out the prior options clearly:

> ...managers should consider [an activity thought potentially suitable] in detail, and
> - confirm whether it needs to be performed. If not it should cease
> - confirm whether it is a suitable candidate for privatization, and, if so, act accordingly
> - when the Government wishes to retain responsibility for a service, consider whether competition for its provision should be introduced. The possibility of a Next Steps Agency should also be considered at this stage
> - in considering how to introduce competition a key decision will be whether for policy or management reasons the work should be done by the private sector (in which case strategic contracting-out without an in-house bid would be the appropriate way forward) or whether to have an in-house bid (market testing) (Efficiency Unit, 1993a, para. 1.5).

Market Testing 'compares with "make or buy" decisions in the private sector, and exists to ensure the efficient provision of services to the public' (para. 1.10). The language of the Market Testing programme is framed in such a way that casual observers might simply believe that it is a common sense approach to management. For example:

The aim of market testing ... is to promote fair and open competition so that Departments and Agencies can obtain the best value for money for the customer and for the tax payer (Efficiency Unit, 1993a, para. 1.3).
Or again:

The advantages of market testing are
* competition helps ensure value for money
* focusing on performance outputs will produce clearer standards and improved QUALITY of service
* an explicit customer/supplier relationship
* external and in-house bidders will be given the opportunity to be more INNOVATIVE in their field; and
* monitoring of contracts and service level agreements will focus on the outputs, objectives and targets required in improving the efficiency and effectiveness of targets (para. 1.4).

This new emphasis on market testing raises the issue of the relationship between that approach and the idea of agencies. Ministers tend to speak as if they are fully complementary but controversy about this may been the area that prompted the remarkable removal of Peter Kemp in 1992. Are agency chief executives really autonomous (as Kemp advocated) or are they subject to centralist imposition of policies such as market testing?

As noted earlier the Market Testing Initiative comes from the White Paper *Competing For Quality* in November 1991 (Cm 1730). This was produced within the Treasury and this source may be significant: there are at the very minimum some tensions between the market testing approach and the Next Steps developments. Cm 1730 stated that there would be a new Public Competition and Purchasing Unit based in the Treasury to promote the work of the White Paper. This read as a challenge to the Cabinet Office and it may be that there is a need to explore how it was resolved.

In the Preface to *Competing For Quality*, the then Chancellor, Norman Lamont, argued that the initiative stemmed from the Citizen's Charter: 'we aim to make public services respond better to the wishes of the users - above all by expanding choice and competition'. Though the connection between Next Steps and the Citizen's Charter were asserted, to those outside the centre of Government the links between Next Steps, the Charter approach and Market Testing are not clear below a very general level of assertion that they are designed to introduce efficiency. Do they support or contradict each other? They may all be aimed at improving the delivery of services, but it is less obvious that they dovetail together in a co-ordinated way. That they do not sit so comfortably was perhaps demonstrated by November 1993 when 'Whitehall in Crisis' was the headline in *The Independent*

(15th November).

Competing For Quality stated that hitherto market testing procedures had been cumbersome because, 'the procedure has often involved a prolonged exercise to bring the in-house operation to maximum efficiency before competitive tendering can begin. After a decade of efficiency reform there should no longer be a need to delay in this way.' Of course if there was a real confidence in the benefits of the efficiency reform, then there would be no wave of market testing ...

As Sue Richards and Jeff Rodrigues point out the 'hero' of Next Steps (i.e. Peter Kemp) was 'thrown out on his ear'. They asked, 'Why has there been such a sharp change in direction: the Agency initiative ... seems in danger of being derailed by market testing, providing solutions from the private sector to achieve improvement.' They complain that there is no 'reasoned critique' that explains why the management reforms of the Next Steps agencies have been overtaken by what they regard as the fundamentally different market testing idea.

Ministers assert that there is no conflict. As Richards and Rodrigues say:

> Whitehall does not let ordinary citizens in on its family arguments, so we have to deduce what we can from the evidence available if we want to understand these events ... in the absence of more open government the old art of Kremlinology comes in useful (1993, p. 33).

Given the Treasury suspicion of Next Steps in the Lawson era it is therefore perhaps significant that *Competing for Quality* was a Treasury document. Perhaps it can be seen as the Treasury's *alternative* to Next Steps rather than a cosy supplement. While Lamont gave the genesis as the Citizen's Charter it is more realistic to trace it back to the Treasury-led exercise that culminated in *Using Private Enterprise in Government; a report of a Multi-Departmental Review of Competition, Tendering and Contracting for Services in Government Departments* (HM Treasury, 1986). That document argued that:

> Competition should be a regular part of every Department's efficiency drive ... Departments should review all their activities to see if they offer scope for contracting out.

If market testing is the future we can surely learn from the experience of competitive tendering in other areas particularly local government. The relevant arguments are set out by Parker and Hartley (1990, p. 9). The arguments for are:

- private firms in competitive markets are better managed, more innovative and more responsive to customer requirements
- private firms are threatened with bankruptcy

- regular recontracting means that a contractor and service levels can be reviewed
- result is efficiency gains and cost saving.

The arguments against are:

- poor quality, unreliable service - for example dirty streets, schools and hospitals
- private industry is monopolistic and not competitive
- hidden costs of contractors - for example organizing and evaluating bids and monitoring contracts
- equity - the poorly paid lose out.

Parker and Hartley stress the need to ensure the creation and maintenance of contestable markets -with the obvious dangers of cartels and collusive tendering. They also note that pressures need to be put on in-house units otherwise they will bid low to eliminate rivals with increases coming later (1990, p. 15). While there are, as Stewart argues effectively, strong arguments in favour of government by real contract as in market testing, what is not convincing is that:

> contacts are the appropriate form of organizational control in the public sector in all conditions and for all services, contracts as a means of organisational control are unproblematic (1993, p. 9).

Conclusion

All these arguments seem to be 'management' questions, using the vocabulary of the management theorists. However it may reasonably be asked whether the debate about changing the scope of government should be couched in such management terms. Are the issues and problems raised not *political* and *constitutional* in nature? What are the implications of major privatizations of activities previously at the heart of government for the society in which we live, for example the prison service? Is it really 'less compelling' to consider support services as being vital to the proper and efficient operation of government as a whole? What are the ramifications of contracting out services such as the computer operations of the Home Office? How might the rights of individual citizens be affected by management changes of the sort being introduced without much debate? What powers might private sector organizations have over the rights of individual citizens? How might equity of treatment between citizens be maintained if, for example, different private sector organizations were providing similar services? What levels of control would ministers be able to exercise over contracted out services? What are the implications for Parliamentary accountability and indeed for the role of Parliament itself? The questions could go on. They are fundamentally important questions; yet there are no signs of any carefully considered and relevant answers. The only responses are phrased in emotive assertions: competition is a good thing; private sector practices are inevitably better; the rigours of the market will unquestionably bring benefits; efficiency will certainly result. Yet even in these terms little attempt is made to indicate the meanings of the benefits which it is promised will accrue, nor how they are to be brought about. What, for example, is meant by competition? What is better? What is efficiency? Is the competition which the government has in mind the same kind of competition which private sector organizations are meant to be subject to? Is it better for services to be provided by organizations which can go bankrupt and over which control by ministers and, through ministers, control by Parliament has been jettisoned? Is it more efficient for the workforce to have it constantly implied that their work is inferior by comparison to a private sector which has signally failed to provide an economic miracle? These are questions which public debate would have thrown up.

All this is not to say, of course, that there has been no discussion. However, what debate there has been has been low-key and generally expressed in managerialist language. To some extent this is because public administration is not a high profile political issue. It is also because there has been little contention between the parties about it. The Labour Party has failed to defend the traditional civil service organization for fear of seeming to be against 'efficiency'. The parameters of political discussion in this area, as in so many others, have been conditioned by the existence of a strong, long standing and ideologically committed government and by the lack of an effective opposition. The consequence is a sort of consensus based around terms such as 'efficiency', 'value-for-money', 'performance', and 'quality', with little attention being given either to the practical meanings of these words, or to the political and constitutional consequences of the reforms.

In Parliamentary terms the most important contributions to the debate have been the considerations of the Treasury and Civil Service Committee, in particular of the Next Steps programme. There have been four reports by the Committee based upon its investigations into that programme, with an interim report based upon its investigation into the future of the civil service (which is proceeding as this book is being completed). Even here, however, the basic premise has always been that the Next Steps programme in particular is both welcome and to be encouraged. Witnesses, too, have generally been supportive, with the exceptions of one or two academics and the trade unions. Only recently has there been much concern that the changes were bringing adverse consequences. The most significant expression came in February 1994, when the Comptroller and Auditor General argued to the

Treasury and Civil Service Select Committee that corruption and waste on an unprecedented scale are being introduced into the civil service by government reforms and the war against bureaucracy. Sir John condemned the prevailing contempt for what he said was seen as 'unnecessary red tape and bureaucracy' in the drive for change and value for money. He was reported as saying that businessmen and other outsiders were being brought in to run newly created semi-autonomous agencies without due regard to traditional public service values and rules (*The Daily Telegraph*, 2nd February, 1994).

At the end of January 1994, John Sheldon of the National Union of Civil and Public Servants argued that the impact of privatization, contracting out, import of private sector managers and methods was leading to the 'Italianisation' of the public services. He said that the PAC Report of January which revealed waste and corruption had shown that,

> After almost 15 years of constant ministerial attacks on civil servants and the civil service as being 'old-fashioned', it now appears that these 'old-fashioned' ideas of accountability, integrity and probity are not so bad after all (*The Independent*, 31st January, 1994).

To date, even the unions have been cautious in their criticisms. They have always phrased them in such a way as to suggest that they will co-operate with the government in changing the management of the civil service so long as the intention is to improve the quality of the services provided. They have also said that they would co-operate so long as there was little chance of those services being privatized and contracted out:

> We wish to emphasize our deep interest in improving the quality of service given to the public ... We see the Ibbs Report as being an important opportunity to improve generally and permanently the quality of services given to the public. [However] ... in the view of the Council [of Civil Service Unions] staff in ... agencies must remain as civil servants and part of the Civil Service. There will be serious morale and industrial relations problems if they are removed from the Civil Service ... The Council wishes to stress, however, that if the exercise is a disguised attempt to break up the Civil Service, to reduce resources, to impose further cuts, to provide an enabling route to privatization or to attack national and departmental pay and conditions of service it will meet with the total opposition of the Council (Treasury and Civil Service Committee, 1988; memorandum submitted by the Council of Civil Service Unions, paras. 3.4, 4.1 and 5).

From a union perspective it may well seem that the worries expressed by them in

1988 were very prescient, and the changes that have since been wrought have presumably spurred them into their 1993 low-key campaign of industrial action. The Government will no doubt suggest that the current concerns of the unions are their traditional priorities of jobs and pay. However, there may surely be some grounds for believing that, even if we do take into account the natural intentions of trade unions to protect the employment conditions of their members, other views they expressed in 1988 and subsequently were legitimate concerns about the management of the civil service. For example:

> our members see the [civil service], and I would hope Parliament sees it, as a national Civil Service with equality of treatment all over the country, equal standards of recruitment and equal service being provided, indeed equal pay being provided as well. The real fear that our members have is that if we do get into so many self contained agencies with different conditions of service ... the ability to move talent around will become restricted. A lot of our members are particularly concerned about that ... our members are concerned that if there are different conditions of service and different rates of pay, their ability to move might be there in theory but might not be there in practice (Treasury and Civil Service Committee, 1988, oral evidence of Mr Leslie Christie, General Secretary of the National Union of Civil and Public Servants and Chairman of the Major Policy Committee of the Council of Civil Service Unions, Q. 220).

The creation of agencies, with the freedoms given to their management, particularly after the Civil Service (Management Functions) Act 1993, which delegates the details of pay negotiations to departments and agencies, may have made these concerns more real. Contracting out and privatization take matters one stage further, perhaps beyond the purview of the unions. The unions have consistently warned against the management problems inherent in the demise of a unified career civil service, and their warnings now seem not to have been fanciful. Not only has the creation of agencies in itself thrown into question the nature of the career civil service, but the agencies are to have their status as civil service organizations continuously reviewed. In other words, there is always the possibility that at some future stage any agency could be a candidate for privatization. In addition, the agencies are being used as a major vehicle for pushing forward the market testing programme perhaps even against the wishes of their chief executives. Even Sir Robin Butler's description of the civil service being 'unified but not uniform' with the creation of the agencies seems to be rather out of touch with what has actually happened.

This state of affairs has led the Council of Civil Service Unions to suggest that the civil service is in a state of 'profound crisis':

The introduction of market testing and plans by ministers for a 'long march through Whitehall' to extend privatization to every area of government responsibility, will, we are convinced, erode the level and quality of services upon which the public depend for their quality of life. Privatization and contracting out are not new to the Civil Service but the scale by which they are now being pursued along with the additional policy of market testing is new. Opening up such an extensive range of Civil Service activities to the 'market place' goes far beyond simple competition and anything seen by the Civil Service before and we believe that the Government's severe bias in favour of private provision is a cause for growing and legitimate concern amongst the public, Parliament and the Civil Service. It seems to us that the drive for private provision is being put before delivering a quality public service (Treasury and Civil Service Committee, 1993, Memorandum submitted by the Council of Civil Service Unions, para. 3).

The creation of the Next Steps agencies, the Citizen's Charter and the Market Testing programme have all been primarily concerned with the operational aspects of government, with the actual delivery of services. They have largely been based upon the premise of a distinction between strategic policy making and the administration of policies. Increasingly, however, there are suggestions that organizational forms considered appropriate for the delivery of services might also be appropriate for the policy functions of government. In other words, either the emphasis on objective setting, performance measurement and openness associated with Next Steps agencies should be applied to the core departments, or ministers should contract out the policy advice function. In New Zealand such changes have already taken place, and permanent secretaries there are subject to performance related pay. Performance in each department is measured in relation a) to the permanent secretary's personal performance, b) to the permanent secretary's responsibilities in relation to the department, and c) to the tasks of the department as a whole. There are, of course, problems with such a system, and Richard Mottram is succinct in suggesting what they might be:

> There may be difficulty in framing key objectives at the departmental level for which the Permanent Secretary can genuinely be held accountable and which are measurable, a price in terms of more mechanistic and inflexible decision making, and a risk that the organization will be steered towards areas which score in the agreement. An additional layer of organization may be needed to advise the Minister on his or her side of the aims and target setting process if there is to be an effective debate with the head of the department (Mottram, 1993, p. 8).

Some of the problems identified by Mottram in relation to the work of core advisers may be similarly found in the operational aspects of a department's work. This is especially the case if it is accepted that there is no such thing as the policy/administration dichotomy. All civil servants operate within policy and resource frameworks set by ministers. They are not separate from them. Even Mottram himself denies that the Next Steps reforms were 'intended to recreate Trevelyan's distinction between intellectual and mechanical tasks' (Mottram, 1993, p. 7). In denying that, there is surely an implicit recognition that it is invidious to apply rigorously the management techniques associated with the Next Steps. While 'Enabling the Chief Executive to manage as freely as possible has always been a key theme' (Mottram, 1993, p. 7), he or she can only be as free as the dictates of ministerial policy allow. As we all know, ministerial policy can, and does, change.

Notwithstanding Mottram's reservations about the application of Next Steps principles at the very heart of government, there are now clear signs that the government intends radical changes even there. In particular, it now seems that, as is the case for agency chief executives, recruitment to the most senior grades of the civil service may be by open competition (Efficiency Unit, 1993c). It may well be that in the future permanent secretaries and deputy secretaries could even be appointed on fixed term contracts, and that they may be subject to performance measurement. Those who consider such changes to be appropriate may genuinely believe that those positions will be filled by the best possible people, from whatever walk of life. It is to be assumed, however, that salary levels will be set at private sector, market determined, rates, otherwise the 'best' people may not apply.

At face value such views may seem perfectly reasonable. Why should senior positions in the civil service not be filled by open competition? New blood would surely mean innovation and imagination, the buzz words of the management gurus, being infused into government policy making. The best practices of the business sector, or the voluntary sector, or the education sector, would all add to the quality of the public service. On the other hand questions must be raised about the nature of civil service work and about the applicability of private sector practices in organizations dominated by the requirements of a Parliamentary democracy. Would business practices really be appropriate in such circumstances? Might people who are recruited from the private sector be frustrated at the 'inefficiency' of the requirements of democratic accountability? Could it be that ministers might feel frustrated if they do not continue to get the service, the 'Rolls Royce' service as it is sometimes called, of the mandarins who know the government machine, are familiar with the political environment and have highly developed professional sensitivities?

These are important questions. More important might be questions relating to the continuation of an impartial career civil service. Will competition for such jobs genuinely be open? Or is there the possibility that they will be filled by placemen?

Might there be scope for corruption of a more overt kind? Will not those people who have been recruited into the fast stream administrative grades, by rigorous open competition, feel cheated, even if the people who are appointed are not partisan appointees? Will those who are thinking of a career in the civil service be deterred by the idea that it might no longer be a 'career' civil service? Besides raising doubts about the managerial efficiency of introducing open competition at the top of the civil service some of these questions are of enormous constitutional importance. Yet once again the changes are being considered with hardly any public debate or comment. While present ministers may be behaving honourably, what of the future?

It has often been stated that civil servants have frustrated the wishes of government in relation to civil service reform. This, however, cannot be alleged in relation to the present government's reform programme. The pace of change since the publication of the Ibbs Report, recommending the creation of Next Steps agencies, has been truly breathtaking. Within only five years of that report most civil servants are now working in agencies. More staggering yet has been the ability of the government to place on the agenda the possible wholesale privatization or contracting out of many government activities, and to submit large areas of activity to a market testing programme. These reforms have taken place with hardly any public comment and with little dissension from parliamentarians or others. The reforms that have taken place, and those that are yet to be put into effect, are of major constitutional and political importance. What is the scope of government? What is the role of Parliament? What is the role of ministers? Are citizens really citizens or are they merely customers? These are questions fundamental to the nature of our democracy. If citizen's are to be treated simply as 'customers' the ultimate question could be: what is the point of democratic government? The Government and civil servants (in post) have consistently presented the changes of the past decade as cost saving without costs: improvements without disadvantages. Such a version of events is incredible. Difficult matters are not resolved so easily. To be critical of the changes is, respectable and responsible. These issues are sufficiently important to merit aggressive scrutiny.

In October 1993 at the Conservative Party Conference the Foreign Secretary, Douglas Hurd, made a noteworthy speech to the Conservative Reform Group. 'We must show', he said:

> that we value those we rely upon to provide the service. The teacher, the nurse, the serviceman, the doctor, the postmaster, the police officer, the civil servant, are not relics ... whom we should periodically despatch to the rice fields for thought reform and indoctrination. They are not entitled to special privileges or immunity from sacrifices, for example on pay. But they, and those whom they serve, rightly distrust any whiff of dogma which they may

detect in the way governments tackle the problems of their profession.

He said that he was against the impression that the Conservative Party believed in a

> permanent cultural revolution in the style of Trotsky or chairman Mao ... We must show that we are not driven by ideology to question every function of the state, to make impossible the life of our public servants, or to depreciate the worth and quality of the different public services (*The Independent*, 8th October).

His case seemed clear. The reform of government by current methods is at risk of destabilizing traditional structures and demoralizing the staff. These are the worries that thread through this volume. Reform should be based on the rigorous identification of weaknesses and a coherent and considered plan to remedy those defects. It should consider the positive and negative effects of change before proceeding. It then needs to be implemented with some skill; and with some recognition of the need to establish support for the goals. Even then reforms may have unintended effects. Without such deliberation the search for efficiency can be vitiated by change that asserts improvement but does not deliver it.

References

Adonis, A. (1991), 'The Leviathan Limbers Up', *Financial Times*, 26 July.

Aglietta, M. (1979), *A Theory of Capitalist Regulation*, Verso.

Aoiki, M., Gustafsson, B. and Williamson, O.E. (1990), *The Firm as a Nexus of Treaties*, Sage.

Aucoin, P. (1990), 'Administrative Reform in Public Management: Paradigms, Principles, Paradoxes and Pendulums', *Governance*, 3, pp. 115-37.

BBC (1993), *Public Eye* 'Profits for Punishment', BBC Publications.

Barberis, P. (1989), *Permanent Secretaries in the British Civil Service: An Historical and Biographical Survey*, Unpublished Ph.D. Thesis, University of Manchester.

Bellamy, C.A. and Henderson, A.M.C. (1992), 'The UK Social Security Benefits Agency: a Case Study of the Information Polity?', *Informatization and the Public Sector* , 2(1), pp. 1-25.

Benefits Agency (1992a), *One-stop: Benefits Agency Service Delivery*.

Benefits Agency (1992b), *Annual Report 1991-2*.

Bevins, A. (1993), 'Mandarins Outwit Major On Reform', *The Observer*, 15 August.

Boston, J. (1992), 'Assessing the Performance of Departmental Chief Executives: Perspectives from New Zealand' *Public Administration*, 70, pp. 405-28.

Boston, J., Martin, J., Pallot, J. and Walsh, P. (Eds) (1991), *Reshaping the State:*

New Zealand's Bureaucratic Revolution, Auckland: Oxford University Press.

Bozeman, B. and Straussman, J.D. (1990), *Public Management Strategies,* San Francisco: Jossey-Bass.

Brindle, D. (1991), 'Leak "Reveals Bias" By Benefits Agency', *The Guardian,* 5 September.

Brindle, D. (1992), 'PM Prompts Rethink on Benefit Jobs', *The Guardian,* 14 January.

Bryman, A. (1989), 'Leadership and Culture in Organizations', *Public Money and Management,* 9, 3, pp. 35-41.

Burns, T. (1966), 'On the Plurality of Social Systems', in J. Lawrence (ed), *Operational Research and the Social Sciences,* Tavistock Publications, pp. 165-78 .

Butler, R. (1991), 'New Challenges or Familiar Prescriptions?', *Public Administration,* 69, pp. 363-71.

Cant, S. (1992), 'Information Management Systems in the DSS', Paper to PAC/PICT Seminar on Informatisation in Public Administration: UK and European Perspectives, April.

Carey, Sir P. (1984), 'Management in the Civil Service', *Management in Government,* 39, pp. 81-85.

Carter, N. (1989), 'Performance Indicators: "Backseat Driving" or "Hands-off Control"', *Policy and Politics,* 17, pp. 13-18.

Carter, N. (1991), 'Learning to Measure Performance: the Use of Indicators in Organizations', *Public Administration,* 69, pp. 85-101.

Carter, N., Klein, R. and Day, P. (1992), *How Organizations Measure Success: the Use of Performance Indicators in Government,* Routledge.

Carvel, J. (1992), 'Prison Service To Be Given a Freer Hand', *The Guardian,* 12 March.

Cave, M., Hanney, S., Kogan, M. and Trevett, G. (1988), *The Use of Performance Indicators in Higher Education,* Jessica Kingsley.

Cave, M., Kogan, M. and Smith, R. (1990), *Output and Performance Measurement in Government,* Jessica Kingsley.

CCSU (1991a), *Next Steps Newsletter* No 3, March.

CCSU (1991b), Memo from John Ellis to Peter Jones dated 18 September, found in CCSU file Next Steps 280.58.

CCSU (1991c), Note of a Meeting between the Next Steps Project Manager and CCSU, held on 17 December 1991, in CCSU file Next Steps 280.58.

CCSU (1991d), Letter from Peter Jones to Sir Peter Kemp, dated 13 August (sent under instruction from the Major Policy Committee, meeting held 6 August 1991, MP 184/91), CCSU file Next Steps 280.58.

CCSU (1991e), Internal memorandum on Pay and Management Flexibilities, dated 23 July. For discussion at Major Policy Committee 134/91, in CCSU file Next

Steps 280.58.

CCSU (1992), Next Steps Newsletter No 13, April.

CCTA (The Government Centre for Information Systems) (1992a), Market Testing IS/IT Provision.

CCTA (1992b), *The Intelligent Customer*.

Cellan-Jones, R. (1992), 'The Business of Benefits', *The Guardian*, 23 June.

Chancellor of the Exchequer (1991), H.C. Debs 6s, Vol. 195, 61, col. 604-5, 24 July.

Chandler, A.D. (1962), *Strategy and Structure: Chapters in the History of the Industrial Enterprise*, MIT Press.

Chapman, L. (1979), *Your Disobedient Servant: The Continuing Story of Whitehall's Overspending*, Penguin.

Chapman, Richard A. (1973), 'The Vehicle and General Affair', *Public Administration* 51.

Chapman, Richard A. (1988), 'The Next Steps', *Public Policy and Administration* 3, 2, pp. 3-10.

Chapman, Richard A. (1991a), 'New Arrangements for Recruitment to the British Civil Service: Cause for Concern', *Public Policy and Administration* 6, 3, pp. 1-6.

Chapman, Richard A. (1991b), 'Concepts and Issues in Public Sector Reform: The Experience of the United Kingdom in the 1980s' in *Public Policy and Administration*, 6, 2, pp 1-21.

Chapman, Richard A. (1992), 'The End of the Civil Service?', *Teaching Public Administration*, xii, 2, pp. 1-5.

Chapman, Richard A. (1993), 'Civil Service Recruitment: Fairness or Preferential Advantage?', *Public Policy and Administration*, 8, 2, pp. 68-73.

Chapman, Richard A. and Greenaway, J.R. (1980), *The Dynamics of Administrative Reform*, Croom Helm.

Chapman, R. (1989), 'Core Public Sector Reform in New Zealand and the United Kingdom', *Public Money and Management*, 9, 1, pp. 43-9.

Child, J. (1987), 'Information Technology Organisation and the Response to Strategic Challenges', *California Management Review*, 30 (Fall), pp. 33-50.

Clarke, R. and McGuinness, T. (1987), *The Economics of the Firm*, Blackwell.

Cmnd. 8616 (1982), *Efficiency and Effectiveness*, HMSO.

Cohen, S. (1988), *The Effective Public Manager*, San Francisco: Jossey-Bass.

Colville, I. and Tompkins, C. (1989), 'Appendix 11', *Treasury and Civil Service Committee, Fifth Report, Session 1988-9, Development in the Next Steps Programme, HC-348*, HMSO.

Committee of Public Accounts (1990), *Second Special Report, Session 1989/90 - Accounting Officer Memorandum, HC 527*, House of Commons.

Coote, A. and Pfeffer, N. (1991), 'Quality and the Equality Gap', *The Guardian*, 17

July.

CSCA (1962), *Red Tape* Vol. 51.

CSCA (1963), *Red Tape* Vol. 52.

CSCA (1968), *Red Tape* Vol. 57.

Davies, A. and Willman J. (1991), *What Next? Agencies, Departments and the Civil Service*, Institute of Public Policy Research.

Dell, Edmund (1974), Letter to the Editor of *The Times*, 22 February.

DSS (1989), *Social Security Agency Study: Report of the Project Team*.

DSS and HM Treasury (1993), *Social Security Departmental Report*, Cm 2213.

Duncan, I. and Bollard, A. (1992), *Corporatization and Privatization: Lessons from New Zealand*, Auckland: Oxford University Press.

Dunleavy, P. (1989), 'The Architecture of the British Central State, Part I: Framework for Analysis', *Public Administration*, 67, pp. 249-275.

Dunleavy, P. and Francis, A. (1990), 'The Development of the Next Steps Programme 1988-90', *Memorandum submitted to the Treasury and Civil Service Select Committee - Eight Report, Session 1989/90: Progress in the Next Steps Initiative,* HC. 481, pp. 69-77.

Dunleavy, P. (1991), *Democracy, Bureaucracy and Public Choice*, Harvester Wheatsheaf.

Dyerson, R. and Roper, M. (1990a), 'Computerisation at the DSS, 1977-89: the Operational Strategy', *Technology Project Paper 4*, London Business School.

Dyerson, R. and Roper, M. (1990b), 'Implementing the Operational Strategy at the DSS', *Technology Project Paper 8*, London Business School.

Earl, M. J. (1989), *Management Strategies for Information Technology*, Prentice Hall .

Earl, M. J. (1991), 'Outsourcing Information Services', *Public Money and Management*, 11, 3, pp. 17-21.

Efficiency Unit (1988), *Improving Management In Government: The Next Steps*, HMSO.

Efficiency Unit (1991), *Making The Most Of Next Steps: The Management of Ministers' Departments and their Executive Agencies*, HMSO.

Efficiency Unit (1993a), *The Government's Guide to Market Testing*, HMSO.

Efficiency Unit (1993b), *Next Steps Briefing Note*, April.

Efficiency Unit (1993c), *Career Management and Succession Planning Study*, HMSO

Employment Service (1990a), A *Framework Document for the Agency*, HMSO.

Employment Service (1990b), *Employment Service Annual Performance Agreement, 1990-91*, HMSO.

Employment Service (1991a), *Annual Report and Accounts 1990-91*.

Employment Service (1991b), *ES in the 90's: Forward as an Agency*.

Employment Service (1993a), *Annual Report and Accounts 1992-93*.

Employment Service (1993b), *Memorandum of Financial Arrangements.*

Ewart, B. and Boston, J. (1993), 'The Separation of Policy Advice from Operations: The Case of Defence Restructuring in New Zealand', *Australian Journal of Public Administration,* 52, pp. 223-40.

FDA (1926), Letter dated 5 May from the Joint Consultative Committee to Secretaries of Departmental Whitley Councils, members of the NSS and Secretaries of the constituent organisations of the NSS, File I80 623.

FDA (1973), *Second Report of the Sub Committee on Tribunals of Enquiry, Ministers and the Civil Service,* 9 March, filed under A00077, part 5.

FDA (1980), 61st *Annual Report.*

Feeny, D., Willcocks, L., Rands T. and Fitzgerald G. (1991), 'Managing IT; When Outsourcing Equals Rightsourcing', in, S. Rock (ed.), *The Director's guide to outsourcing,* Institute of Directors.

Financial Management Unit (1985), *Policy work and the FMI,* HM Treasury.

Flynn, A., Gray A. and Jenkins, W.I. (1990), 'Taking The Next Steps: The Changing Management of Government', *Parliamentary Affairs,* 43, 2, pp. 159-78.

Flynn, A., Gray A., Jenkins W. and Rutherford, B. (1988), 'Making Indicators Perform', *Public Money and Management,* 8, 4, pp. 35-41.

Flynn, A., Gray A., Jenkins W. and Rutherford, B. (1988), 'Implementing the "Next Steps"', *Public Administration,* 66, pp. 439-45.

Flynn, N. (1990), *Public Sector Management,* Harvester Wheatsheaf.

Francis, A., Turk J. and Willman, P. Eds. (1983), *Power, Efficiency and Institutions: a Critical Appraisal of the 'Markets and Hierarchies' Paradigm,* Heinemann Educational.

Fry, G.K. (1988), 'Outlining "The Next Steps" ', *Public Administration,* 66, pp. 429-438.

Fulton Report (1968), *The Civil Service - Vol. I: Report of the Committee, 1966-68,* Cmnd. 3638, HMSO.

Gladden, E.N. (1956), *Civil Service or Bureaucracy,* Staples Press.

Goldsworthy, D. (1991), *Setting up Next Steps,* HMSO.

Gray, A.G. and Jenkins, W.I. (1982), 'Policy Analysis in British Government: the Experience of PAR', *Public Administration,* 60, 429-50.

Gray, A. and Jenkins, B. (1991), in Bill Jones (Ed.), *Politics UK,* Philip Allan.

Gray, A.G. and Jenkins, W.I. With Flynn, A.C. and Rutherford, B.A. (1991), 'The Management of Change in Whitehall: the Experience of the FMI', *Public Administration,* 69, 41-59.

Greer, P. (1992a), 'The Next Steps Initiative: An Examination of the Agency Framework Documents', *Public Administration,* 70, pp. 89-98.

Greer, P. (1992b), 'The Next Steps Initiative: The Transformation of Britain's Civil Service', *Political Quarterly,* 63, pp. 222-27.

Hambleton, R. (1988), 'Consumerism, Decentralisation and Local Democracy', *Public Administration*, 65, pp. 161-77.

Hambleton, R. (1992), 'Decentralization and Democracy in UK Local Government', *Public Money and Management*, 12, 2, pp. 9-21.

Harvey-Jones, J. (1991), *Trouble Shooter*, BBC Publications.

Headey, B. (1974), *British Cabinet Ministers: The Roles of Politicians in Executive Offices*, Allen and Unwin.

Heath (1919), *Report of the Sub-Committee of the Inter-Departmental Committee on the Application of the Whitley Report to the Administrative Departments of the Civil Service* Cmd. 9.

Hencke, D. (1991a), 'Civil Service to be Put to Market Test', *The Guardian*, 16 November.

Hencke, D. (1991b), 'Sun Shines For High-Pressure Met Office', *The Guardian*, 31 December.

Hencke, D. (1991c), '100 Whitehall Pieces', *The Guardian*, 30 January.

Hencke, D. (1991d), 'Testing Times For Laboratory', *The Guardian*, 12 November.

Hencke, D. (1991e), 'Charter Can Benefit Citizen Juggernaut', *The Guardian*, 3 December.

Hencke, D. (1991f), 'Mrs Thatcher's Strangest Legacy', *The Guardian*, 2 December.

Hencke, D. (1992a), 'Private Companies Ousting Civil Service Job Recruiters', *The Guardian*, 7 February.

Hencke, D. (1992b), 'More Whitehall Staff Face Market Test For Jobs', *The Guardian*, 21 July.

Hencke, D. (1992c), 'MOT Test Agency Faces Sell-Off', *The Guardian*, 19 February.

Hennessy, P. (1989), *Whitehall*, Secker & Warburg.

Hennessy, P. (1991a), in Bill Jones (Ed.), *Politics UK*, Philip Allan.

Hennessy, P. (1991b), 'Civil Service "Sahibs" Cling to Past', *The Independent*, 8 April.

Hennessy, P. (1991c), 'Drawing Up New Rules For Players in a Power Game', *The Independent*, 21 October.

Hepworth, M. (1989), *The Geography of the Information Economy*, Francis Pinter.

Heseltine, M. (1990), *Where There's a Will*, Arrow Books.

HM Treasury (1986), *Multi-Departmental Review of Budgeting*, HMSO.

HM Treasury (1989a), *The Financing and Accountability of Next Steps Agencies*, Cm. 914, HMSO.

HM Treasury (1989b and updates), *Guide to Accounting and Financial Procedures for the Use of Government Departments*, HMSO.

HM Treasury (1991a), *Pay and Management Flexibilities in the Fields of Personnel Management, Pay and Allowances available to Departments and Agencies*, HM

Treasury and Office of the Minister for the Civil Service.

HM Treasury (1991b), *Competing for Quality*, Cm 1730.

HM Treasury (1992), *Executive Agencies: a Guide to Setting Targets and Measuring Performance*, HMSO.

Hoggett, P. (1991), 'A New Management in the Public Sector?', *Policy and Politics*, 19, 4.

Hogwood, B.W. and Gunn L.A. (1984), *Policy Analysis for the Real World*, Oxford University Press.

Hogwood, B.W. (1993), 'The Uneven Staircase: Measuring up to Next Steps', *Strathclyde Papers on Government and Politics*, No. 92, University of Strathclyde.

Hood, C. (1976), *The Limits of Administration*, John Wiley.

Hood, C. (1990), 'De-Sir Humphreyfying the Westminster Model of Bureaucracy: A New Style of Governance?', *Governance*, 3, pp. 205-14.

Hood, C. (1991), 'A Public Management For All Seasons?', *Public Administration*, 69, pp. 3-19.

Hood, C. and Jackson, M. (1991), *Administrative Argument*, Dartmouth.

Hood, C. and Jones, G. (1990), 'Progress in the Government's Next Steps Initiative' *Memorandum submitted to the Treasury and Civil Service Committee - Eighth Report, Session 1989/90: Progress in the Next Steps Initiative*, HC 481, pp. 78-83.

Humphreys, B.V. (1958), *Clerical Unions in the Civil Service*, Blackwell and Mott.

Hunn, D. (1991), 'Chief Executive's Overview', in *Annual Report of the State Services Commission for the Year Ended 30 June 1991,* Wellington: GP Print.

Hutton, W. (1991a), 'Tories' More Means Less For The Public', *The Guardian*, 4 November.

Hutton, W. (1991b), 'All Is Set Fair For Election About Rights and Wrongs', *The Guardian*, 29 July.

Independent (1990), 'Whitehall Learns To Take a Business-like Approach', 31 October.

Information Technology Services Agency (1993), *Business plan 1992-3*.

Inland Revenue IT Office (1992), 'Partnership briefing', *Online*, December, 2-3.

Inland Revenue IT Office (1993), 'Partnership briefing', *Online*, January 2-4.

IPPR (1991), *What Next? Agencies Departments and the Civil Service*.

Jackson, P. (1988), 'The Management of Performance in the Public Sector', *Public Money and Management*, 8, 4, pp. 11-16.

Jenkins, L., Bardsley, M., Coles, J., Wickings, I. and Leow, H. (1987), *Use and Validity of NHS Performance Indicators: a National Survey*, CASPE, King Edwards Hospital Fund.

Jennings, Sir W. Ivor (1959), *Cabinet Government*, (3rd Edition), Cambridge University Press.

Johnstone, R. and Lawrence, P.R. (1991), 'Beyond Vertical Integration - the Rise of the Value Adding Partnership', in Thompson, G. et al., *Markets, Hierarchies and Networks*, Sage.

Jones, P.D. (1982), Article in *Management in Government*, 37, 3.

Jones, P. D. (1991), 'The Search for Good Management in the Civil Service - A Union Perspective', *The Bulletin of the Council of Civil Service Unions*, 11, 2, pp. 21-27.

Jordan, G. (1992), 'Next Steps Agencies: from Management by Command to Management by Contract?', *Aberdeen Papers in Accountancy, Finance and Management*, University of Aberdeen.

Kanter, R.M. (1990), *When Giants Learn to Dance*, Unwin Paperbacks.

Kellner, P. and Lord Crowther-Hunt (1980), *The Civil Servants*, Macdonald Books.

Kelly, Michael P. (1980), *White Collar Proletariat: The Industrial Behaviour of British Civil Servants*, Routledge & Kegan Paul.

Kemp, Sir Peter (1990a), 'Can the Civil Service Adapt to Managing by Contract?', *Public Money and Management*, 10, 3, pp. 25-31.

Kemp, Sir Peter (1990b), 'Next Steps for the British Civil Service', *Governance*, 3, pp. 186-96.

Kemp, Sir Peter (1993), *Beyond Next Steps: a Civil Service for the 21st Century*, Social Market Foundation, Paper No. 17.

Lacity, M. and Hirscheim, R. (1993), *Outsourcing Information Systems*, John Wiley and Sons.

Lawton, A. and Rose, A. (1991), *Organisation & Management in the Public Sector*, Pitman.

Lewis, S. and Jones, J. (1990), 'The Use of Output and Performance Measures in Government Departments' in M. Cave et al., pp. 39-55, *op. cit.*

Lipietz, A. (1987), *Miracles and Mirages*, Verso.

Mackenzie, W.J.M. and Grove J.W. (1957), *Central Administration in Britain*, Longmans.

Madnick, S. E. (Ed.) (1987), *The Strategic Use of Information Technology*, Oxford University Press.

Margetts, H. (1991), 'The Computerisation of Social Security: a Step Forwards or a Step Backwards?', *Public Administration*, 69, pp. 325-364.

Margetts, H. and Willcocks, L. (1992), 'Information Technology as Policy Instrument in the UK Social Security System: Delivering an Operational Strategy', *International Review of Administrative Sciences*, 58, 3, pp. 329-347.

Matthews, R. S. (1979), 'Accountable Management in the DHSS', *Management in Government*, 34, 3, pp. 125-132.

Mellon, E. (1991), *The Next Steps Initiative*, Memorandum Submitted to the Treasury and Civil Service Committee, published as Appendix A in HC. 496, HMSO.

Metcalfe, L. and Richards, S. (1987), *Improving Public Management*, Sage.

Metcalfe, L. and Richards, S. (1990), *Improving Public Management*, (second edn.), Sage.

Ministry of Labour (1917), *Report by the Ministry of Labour on the Attitude of Emloyers and Employed to the Whitley Report*, 26 September, Paper G.T. 2176, PRO/CAB 24/27.

Mintzberg, H. (1979), *The Structuring of Organisations*, Prentice Hall

Mintzberg, H. (1983), *Power in and around Organisations*, Prentice Hall.

Moe, T. (1984), 'The New Economics of Organization', *American Journal of Political Science*, 28, pp. 739-75.

National Audit Office (1986), *The Financial Management Initiative*, HC 588.

National Audit Office (1991a), *Performance Measurement in the Civil Service: Experience in the Foreign and Commonwealth Office, HM Customs and Excise and Department of Education and Science*, HC 399.

National Audit Office (1991b), *National Insurance Contributions*, HC 665.

National Audit Office (1992), *The Vehicle Inspectorate: Progress as an Executive Agency*, HMSO.

NUCPS (1991), *Motions for Debate at the Annual Delegate Conference*, May.

OECD (1990), *Public Management Developments: Survey-1990* Paris: OECD.

OECD (1992), 'Complex Contracting out for Information Technology', PUMA Occasional Papers, Market-type Mechanisms series, 5.

Office of the Minister for the Civil Service (1988), C*ivil Service Management Reform: The Next Steps - The Government Reply to the Eighth Report from the Treasury and Civil Service Committee, Session 1987/88 HC 494-I*, Cm 524.

Office of the Minister for the Civil Service (1989), *Developments in the Next Steps Programme - The Government Reply to the Fifth Report from the Treasury and Civil Service Committee, Session 1988/89, HC 348*, Cm 841.

Office of the Minister for the Civil Service (1990), *Progress in the Next Steps Initiative - The Government Reply to the Eight Report from the Treasury and Civil Service Committee, Session 1989/90, HC 481*, Cm 1263.

Office of the Minister for the Civil Service (1991), *The Next Steps Initiative - The Government Reply to the Seventh Report from the Treasury and Civil Service Committee, Session 1990/91, HC 496*, Cm 1761.

Office of Public Service and Science (1991), *The Citizens Charter: Raising the Standard*, Cm. 1599, HMSO.

Office of Public Service and Science (1993), *Next Steps Review*, Cm. 2430, HMSO.

Official Report (1971-72), Fifth Series, Volume 836, House of Commons.

Official Report (1987-88), Sixth Series, Volume 17, House of Commons.

Official Report (1990-91), Sixth Series, Volume 191, House of Commons.

O'Halpin, Eunan (1989), *Head of the Civil Service : A Study of Sir Warren Fisher*, Routledge.

Optimum (1991/2), 'A Theme Issue on Special Operating Agencies', 22(2), Ministry of Supply and Services Canada.

Osborne, David and Gaebler, Ted (1992), *Reinventing Government*, Addison-Wesley.

O'Toole, Barry J. (1989a), *Private Gain and Public Service : The Association of First Division Civil Servants*, Routledge.

O'Toole, Barry J. (1989b), 'The Next Steps : A Historical Perspective', *Public Policy and Administration*, 4, 1, pp. 41-52.

O'Toole, Barry J. (1989c), 'The FDA and the GCHQ Affair: a Prediction Made Manifest', *Public Policy and Administration*, 4, 3, pp. 22-31.

O'Toole, Barry J. (1990), 'T.H. Green and the Ethics of Senior Officials in British Central Government', *Public Administration*, 68, pp. 337-352.

Painter, C. (1989), 'Thatcherite Radicalism and Institutional Conservatism', *Parliamentary Affairs*, 42, 4.

Painter, C. (1991), 'The Public Sector and Current Orthodoxies: Revitalisation or Decay?', *The Political Quarterly*, 62, 1, pp. 75-89.

Parker, D. and Hartley, K. (1990), 'Competitive Tendering: Issues and Evidence', *Public Money and Management*, 13, 2.

Parris, Henry (1973), *Staff Relations in the Civil Service : Fifty Years of Whitleyism*, Allen and Unwin.

Perrow, C. (1977), 'The Bureaucratic Paradox: the Efficient Organization Centralizes in order to Decentralize', *Organizational Dynamics*, pp. 3-14.

Perrow, C. (1986), *Complex Organizations: A Critical Essay*, New York: Random House.

Peters, T.J. and Waterman, R.H. (1982), *In Search of Excellence*, New York: Harper & Row.

Peters, T.J. (1989), *Thriving on Chaos*, Pan Books.

Pettigrew, A. and Whipp, R. (1991), *Managing Change for Competitive Success*, Blackwell.

Phillips, M. (1992), 'The Tenders Trap of Civil Service plc', *The Guardian*, 21 July.

Piore, M. J. and Sabel, C.F. (1984), *The Second Industrial Divide*, Basic Books.

Pliatzky, L. (1992), 'Quangos and Agencies', *Public Administration*, 70, pp. 555-576.

Plumptre, T.W. (1988), *Beyond The Bottom Line: Management in Government*, Nova Scotia: The Institute for Research in Public Policy.

Pollitt, C. (1984), *Manipulating the Machine: the Changing Pattern of Ministerial Departments 1960-83*, Allen & Unwin.

Pollitt, C. (1986), 'Beyond the Managerial Model: the Case for Broadening Performance Assessment in Government and the Public Services', *Financial Accountability and Management*, 2 (3) pp. 155-70.

Pollitt, C. (1990a), in M. Cave, M. Kogan and R. Smith (Eds.), *Output and Performance Measurement in Government: The State of the Art*, Jessica Kingsley.

Pollitt, C. (1990b), *Managerialism and the Public Services: The Anglo-American Experience*, Basil Blackwell.

Pressman, J.L. and Wildavsky, A.B. (1973), *Implementation*, University of California Press.

Price Waterhouse (1992), *Executive Agencies: Update*, (Edition 5), Price Waterhouse.

Prime Minister (1988), *Civil Service Management Reform: The Next Steps*, Cm. 524, HMSO.

Prime Minister (1990), *Progress in the Next Steps Initiative*, Cm. 1263, HMSO.

Prime Minister (1991a), *The Next Steps Initiative*, Cm. 1761, HMSO.

Prime Minister (1991b), *The Citizen's Charter*, Cm. 1599, HMSO.

Prime Minister (1992), *The Citizens Charter First Report*: 1992, Cm 2101, HMSO.

PRO (1920), T1/12564/20935, Cabinet Finance Committee, Council of Financial Officers (the Baldwin Council), *Interim Report on the Position of Accounting Officers*, FC 33, December 1919.

Quinn, J.B. (1980), *Strategies for Change: Logical Incrementalism*, Irwin

Radcliffe, J. (1991), *The Reorganisation of British Central Government*, Dartmouth.

Ramsay (1919), *Report of the National Provisional Joint Committee on the Application of the Whitley Report to the Administrative Departments of the Civil Service* Cmd. 198.

Rayner, Lord (1991), 'Twin Track at the Top', *Financial Times*, 4 February.

Recruitment and Assessment Services (1992), *Annual Report and Accounts, 1991-1992*.

Rhodes, R.A.W. (1991), 'Theory and Methods in Public Administration: The View From Political Science', *Political Studies*, 39, pp. 533-554.

Richards, S. and Rodrigues, J. (1993), 'Strategies for Management in the Civil Service', *Public Money and Management*, 13, 2.

Rogers, E. (1983), *The Diffusion of Innovation*, 3rd Edition, Free Press.

Rogers, E. and Kim, J. (1985), 'Diffusion of Innovations in Public Organisations', Ch. 4 in R. Merritt & A.J. Merritt (eds), *Innovation in the Public Sector*, Sage.

Rose, R. (1985), 'Accountability to Electorates and the Market: the Alternatives for Public Organizations', *Studies in Public Policy No. 144*, Centre for the Study of Public Policy, University of Strathclyde.

Royal Institute of Public Administration (1992), *The Civil Service Reformed: the Next Steps Initiative*, Royal Institute of Public Administration.

Scott, G. and Gorringe, P. (1989), 'Reform of the Core Public Sector: The New Zealand Experience', *Australian Journal of Public Administration*, 48, pp. 81-92.

Scott, G., Bushnell, P. and Sallee, N. (1990) 'Reform of the Core Public Sector: New Zealand Experience', *Governance*, 3, pp. 138-67.

Scott Morton, M. S. (1991), *The Corporation of the 1990s: Information Technology and Organizational Transformation*, Oxford University Press.

SCS (1970), *Minutes of the Annual Conference of the Society of Civil Servants*.

Select Committee on Procedure (1991), *Third Report from the Select Committee on Procedure, Session 1990-91, Parliamentary Questions HC-178*, House of Commons.

Smith, J. (1991), 'The Public Service Ethos', *Public Administration*, 69, 4, pp. 515-23.

State Services Commission (1991), *Review of the Purchase of Policy Advice from Government Departments*, Wellington: State Services Commission.

Steering Group (1991), *Review of State Sector Reforms*, Wellington: State Services Commission.

Stewart, J. and Ranson, S. (1988), 'Management in the Public Domain', *Public Money and Management*, 8, 2, pp. 13-19.

Stewart, J. (1993), 'The Limitations of Government by Contract', *Public Money and Management*, 13, 3.

Stowe, Sir K. (1992), 'Good Piano won't play Bad Music', *Public Administration*, 70, 3.

Theakston, K. (1987), *Junior Ministers in British Government*, Blackwell.

Thompson, G., Francis, J., Levacic R. and Mitchell, J. (1991), *Markets, Hierarchies and Networks: the Coordination of Social Life*, Sage.

Tomkins, C. and Colville, I. (1989), 'Managing for Greater Innovation in the Civil Service: Customs & Excise', *Public Money and Management*, 9, 4, pp. 15-20.

Treasury (1984), *Economic Management*, Wellington: Government Printer.

Treasury (1987), *Government Management*, Wellington: Government Printer.

Treasury and Civil Service Committee (1988), *Civil Service Management Reform: The Next Steps, HC. 494-I and II*, House of Commons.

Treasury and Civil Service Committee (1989), *Developments in the Next Steps Programme, HC. 348*, House of Commons.

Treasury and Civil Service Committee (1990), *Progress in the Next Steps Initiative, HC. 481*, House of Commons.

Treasury and Civil Service Committee (1991), *The Next Steps Initiative, HC. 496*, House of Commons.

Treasury and Civil Service Committee (1991), *The New System of Departmental Reports HC. 290*, House of Commons.

Treasury and Civil Service Committee (1993), *The Role of the Civil Service: Interim Report 1992-3 HC. 390 I and II*, House of Commons

Tyson, S. (1990), 'Turning Civil Servants into Managers', *Public Money and Management*, 10(1), pp. 27-30.

Vehicle and General Tribunal (1972), *Report of the Tribunal Appointed to Inquire into Certain Issues in Relation to the Circumstances Leading to the Cessation of Trading by the Vehicle and General Company Ltd HL. 80 and HC. 133*, House of Lords and House of Commons.

Waldegrave, W. (1993), 'The Reality of Reform and Accountability in Today's Public service', Public Finance Foundation/BDO Consulting Inaugural Lecture 5 July.

Walsh, K. (1991), 'Quality and Public Services', *Public Administration*, 69, pp. 503-14.

Wass, Sir Douglas (1984), *Government and the Governed*, Routledge and Kegan Paul.

Webb, A. (1991), 'Co-ordination: A Problem in Public Sector Management', *Policy and Politics*, 19, 4.

White, L.D. (1933), *Whitley Councils in the British Civil Service : A Study in Conciliation and Arbitration*, University of Chicago Press.

Whitley (1917), *Sub-Committee on Relations between Employers and Employed (Whitley Committee) Interim Report on Joint Standing Industrial Councils* Cd. 8606.

Willcocks, L. (1993), 'Managing Information Systems in UK Public Administration: Issues and Prospects', Paper to ESRC Study Group on Informatization in Public Administration, April.

Williams, W. (1989), 'Central Government Capacity and the "British Disease"', *Parliamentary Affairs*, 42, pp. 250-264.

Williamson, O. E. (1975), *Markets and Hierarchies: Analysis and Antitrust Implications*, Collier Macmillan.

Williamson, O. E. (1985), *The Economic Institutions of Capitalism: Firms, Markets, Relational Contracting*, Collier Macmillan.

Wilson, G.K. (1991), 'Prospects For The Public Service in Britain: Major To The Rescue?', *International Review of Administrative Sciences*, 57, 3.

Wistrich, E. (1992), 'Restructuring Government New Zealand Style', *Public Administration*, 70, pp. 119-35.

Biographical Notes

Peter Barberis is a Senior Lecturer in Politics, Manchester Metropolitan University. He is the co-author (with Timothy May) of *Government, Industry and Political Economy* (Open University Press, 1993) and is currently preparing what will be the first ever book on permanent secretaries in the British civil service.

Chris Bellamy is Head of Politics and Public Administration at Nottingham Trent University. She has published on the subject of central government-local government relations, and is now researching and writing on 'public administration in the information age'. Chris Bellamy is the current Chair of the Joint University Council's Public Administration Committee.

Jonathan Boston is Associate Professor of Public Policy at Victoria University of Wellington. He has previously worked for the New Zealand Treasury and taught in the Political Science Department at Canterbury University. He has undertaken research in a variety of areas including central government administration, incomes policy, the funding of higher education, and moral theology. Among the books he has written or co-edited are *Incomes Policy in New Zealand, The Future of New Zealand Universities, The Fourth Labour Government,* and *Reshaping the State.*

Neil Carter is a Lecturer in Politics at the University of York. He is the co-author (with Rudolf Klein and Patricia Day) of *How Organisations Measure Success: the Use of Performance Indicators in Government* (Routledge, 1992) and a number of journal articles on performance evaluation. His current research interest is in environmental policy and politics.

Richard A. Chapman is Professor of Politics, University of Durham. He previously taught at Carleton University and the Universities of Leicester, Liverpool and Birmingham; before that he was a civil servant. He was Chairman of the Public Administration Committee of the Joint University Council 1977-81. His most recent monograph is *Ethics in the British Civil Service* (Routledge, 1988); he also edited *Ethics in Public Service* (Edinburgh University Press, 1993). He is currently writing a book on The Treasury which includes case studies of Treasury control of Next Steps agencies.

Andrew Gray is Reader in Public Accountability and Management at the University of Kent, and Co-Director of the Public Sector Management Unit at the Business School. He is a specialist in decision making, control and accountability in public sector organizations.

Patricia Greer is now a Senior Consultant with Price Waterhouse. She is the author of *Transforming Central Government: the Next Steps Initiative* (Open University Press, 1994) and a number of articles in leading journals on the Next Steps Initiative.

Michael Hunt is a Senior Lecturer in Public Administration at Sheffield Hallam University. As well as the Next Steps Agencies he has research interests in the area of open government, and was joint editor (with Professor Richard Chapman) of *Open Government: a study of the prospects of open government within the limitations of the British political system* (Croom Helm, 1987). He is the current editor of *Teaching Public Administration*.

William Jenkins is Reader in Public Policy and Management at the University of Kent. He is Associate Editor of *Public Administration* and is a specialist in the management of change within central and local government, and the Health Service.

Grant Jordan is a Professor of Politics at the University of Aberdeen. His major research interest is policy making in Departments, and relations with outside interests. Recent publications include *The Commercial Lobbyists* (Aberdeen University Press, 1991); *Engineers and Professional Self Regulation* (Clarendon Press, 1992); (with N. Ashford, eds.) *Public Policy and the Impact of the New Right*

(Pinter, 1993).

Barry J. O'Toole is a Lecturer in Politics at the University of Liverpool. He has published widely on industrial relations in the civil service and on ethics in government. He is editor of *Public Policy and Administration*.

Chris Painter is a Principal Lecturer in the Institute of Public Policy and Management, University of Central England Business School. Apart from articles in a number of professional and academic journals, recent publications include the editorship with Kester Isaac-Henry and Chris Barnes of *Management in the Public Sector* (Chapman & Hall, 1993). Current research interests centre on public service reform, including a joint project partly funded by the West Midlands Joint Committee of District Councils on appointed agencies and their publics.

Index